ROOTS OF REVOLUTION

University of Nebraska Press: Lincoln and London

SHELDON B. LISS

Roots of

Revolution

Radical
Thought
in Cuba

The paper in this book meets the
minimum requirements
of American National Standard for
Information Sciences —
Permanence of Paper for Printed
Library Materials,
ANSI Z39.48-1984.

Library of Congress Cataloging
in Publication Data
Liss, Sheldon B.
Roots of revolution.
Bibliography: p.
Includes index.
1. Cuba — Politics and government —
Philosophy.
2. Radicalism — Cuba — History.
3. Cuba — Intellectual life.   I. Title.
F1778.L57   1987
972.91'063   86-7109
ISBN 0-8032-2873-2 (alkaline paper)
ISBN 0-8032-7920-5 (paperback)

For the courageous academicians in the
anti-imperialist movement in the Americas who
sacrifice themselves to sustain others

CONTENTS

ACKNOWLEDGMENTS

Since the late 1950s scholarly materials from Cuba have not been readily available in most major United States research centers, and access to Cuba for United States investigators has frequently been hindered by travel bans imposed by their government. Despite various obstructions and inconveniences, I have obtained most of the articles, documents, collected works, and books I needed and have accomplished the exchange of ideas vital to this volume.

Individuals in Cuba and the United States, some unknown to me, facilitated my work. Among those I know, Naomi Friedman and Sandra Levinson from the Center for Cuban studies in New York City periodically obtained difficult to locate materials. Their greatest contribution occurred in Havana, where in December 1981, I presented them with an extensive list of somewhat esoteric publications, and they, in conjunction with representatives of Cuba's Ministry of Education, managed to procure them by January 1982.

During my travels across Cuba, bookshop workers in every major city graciously waded through dusty stacks of volumes searching for, and often finding, copies of out-of-print works by, and biographies of, well-known Cuban and Latin American thinkers and writers.

Surprised members of the staff of the University of Havana Library never flinched or said a word when this somewhat clumsy, unannounced, unescorted, and unintroduced Yankee accidentally dismantled and knocked over part of the card catalog in an overzealous attempt to uncover new sources. Members of the Hispanic Division of the Library of Congress in Washington, D.C., complied with my occasional pleas for assistance. Valerie Johnson and Sarah M. Lorenz of the Bierce Library at the University of Akron efficiently processed my countless, and often illegible, interlibrary loan requests for obscure books and articles.

Through his correspondence, Harold Eugene Davis sent encouragement and also pointed out aspects of Cuban thought that had not occurred to me but proved worthy of investigation. Louis A. Pérez, Jr., examined the entire manuscript; he offered thoughtful suggestions for its improvement, corrected my errors, and put his store of historical knowledge and scholarly analyses of Cuba at my disposal. My longtime colleague and friend Barbara Evans Clements once again subjected herself to a manuscript of mine, and as in the past I benefited from her good common sense, command of the English language, and extraordinary familiarity with socialist theory in general and the machinations of Soviet communism in particular.

Garnette Dorsey, Inez Bachman, and Mia Hahn deciphered my longhand and expertly typed and retyped the manuscript, while continuously expressing delight at seeing "our" project come to fruition.

Contrary to the beliefs of the skeptics who doubted it could be done, I completed this project with considerable joy, and without requesting or receiving the benefit or detriment of grants or advice from philanthropic, research, scholarly, or government foundations or institutions here or abroad.

Finally, I am indebted to many inquisitive undergraduates and graduate students who, along with my perspicacious friends in the anti-interventionist movement, have bombarded me with questions about the intellectual origins of the Cuban revolution and have forced me to come to grips with the history of that nation's ideological development, its national and international character, and its creative, destructive, repressive, and emancipatory processes.

A radical is no more than this: he who goes to the roots. Let him who fails to arrive at the bottom of things call himself not a radical; nor let him who fails to help other men obtain security and happiness call himself a man.

José Martí

INTRODUCTION

Spanish colonial rule existed in Cuba for over four centuries. Immediately after independence from Spain in 1898, the 750-mile-long Caribbean island came under the political hegemony of the United States, and its middle and upper classes became economically, and to a lesser extent culturally, dependent on its more powerful neighbor 90 miles to the north. Cuba remained in that neocolonial situation until 1959, when it began the process of building a revolution—a phenomenon often spoken about but rarely carried out in Latin America.

Throughout their history Cubans have used the printed word as a weapon in the struggle for liberty, protesting the oppressive acts inflicted, and the myths perpetuated, by Spanish overlords, Yankee entrepreneurs, and native gentry. In the colonial and neo-colonial eras, Cuban politics were marked by administrative corruption, lack of civic accountability, and little sensitivity to the plight of the masses. At the same time, Cuba's literature frequently assumed a polemic quality as writers placed it at the service of society. Cuban intellectuals, especially essayists, imparted pro-gressive, often radical and revolutionary ideas to their disen-chanted countrymen. By the nineteenth century, Cuba's

historically oriented writers who focused on social and political themes, although often an alienated minority, played an important role in the country's intellectual life.

Subsequent chapters show that even during the colonial epoch middle-class Cuban intellectuals identified with the concept of *Cuba Libre* (free Cuba) and searched, sometimes in radical or utopian fashion, for reforms designed to benefit the masses with- out changing the fundamental institutions of society. *Cuba Libre* was later embraced by socialist *pensadores* (thinkers) who believed that changes benefiting most Cubans could be effected only by identifying and analyzing political, economic, and social abuses and working to restructure the basic institutions of society.

Socialist and nonsocialist advocates of *Cuba Libre* have generally believed that social and political progress in the country depended on their ability to communicate with the elites who controlled the island's economy and the masses whom the elites' decisions affected. Historically there has existed in Cuba a working relationship between the economic elites and those who have presided over intellectual activities. Fortunately, even under the harshest of dictatorships some freedom of expression, particularly in the publication of scholarly, politically oriented books and pamphlets, has usually existed in Cuba, where cen- sorship has most often been reserved for lower-level mass pub- lications such as newspapers and fliers. Unlike the situation in the United States, where social and political criticism, both writ- ten and oral, has been a discipline unto itself, in Cuba such commentary became an integral part of the literary world. Cuban volumes frequently integrate poetry, fiction, and fantasy with collections of political speeches and even polemics stress- ing nationalism.

In Cuba, where the indigenous population was killed by the Spanish conquerors, died in forced labor, or was absorbed through miscegenation, writers—in contrast to their colleagues in Bolivia, Mexico, or Peru—have not frequently looked to their

Indian heritage for revolutionary inspiration. Instead, they have emphasized nationalism in their quest for independence. Since the nineteenth century, progressive Cuban writers and thinkers have continuously tried to create a populist following by examining the past to interpret the present, by endeavoring to build a sense of community or *Cubanidad* (Cubanness), and by working to imbue their people with a belief in progress. In so doing they have built rich historical and historiographic traditions.

To gain an audience for their ideas, Cuban thinkers have frequently convened public conferences where they have delivered papers on topics of social and political concern. Cuba's intelligentsia has emphasized the publication of conference papers, the cataloging of public documents and personal archives, and the compilation of the works of essayists. In proportion to its size, Cuba has probably given more attention to the preservation of the history of its thought than any Latin American nation.[1]

Intellectuals

In Cuba, which has little democratic tradition and a history of poor public education, thinkers or intellectuals as a group belong to a revered elite. However, this book deals primarily with only a segment of that elite, one that adheres to radical persuasions. The contemplative, often creative people presented here work with ideas—they analyze, criticize, and theorize. Italian Marxist Antonio Gramsci (1891–1937) would have defined these intellectuals as those who exercise a directive role in society, including managers, bureaucrats, administrators, politicians, and organizers of culture such as journalists, scholars, and artists. In Gramsci's view every major social group creates its own intellectuals, who are "organically" tied to that group. He believed there exist "traditional" intellectuals, tied to older social groups, who exert some ideological power over all groups. As each new social group emerges, he maintained, its organically linked intellectuals strive to conquer ideologically the traditional intellectuals. Thus intellectuals are involved in a continuing dialectical process.[2] Gramsci saw social structures as undergoing perpetual change, and intellectuals as mobile within those structures. At all times, according to him, intellectuals' ideas reflect their connections to social groups. Thus they are not rootless and classless. In Gramscian terms, the Cuban writers with whom subsequent chapters deal are generally incorporated, consciously or otherwise, into the class struggle because of their political roles and attitudes, not their economic status.

Functionalist theorists claim that most intellectuals affiliate in one way or another with the state and tend to become politically moderate or conservative. On the other hand, sociologist Karl Manheim (1893–1947) asserted that intellectuals examine social and political life from diverse points of view and that their values do not express the beliefs of a particular class,[3] a contention Marxists call a delusion. Conservative thinkers often believe that they significantly influence the establishments they support. Liberals frequently depict the intellectual as existing outside the realm of political power and decision making. Radical sociologist C. Wright Mills (1916–62) called the liberal or capitalist intellectual the political creation of a national economy and a nation-state,[4] a person who has some effect on political power and decisions. Mills would also agree that socialist intellectuals, more so than their capitalist counterparts, would adhere to the necessity of blending theory with practice and thus live in less of a power vacuum. Neo-Marxists adhere to the hypothesis that when some intellectuals lose their independence to the capitalist state, they become intellectual wage laborers who struggle to radically alter the structure of the state, even if it employs them. Most of the radical Cuban intellectuals dealt with in this book would concur with the definitions propounded by Gramsci and share the attitudes of Mills, the functionalists, and the neo-Marxists rather than those of the conservatives, Manheim, or the liberals.

Radicals

Throughout this volume the term radical generally refers to socialist and nonsocialist advocates of progressive left-of-center political and social thought. The definition of "radical" has varied over different epochs and the term must be kept in proper historical context. Late seventeenth-century epistemologists used it to refer to those who advocated progress. By the 1790s it was used in England to connote social attitudes. The term radical, per se, rather than radical-reformist, in reference to political action, initially appeared in France shortly after 1830 when the first well-known radical, Etienne Garnier-Pagès, averred that people must struggle against a government that rejects popular sovereignty and does not uphold the freedoms written in the Declaration of the Rights of Man.[5] Radicalism as a political movement probably began during the French Revolution and was promoted in the 1890s by the French syndicalists, who espoused transferring the ownership and control of the means of production not to the state, but to the trade unions.

Nineteenth-century Cuban radicals fought for democracy, a concept considered as subversive then as is the socialism for which some radicals in the United States struggle today. Early Cuban radicals sought to negate privilege, to strike a better balance between the haves and have-nots. Some Cubans who advocated only independence from Spain might have been labeled radical during the nineteenth century, but they were basically conservatives or moderates.

Radicals go beyond espousals of independence or militance. Radicalism entails a quest for major institutional changes, for equality, social justice, better distribution of wealth, and a healthy skepticism toward those who talk about protecting liberties when such a posture constitutes acceptance of the status quo. Radical attitudes, according to disharmony experts, evolve from numerous sources, such as tension, conflict, social contradictions, and incongruence between environment and values.[6]

Radicals usually state their objectives openly, are not fundamentally fanatics or subversives, and frequently prefer peaceful, rather than forcible, means to achieve change. Rarely do they advocate the degree of violence perpetrated by those they seek to overthrow. The radicals in this volume are for the most part intellectuals—rational, open-minded, and well disciplined. They are not social outcasts or angry people venting their frustrations but are psychologically healthy individuals, sensitive to the human condition.

Radicals do not always choose the safe course. They are often courageous, willing to experiment, and prepared to risk failure. Their actions are not necessarily irrelevant to the mainstream of social and political concerns, but they do not always deal with these concerns in conventional fashion. For example, they respond negatively to the "obedience syndrome"—respect for authority or power simply because it exists.

Contrary to common misconceptions, radicals covet stability. They desire strong yet flexible systems that benefit the majority. They possess an idealistic vision of the good life for all. The Cuban radical intellectuals in this book do not always hold the same ideology, but they are bound together by outrage caused by injustice and by a common recognition of their social and political role in society.

Radicals, often in nonconformist ways, seek a unified interpretation of the world, a philosophy that explains society's problems and structural defects and proposes ways to alleviate the former and replace the latter with stronger, more just institutions. They generally possess a well-defined sense of ideology. They believe that humans can reshape society by persuading the powerholders through rational dialogue to change the system, or by engaging in forceful struggle and sometimes by mobilizing the people against the existing order.

Radicals generally can be classified as "hot" or "cold." The "hot" radical sometimes responds to impulse, raw emotions, or romantic visions, might ignore planning, and does not always consider how to involve the masses in the process of societal change. The "cold" radical plans, devises precise strategy, weighs gains against losses, and endeavors to involve a large portion of society in the process of change.[7] Cuba's radical thinkers discussed in this volume fit into the "cold" category.

Cuba's nonsocialist radicals have been willing to have society undergo temporary upheaval, even illegal actions, to reshape traditional institutions. They have not believed in the preservation of the social order, nor have they necessarily advocated the transfer of power from one class to another. With their Marxist colleagues, they have shared a belief in human malleability, opposed imperialism, understood the function of nationalism, contended that humans cannot attain the possible unless they strive for the impossible, and had confidence that their methods and solutions for society's ills would work. The revolutionaries among them have asserted that the odds have been in their favor, and though they have abhorred bloodshed, they have with trepidation accepted the idea that a hundred might die in the immediate battle so that thousands more could live in the future.

The Writer's Approaches

The writers whose thoughts are analyzed on subsequent pages fall into a number of categories. All exhibit some radical traits. Some simply have a populist bent, others pronounce themselves anticapitalists. A few are utopians or utopian-socialists. Some of them use Marxist tools of analysis merely as heuristic devices, others openly proclaim their adherence to Marxism. Some advocate criticism and moral appeals to man rather than revolution, others take a more dynamic and scientific approach to institutional change—one predicated upon history. Like Marx, the latter espouse determinism, believing it is possible to prove that the existing forces in society will ultimately produce socialism.

Historical studies of ideas usually take one of two approaches. The internal approach analyzes ideas apart from questions of social origin and assumes that ideas have their own lives and do not fit a particular scheme. The external approach traces the relation of ideas to events rather than to each other. Proponents of external analysis see ideas as catalysts for change. Cuba's Marxists disagree with the internal approach, for it usually rejects the proposition that ideas refer to the material facets of human experience, and without reference to material conditions ideas are intangibles and do not fit into a scientific design of history.[8]

The Marxist thinkers concur with the German master that "to be radical is to grasp things by the root. But for man the root is man himself."[9] Some of them believe that theory can capture the masses only through the vehicle of a political party. To them the party must guide the political revolution, which is a precondition for social revolution. They agree with political scientist Richard Fagen that "the transformation of Cuban man into revolutionary man is at the heart of Cuban radicalism."[10]

However, Cuban Marxists do not all think alike. This book deals with Marxists with diverse ideas: it adheres to no ironclad definition of Marxism, often uses the term as a synonym for socialism and does not delve into sectarian arguments over who constitutes the true Marxist. The Marxist thinkers discussed herein all indict capitalism, think dialectically, and espouse socialism, but they represent no single variant within Marxist philosophy. For the most part, they fall into two categories designated by C. Wright Mills: (1) "sophisticated" Marxists, for whom Marxism constitutes a model of society, who shape Marxist ideas to fit new situations and locate Marxist answers for everything, and whose rigidity at times weakens their analyses and substitutes dogmatism for reflection and investigation; and (2) "plain" Marxists who, like Karl Marx, work openly and flexibly, view Marx's ideas as applicable to contemporary situations, but reject forcing realities to conform to immutable rules.[11]

Among intellectuals two basic types of thought exist. One examines our knowledge of the world from the perspective of natural and physical science. The other treats the problems that arise from human situations. The Cuban writers analyzed in this book fall into the second category. Most are humanists who seek to comprehend how man can utilize his potential and overcome his vulnerabilities in order to gain greater control of the world. Like their classical and Renaissance predecessors, the Cubans believe in human advancement. They want to serve people, not academic disciplines. They are not impartial arbiters who rationalize their roles as being above their society. They do not pursue thought for its own sake.

Most of the Cuban writers discussed here have not been overconcerned with their own social standing. Radicals learn rather rapidly about the difficulties of maintaining personal status. They understand that writers who care primarily about their positions generally are more interested in adding to, or slightly modifying, the existing corpus of knowledge than in changing it radically or creating a new one. Non-Marxist Cuban intellectuals who study and pursue radical and revolutionary objectives are idealists for whom thought takes precedence over material reality, while their socialist counterparts regard material reality as more important than ideas. Both groups reject metaphysical analysis of rebellion in favor of historical analysis; but they also know that historical knowledge cannot be complete. They subscribe to the almost universal Latin American concept of humanity moving toward social justice through radical reform or revolution.

To understand the potential for revolution, Cuba's radical *pensadores* strive to know how power works in society and to comprehend the relation of individual liberty to central authority and the state's capacity for social control. They search for the causes of despotism and for ways to overcome it. They endeavor to define and implement legitimate government in a humane fashion. While looking for explanations for the copious problems noted above, as well as for the multifarious contradictions found in Cuban society, the nation's radical thinkers remain aware that objectivity is a property of methodology, which always evolves from an ideological framework.

Cuba's radical thinkers attempt to interpret social reality, but their respective levels of analysis differ. They all examine the facts and evaluate causal connections, and the most profound among them deal with abstract thought and propound new ideas. In unique ways they are all political beings with an activist bent. Cuba's history compels them to study colonialism and then to inveigh against it and its ramifications. Just as Shakespeare used "Caliban" as an anagram for cannibal, Cuba's radical *pensadores* have used "Caliban" as an analogy for colonialism and its perpetrators. Theirs is often referred to as the history and culture of Caliban.[12]

The Author's Approach

Leon Trotsky once wrote of the inability of Anglo-Saxons to understand a revolutionary situation. His words accurately depict the current attitude of most United States citizens with regard to the Cuban revolution led by Fidel Castro. This book is designed to help explain that revolution by tracing the country's radical thought from its origins through the Castro era. It is an examination of various ideas expressed by Cuba's most prolific

authors of radical books and essays. I touch upon the foundations built by the precursors of radical thought in Cuba, then
emphasize the thinking of the nation's writers who represent
major radical points of view. Many students of Cuban thought
will be disappointed because I have chosen to ignore some
thinkers or placed too little or too much stress on the works of
others. Time and space permitting, a full biography could be
written on each *pensador* whose ideas I mention prominently.

Here I endeavor to show how the thoughts of Cuban radicals
have related to and affected each other. All writing has a political dimension, but this book deals primarily with works specifically in the fields of political and social analysis or theory and
political economy. With the knowledge that it is easier to attack
a thinker's reputation than to discuss his or her ideas, I opt for
the latter and try to emphasize the positive contributions of
Cuba's radical *pensadores*. Fear of radical ideas often causes
people to try to discredit those who create them. This destructive
process occurs frequently in the works on Cuba written recently
in the United States by those who too loudly herald their "value-
free" analysis while simultaneously making subtle ideological
judgments. Unlike them, I acknowledge that my "objectivity"
operates out of nonsectarian socialist and anti-imperialist
perspectives.

Rather than hold out false promises, it might be well to note
briefly what this volume does not contain. Those who seek a
handbook on revolutionary tactics or strategy will find only
cursory allusions to them here. This book explores some of the
thinking of those in power in Cuba since 1959, but it is not a
treatise on contemporary affairs. It does not deal with the day-
to-day mechanics of the Cuban revolution. For example, it is
more likely to delve into abstract theory about material incentives than into the practical aspects of how the revolution han-
dles them.

Cuba has a rich tradition of radical thought expressed in

literature, literary criticism, and poetry. This book gives little or no space to the social commentators and political activists who primarily have used or use those media. Thus the ideas of radicals such as the world-renowned novelist and savant Alejo Carpentier or the poet and "national treasure" Nicolás Guillén are virtually excluded, as are those of the noted chroniclers of Cuban literary thought Roberto Fernández Retamar and José Antonio Portuondo. Nevertheless, the writings of these people of letters have contributed enormously to my understanding of Cuban radical thought.

The following pages touch ever so lightly on organized politics and on political parties and their intrigues. They do not detail circumstances surrounding writers who have fallen out of favor with the revolutionary government. The book does not debate the merits of Cuba's communist, socialist, or anarchist organizations, nor does it criticize non-Cuban seminal thinkers such as Marx and Lenin. Rather, it attempts to explain the contributions of these people to Cuban political groups and the ways the respective organizations' theoreticians have extrapolated from foreigners' ideas in order to contribute to the sociology of knowledge.

This book examines how and what Cuban radicals have thought about their nation's protracted struggle for independence. It looks at each thinker's mode of analysis, position on the class struggle, ideas on reform or revolution, and search for community. It investigates each *pensador*'s views of the state and power and his relation to the means of production and to social and workers' movements, beliefs about ethics, morality, religion, social mobility and control, aesthetics, and the quality of life. Also scrutinized are the thinker's unusual national and international postures, including views on Cuban–United States relations, his role in Cuba's intellectual life, how or whether his ideas were implemented, whether they endured, and their historical significance.

In the course of conveying the ideas of Cuba's radical writers, I have tried to retain, where possible, the unique qualities of their language and thoughts and to characterize the ideological climate of the eras in which they lived and worked. The observant reader can easily separate the ideas and opinions of Cuba's *pensadores* from my comments upon them. The attitudes and perspectives of Cuban radicals and progressives set the tone for the following chapters.

Ignorance is the agent
of tyranny.

Félix Varela y Morales

CHAPTER 1

The Intellectual Precursors of Cuban Radicalism

During its long colonial rule, Spain left its economic and cultural
imprint on Cuba. Through the corrupt Spanish administrative
system a select few prospered, particularly the oligarchy that
controlled the island's sugar mills and estates. Under the dominance of the plantation economy no strong manufacturing sector
emerged, and the small local capitalist sector, fearful of the
potential strength of a growing working class, maintained an
alliance with, and subservience to, foreign—especially sugar—
interests.[1] Nevertheless, between 1492 and 1898 a spirit of
progress, sometimes predicated on nationalism, grew among
the members of the island's tiny intelligentsia, who contributed
significantly to the development of Cuban culture.

Cuba's first native literature appeared in 1608—a series of
sonnets by Silvestre de Balboa Troya y Quesada. Intellectual
ferment, in the form of political and social thought, did not
emerge in Cuba until the eighteenth century. It did so as a result
of native and European revolutionary ideas. Some Cuban intellectuals, whose attitudes belied their upper-class and middle-

class origins and ties, began to espouse independence or some type of separation from Spain. Those who substituted Enlightenment rationalism for Spanish thought predicated on mysticism or the teachings of the church found themselves censored and ostracized or exiled.

Pope Innocent XII authorized the Dominicans to establish a university in Havana in 1721, and the following year the governing body of the Spanish colonies, the Council of the Indies, approved the project. While preparations were being made for creating the university, in 1723 private printing was introduced in Havana. This made it easier for native writers to have their works published, which occurred with greater frequency after 1728 when the University of Havana opened.

The university, dominated by the Scholastic philosophy of the day and primarily designed to train priests, taught Thomist theology, canon and civil law, Aristotelian thought, and foreign languages. Although it had a greater interest in communicating dogma than in generating ideas, through the efforts of the more liberal priests it branched out into diverse and less rigid areas of thought.

Freemasonry entered Cuba in 1762 and brought with it French Enlightenment ideas of sweeping social change and intellectual reform. At that time Cubans began to write non-analytic histories. The island's first newspapers *La Gazeta* (The Gazette) and *El Pensador* (The Thinker) appeared in 1764.[2] Soon a few Cuban intellectuals broke with Thomist philosophy and medieval Scholasticism in favor of French rationalism, which they thought provided a more direct means of attaining technological growth and political independence. Also, Jean-Jacques Rousseau's concept of the natural virtue of prelapsarian man became popular among Cuba's radical intellectual elite. They believed that Rousseau's idea of man's natural state of goodness enabled them to retain Christian principles and yet reject the church.[3]

By the last decade of the eighteenth century Cuba had witnessed a slave insurrection in nearby Haiti, sampled new intellectual currents, and undergone an economic transformation.
There existed large landholdings, enormous profits, an ever-
present quest for better marketing, and a huge cheap labor
force. Agribusiness, with sugar as its anchor, took hold in Cuba
and expanded for over four decades, a period of vast personal
capital formation in a colony whose commerce and industry
were attuned to an export-oriented economy.[4] At this time Cuba
provided no political or civil liberties or economic security for
most of its inhabitants.

With the growth of personal fortunes and material opulence
came Cuba's first great awakening in the area of political,
social, economic, and scientific change. Men such as economist
and statesman Francisco Arango y Parreño, physician and scientist Tomás Romay, philosopher José Agustín Caballero, and
poet Manuel de Zequeira introduced a new era of philosophical
thought to the island.[5] This era was formally launched in 1793
when a group of reform-minded Cuban intellectuals established
the Sociedad Económica de Amigos del País (the Economic
Society) to promote good teaching, trade, agriculture, science,
literature, the fine arts, and sound government.

The early nineteenth century witnessed the growth of independence movements in most of Latin America. Cuba, though
cognizant of events elsewhere, remained *la isla siempre leal* (the
ever-faithful island or colony). When Napoleon Bonaparte
invaded and took over the Iberian Peninsula in 1807 and 1808,
the rest of Latin America prepared to fight for its freedom from
the mother country, but little mass support for independence
existed in Cuba, where the *criollo* (native white) elites hesitated
to engage in a rebellion that might end up controlled by the
island's large black slave population.

A century of intellectual emancipation and evolution of social
conscience in literature preceded political independence in

Cuba. The island's outstanding thinkers of the first half of the nineteenth century, José Agustín Caballero, Félix Varela y Morales, José Antonio Saco, and José de la Luz y Caballero strengthened the trend toward examining the political role of the individual in society. In their writings about human rights, reform, autonomy, and independence, they expressed the idea that freedom meant more than just breaking political ties to Spain. They searched for more scientific and precise language and for new methods and social ideologies to use in political writing. They made their readers aware of the class divisions in Cuba, the effects of economic relations in a predominantly slave society, and in embryonic fashion they began to depict Cuba in terms of imperialism, as a satellite of Spain.

Cuba's early nineteenth-century thinkers, usually lawyers, liberal priests, and university students, for the most part discussed the quest for nationhood with each other. Unlike what happened elsewhere in Latin America, in Cuba no liberal versus conservative debate attracted the masses. Very few workers were drawn to the ideas of a handful of native labor-oriented writers. Poems, stories, essays, polemics, and speeches were generally read and discussed only by the educated men who frequented the island's few bookshops, coffeehouses, and literary and political clubs.

Liberal thought, expressed as resistance to absolutism, began to appear among these intellectual elites during the 1820s. Inspired by the Colombian independence movement led by Simón Bolívar, Francisco Lemus, a Cuban who had served with "The Liberator," organized in 1823 the Rayos y Soles de Bolívar (Sun and Rays of Bolívar) a secret society advocating rebellion against Spain and the establishment of the Republic of Cubanacán. Assisted by a few Mexican freedom fighters, the group set up cells in Masonic lodges throughout Cuba. Under the motto "Independence or Death," the organization appealed to students and poor whites, who were urged to unite with slave and free blacks to fight against Spain. Although the Spanish captured Lemus, his abortive conspiracy aroused the consciousness of a small portion of Cuba's previously apolitical population.

Philosophically oriented polemics began to appear with regularity in Cuba during the mid-1820s. Thinkers started to use Cartesian methodology, with its emphasis on mathematical certitude and radical doubt, to examine the island's social problems and in their condemnations of colonial absolutism[6] and the exploitation of labor. The island's social critics began occasionally to galvanize some of the laboring masses into action. For example, in 1829 the Gremios de Mareantes y Pescadores (Society of Sailors and Fishermen), a mutual help and beneficial society, was founded in Havana. An embryonic labor movement gradually evolved in Cuba.

By 1830 young liberal thinkers, influenced by the successful independence movements of Latin America, explored ways to liberate Cuba. Many of them believed that the United States opposed this and preferred the stability of Spanish colonialism to the potential instability of a Caribbean region composed of independent nations. Talk frequently arose in intellectual circles about the annexation of Cuba by the United States, which some Cuban writers viewed as a way of fostering the progressive goals of the Economic Society. Others, most notably the humanist poet and literary critic Domingo del Monte y Aponte, pointed out that life under a United States protectorate would be no better than under Spain. The *Revista Bimestre Cubana* (Bimonthly Cuban Magazine), published between 1831 and 1834 under the auspices of Cuba's Economic Society and directed by Mariano Cubí and José Antonio Saco, discussed the annexation question and helped sow the seeds of independence, as did the liberal Club de los Habaneros (Club of Havanans), which also organized, in 1837, a movement to end slavery.[7]

Cuban thinkers interested in links between the island's plantation system and its political administration inaugurated a professorship at the University of Havana in 1840 in the field of political economy, but those who held it made few immediate creative contributions. Two years later the university was secularized and became a source of nationalist sentiment and a distribution point for political polemics with a historical orientation.

Radical ideas of a homegrown variety developed among Cuba's thinkers by midcentury, but the philosophies of Europe's 1848 revolutions barely touched the island. Mutual aid and professional societies sprang up throughout the colony during the 1840s, slowly laying foundations for future trade unions. Although the ideas of Karl Marx about Spanish colonialism and potential United States imperialism were virtually unknown in Cuba, the island's *pensadores* understood the expansionist tendencies of the United States as expressed in its 1853 Ostend Manifesto, which stated that the United States would eventually either purchase Cuba or take it by force.

Spanish tolerance between 1862 and 1867 permitted Cuban intellectuals more latitude to speak out on behalf of the interests of their fellow colonists. The newspaper *El Siglo* (The Century) appeared in 1862, stressing political, literary, and economic themes and containing some articles by writers with radical views. Radical thought now reached Cuba through a few Spanish anarchosyndicalist laborers who had fled the mother country in search of a better life. A tiny core of them, mostly from Catalonia, a region with strong radical traditions, believed in the necessity and inevitability of class struggle and worker/employer conflict. They remained an influential part of Cuba's labor movement, particularly in the tobacco industry, until the emergence of the Communist party in the 1930s.[8]

While the anarchosyndicalists struggled to make their ideology known, the ideas of the First International of Labor, for which Marx wrote the declaration of principles, were spread to Cuba by a few Argentine intellectuals.[9] Anarchosyndicalist and Marxist thought inspired Cuban writers such as poet and dramatist Alfredo Torroella (1845–79) to write about the plight of the proletariat, a group he believed viewed the philanthropy and compassion of the bourgeoisie as disingenuous.[10] Torroella's ideas dovetailed nicely with the ideas of the popular *costumbrista* (followers of custom) school of literature, whose novels and short stories depicted, through thinly disguised satire, revolutionary life in early nineteenth-century Cuba and often severely criticized the Spanish upper classes.

Labor union activities increased rapidly in Cuba about 1865, especially among tobacco workers. In 1865 anarchosyndicalist intellectuals Saturino Martínez and José de Jesús Márquez founded *La Aurora* (The Dawn), Cuba's first workers' periodical with a social program. The newspaper, which lasted until 1868, promoted a fraternal type of mutual aid for tobacco workers, explained workers' grievances in easily understood socialist-humanist terms, and advocated trade unionism and a mild form of the anarchist philosophy of the Russian revolutionary Mikhail Bakunin (1814–76). The newspaper also initiated a dialogue between the tobacco growers and their employees and helped improve Cuba's "lector system" whereby artisans in tobacco factories and shops chose literature and paid someone to read it to them while they worked. This system, still used to educate Cuban workers, spread many radical, utopian, and reformist ideas.[11]

The efforts of *La Aurora* led to the founding of the Asociación de Tabaqueros de la Habana (Tobacco Workers' Society of Havana) in 1866, which almost immediately organized Havana's first tobacco workers' strike. Within two years an insurrection against the Spanish, the Ten Years War (1868–78), broke out in Cuba. The Tobacco Workers' Society's local labor struggles came to an abrupt halt. Many tobacco workers moved to Tampa and Key West, Florida, or to New York City, and the movement did not regenerate in Cuba until 1884.[12]

Although new strains of radical thought and philosophy had entered Cuba by the beginning of the Ten Years War, national emancipation remained uppermost in the minds of most Cuban *pensadores*. In their quest for freedom from Spain, Cuban thinkers sought less intellectual guidance from Europe than had their Latin American counterparts a half-century earlier. Three positions dominated the thinking of Cuba's independence seekers. The more traditional *pensadores* favored autonomy from Spain through peaceful evolution. The autonomists believed that Cuba could exist under its own constitution, but with ties to Spain much like those between Canada and Great Britain.[13] Some thinkers favored annexation to the United States. Others advocated winning complete political independence from Spain through what they called revolutionary means. This more radical contingent of political philosophers generally numbered among its ranks those who viewed slavery as a form of class discrimination, which they hoped to abolish along with ties to Spain.

José Agustín Caballero (1762–1825)

Father José Agustín Caballero profoundly influenced the Cuban tradition of political philosophy, which led to the intellectual struggle for emancipation from Spain. Caballero, who held a doctor of theology degree, taught and directed Cuba's San Carlos Seminary, where he became well known for his *Philosophia electiva* (1797) (Elective Philosophy) a treatise on logic written in Latin. An advocate of greater self-government for the island, he also gained considerable recognition by presenting, in 1810, a quasi-autonomist position to Spain's Cortes of Cadíz. But it was as a teacher, writer, and thinker rather than as an emancipator that he, a moderate reformer, contributed to the foundations of radical thought upon which Cuba's *pensadores* built.

A disciple of Descartes' rationalism, Caballero was a product of the European Enlightenment. He strove to develop a method of understanding the causes of human problems. In so doing, during a period of commercial capitalist resurgence he propagated the materialist ideas of Etienne Bonnot de Condillac and John Locke's belief that understanding external and internal sensations comes from reflection that permits one to begin to comprehend the human conscience. He also supported the new scientific and analytical thinking of Francis Bacon and Isaac Newton.

Caballero taught that thought should not be slave to a system and urged his students and colleagues to break with Scholasticism, which dominated higher learning in Cuba. He defied the church and its Scholastic teaching methods, referred to them as sterile, and believed they retarded the progress of the arts and sciences.[14] In his *Memoria* (1795) he advocated greater liberty for university teachers[15] and broader, more probing techniques of inquiry, and he stressed that seminal thinkers such as Galileo and Bacon had broken from Scholasticism.[16] His efforts to supplant that system with rationalism and electicism, which he saw as impartial means of seeking the truth, were considered radical for his day, although on purely political matters his views were considered quite conventional and sometimes rather conservative. Caballero emphasized that new methods of thought had been accepted all over Europe, that rationalism in particular had given rise to major advances in physics and mathematics and was an extremely useful tool to help locate answers to social questions. To him scholarly skepticism also contributed significantly to progress, since it fostered new avenues of approach and thereby aided the expansion of knowledge.

He put his teaching and his exceptional ability as an orator at the disposal of Cuba's Patriotic Society in order to bring his country modernity, in terms of new trends in philosophy. His writing displayed a clear conception of the historical process and the development of culture in Cuba. He explained how the island fit into the pattern of New World discovery and showed the economic, social and political reasons behind the Spanish imperial system. He contributed enormously to the erosion of the colonial mentality of exploitation perpetuated by the crown and its agents and to its replacement by *Cubanidad* (Cubanness)—a state of consciousness connoting a dedication to collective betterment.[17]

Among Caballero's many students were three outstanding *pensadores*—his nephew José de la Luz y Caballero, José Antonio Saco, and Félix Varela—who represented the most perceptive thinking in Cuba and aroused a considerable amount of the class consciousness in their respective epochs. Caballero's eloquent pleas for more flexible political and social philosophies in Cuba influenced and encouraged subsequent generations of thinkers, many of them radicals. He passed his mantel as a teacher and philosopher on through his distinguished students to Diego Vicente Tejera, whose ideas are examined in the next chapter and who subsequently bridged the gap between nineteenth- and twentieth-century Cuba and between capitalist and socialist radical thought.

Félix Varela y Morales (1787–1853)

Philosopher, politician, and priest Félix Varela gained a greater reputation than José Caballero, under whom he earned a bachelor of arts degree at the San Carlos Seminary. A Havana-born son of a soldier, Varela adopted his mentor's desire to distinguish between philosophical doctrines and church dogma and his penchant for Descartes's rationalism.[18] He too sought to apply European ideas to Cuba, and he devoted his life to reflection, the development of philosophy, and the application of it to existing problems. He pursued three basic philosophical objectives: to move away from the genuflection and fantasy of medieval thought; to delve deeply into the realm of reason; and to change the ways the natural and physical sciences were taught in order to attain the well-being of humanity.[19]

Using elegant prose, Varela wrote numerous books, often in Latin. His best-known work, the three-volume *Lecciones de filosofía* (1818–19) (Philosophy Lessons), deals with ethics, logic, natural philosophy, chemistry, and metaphysics. It has stood the test of time and was republished in Cuba in 1961.[20] His writings, as well as his excellent orations, were filled with classical allusions and marked by a sense of humor, and they displayed the elasticity of mind one might expect from a successful practitioner of the eclecticism of French philosopher Victor Cousin, Cartesian thought, and scientific sensualism.

Varela read, and for the most part rejected, the work of Immanuel Kant, the founder of critical or transcendental idealism, for whom practical knowledge was more important than theory, in favor of the methods of Locke, Condillac, and Caballero. He followed Caballero's views and championed social Christian doctrine, criticized religious institutions and Thomist thought, and pointed out the errors of Scholasticism, with its dependence on dogma and theology. He and Caballero also followed aspects of Jeremy Bentham's utilitarianism that purported to create a conscience oriented to social well-being.[21]

Varela's political and social thought and postures changed and expanded over time. For example, soon after receiving the chair of philosophy at the San Carlos Seminary, he defended Spain's new liberal constitution of 1812. He then created a minor uproar in academic and church circles by defying classical tradition and teaching in Spanish rather than Latin.

After absorbing some of the independence ideas flowing southward from the United States, in 1816 he joined the Sociedad Económica de Amigos del País (The Economic Society), a center of intellectual discourse that agitated for political liberalization, Cuban autonomy, and the abolition of slavery.[22]

Varela initiated the teaching of politics in Cuba at the San Carlos Seminary in 1820, an act that struck fear into the minds of those in power, who did not relish scrutiny of how they used and abused their position.[23] He examined the political theory operating in Cuba and the relationship of the metropolis (Spain) to its satellite (Cuba), called that relationship arbitrary and detrimental to constitutional rights, and asserted that people deserved guarantees of freedom and social justice.[24] At the San Carlos Seminary and at the University of Havana, Varela's philosophy courses nourished the progressive ideas of Europe within a framework of Cuba's Catholic and Spanish culture. For a decade (1812–22) he asserted vigorously, in conferences sponsored by the Economic Society, that every *pensador* had the right to reevaluate the philosophy of the past and make it more relevant to the present. To him faith was not blind obedience to someone else's concepts but what one learned about humanity from one's own studies.[25]

During the early 1820s Varela served as a Cuban delegate to the Spanish Cortes or Parliament, where he supported ties to Spain and stressed the need for legislation to eliminate slavery in Cuba while compensating the slaveholders for their losses, a move he felt was necessary to ensure public order.[26] He anticipated replacing slavery with other forms of production and vehemently demanded reforms in the colonial system. By 1823 Varela was dissatisfied with the possibilities of reform within the Spanish empire and presented the case for Cuban independence to the Cortes.

The courageous priest fled from the Spanish authorities to

the United States, where he lived the rest of his life, helping to launch a tradition of Cuban intellectuals writing from exile. While serving a parish in New York City, Varela began, in 1824, to publish a newspaper, *El Habanero* (The Havanan), dedicated to the independence of Cuba. For the two years of its existence the paper was regularly smuggled into his country. With José Antonio Saco, Varela edited the review *El Mensajero Semanal* (The Weekly Messenger). He also became enamored of the ideas of Thomas Jefferson and translated his *Parliamentary Manual* into Spanish. Varela and his associates in exile opposed Spain, considered themselves liberals, and believed it was their duty to promulgate ideas on liberty and human dignity. They also shared a sense of commonality with the independent American states, which had successfully broken with European mother countries, and lamented because though Spain had relinquished control over its other colonies in Latin America it retained Cuba and Puerto Rico.[27]

Father Varela maintained that freedom was part of the Latin American ethos and inextinguishable.[28] He understood the independence movements of Colombia, Mexico, and Buenos Aires but saw no need for Cuba to ally formally with other Latin American states to attain independence.[29] He also disdained ties to the United States for purposes of annexation or sovereignty.[30] He proclaimed the right of his people to rebel—to destroy, preferably without bloodshed, the government that prevented national progress, liberty, and justice.

Varela interpreted the Spanish constitution and found the division of powers unequal, since the judiciary had more strength than the legislature that represented the people.[31] He concluded that no political equilibrium existed because the Spanish monarchy had veto power over laws, which contravened the idea of the legislature as representing the national interest.[32] Following the thinking of Montesquieu, he claimed that the citizenry should influence the laws,[33] and that this could best be accomplished by maintaining a separation of powers. He argued that Spain violated the social contract—that the colonial state abridged individual rights. To him, ideally, government represented sovereignty but did not own people or property. He claimed that only people, not governments, have rights.

Varela viewed Cuba as a potential mercantile or trade center because of its strategic position vis-à-vis North, Central, and South America, the Atlantic Ocean, the Caribbean Sea, and the Gulf of Mexico. However, he reasoned that Cuba had failed to progress because it lacked capital and the strength to expand and because Spain could not guarantee commerce for the island.[34] He railed against unthinking patriotism or irrational loyalty to the far-removed, uncaring Spanish crown. In his liberal view, Spain held no commitment to Cuba's well-being, and Cuban society was divided into two classes. One had an international outlook and sought prosperity for its own sake. The other was composed of patriots who sought prosperity for Cuba.[35]

Varela's thought has had considerable impact on the intellectual and political life of Cuba. He represented points of departure for an ideological struggle, for freedom in the field of philosophy, and for *pensadores* working for political change on a practical level. He began the long process of building an independent spirit in the country.[36] The first of Cuba's revolutionary intellectuals, Varela opened up the island to modern ideology, which he claimed had two major thrusts. The first originates and deals with "our" ideas. The second is logic, which shows the defects in "our" thinking.[37] He stressed the need for Cubans to develop their intellect in order to understand and eliminate the defects in their thinking. He accentuated the necessity of clearly expressing a complete analysis of political and social problems and tried to reconcile such analyses with the teachings of the church, thereby interpreting the latter pragmatically.[38]

He believed that intellectuals have a responsibility to involve themselves in national matters, to direct and teach others. By engaging in dynamic progressive endeavors for good govern- ment, he served as a major link between philosophical thought and political thought and between social action and national liberation. In paving the way for Cuba's independence, he rejected the intervention of foreigners in Cuban affairs. Before José Martí, he was the apostle of *Cubanidad.* He represented the Cuban bourgeoisie's quest for independence, a position he passed on to Martí.

He imparted to the Cuban people a tripartite explanation of equality. For Varela and subsequent generations of Cuban thinkers, natural equality meant that the same principles guide all people; social equality connoted that all have the right to the same share of life's benefits; and legal equality signified that all must abide by the same laws and penalties.[39] He proclaimed the right to work and to own what one produced by his labor,[40] and he noted that changes in the relations of production were essential to Cuba's freedom in the individual as well as the col- lective sense.[41] Subsequent pages reveal that his thoughts pre- saged those of Cuba's independence and radical revolutionary movements, which strove to break ties to Spain during the nine- teenth century and to the Spanish worldview in the twentieth century.

José Antonio Saco (1797–1879)

Varela's student and lay successor to the chair of philosophy at the San Carlos Seminary, José Antonio Saco evoked consider- able controversy as a political activist and as a writer. Scholars have always placed him in the pantheon of Cuban *pensadores* but have not been able to agree upon where he belongs on the ideological spectrum. He gained a reputation for his clearly written, intensely critical, and sometimes brilliant pamphlets and books. He considered himself a perpetual student of life, and he wrote on pedagogy, Spanish despotism, slavery, economics, culture, and Cuban relations with the United States.

Early in life he chose to serve Cuba rather than attain personal wealth and power. In 1824, after being forced into exile by the Spanish authorities, Saco was reunited with Varela in the United States, where they published *El Mensajero Semana*. In 1836 he was elected (in absentia) deputy from Santiago de Cuba to the Spanish Cortes. When that body refused to seat him, he protested furiously, thereby widening the conflict between Spain and Cuba and accelerating the termination of Cuban representation in the mother country.

Following his unpleasant reception in Madrid, Saco departed for France, where he pursued a contemplative life, studying colonial structures, examining the roots of slavery, and exploring the possibilities for political reform in Cuba.[42] He then began to write his famous, and basically uncritical, multivolume *Historia de la esclavitud desde los tiempos más remotos hasta nuestros días* (1875–92) (History of Slavery from the Past to the Present), with the following basic objectives: to suppress African slave traffic and prevent racial conflict; to promote white immigration to Cuba as an agent of civilization, which he believed would bring economic and political order; to eliminate Spanish domination of Cuba and the exploitation of the colony's wealth for the benefit of the privileged classes; to encourage Cubans to gradually take control over their own moral and economic development; and to prevent United States annexation of Cuba.[43]

Saco aroused the passions of his countrymen and the Spanish over the issues of slavery and political rights. He cited two types of slaves in colonial Cuba, one black and subservient to the plantation owners, the other white and subordinate to Spain. In his opinion those enslaved were unworthy of political rights.

Both the plantation owners and the Spanish government persecuted him for his views, especially after he advocated the abolition of the slave trade, which would extinguish huge investments in slave property. He called the fears of bankruptcy unfounded and claimed that whites, particularly those born in Cuba, could work the plantations and withstand the tropical heat and diseases. He concluded that, considering slave mortality and maintenance costs, white labor would be less expensive.[44] Saco also wrote a book on Indian slavery in the New World[45] and a volume on the suppression of slave traffic in Cuba.[46] Although he did not develop even a quasi-scientific socioeconomic perspective on slavery, he started a great historical tradition of Cubans writing about slavery, which enabled subsequent generations of scholars to analyze its effects upon the island's political, social, and economic life. In his multivolume work he surveyed slavery from its Egyptian origins to the nineteenth century, placed slavery in a world context, and explained, with great erudition, its relation to Spanish colonialism.[47] He demonstrated how Cuba's wealthy planter class used force, and the threat of it, to maintain social order and political stability, and he protested against the horrible methods, including torture, that the government used to prevent slaves from organizing and rebelling.

Saco represented this planter class, which desired a white Cuba; for him the abolition of the slave trade was a way to rid the island of blacks. Historian Franklin Knight calls him a racist who upheld the apartheid policy of Cuba's governors. Saco undoubtedly feared black dominance and envisioned white immigration, for which he lobbied successfully, as the answer to future progress in Cuba.[48] He was an abolitionist for unconventional reasons. He believed that Cuban nationality was embodied in Caucasian Cubans, and he even advocated segregated occupations. For example, though we do not know whether he believed in the "Africans have rhythm" myth, he thought fields such as music should be set aside for blacks. While he saw slavery as a social menace, he was narrow-minded and even feared having to enlist the aid of black Cubans in an independence movement.[49] He realized that Cuba's white landowners were a small minority and that a rebellion by them against Spain might foster a racial insurrection like the one that had led to a black takeover in Haiti during the 1790s. Though the Cuban aristocracy and Saco disliked Spanish control, they preferred it to black rule. Spain, for a long time, reasoned that if it could keep whites numerically inferior to blacks, it would retain the loyalty of the whites.[50]

Saco's writings illustrated, often indirectly, the rigidity of the Spanish government in Cuba as well as that of the dominant planter class, which contributed to the island's authoritarian tradition and diminished the likelihood of its autonomy or independence.

In the *Revista Bimestre Cubana*, which he directed, Saco analyzed the possibilities for Cuban economic, political, and cultural control over the island. In *Paralelo entre la isla de Cuba y algunas colonias inglesas* (1837) (Parallels between the Island of Cuba and Some English Colonies), he compared the administration of Cuba by Spain to that of Canada by Great Britain and criticized Spain's belief that Cuba fared well under its dominion.[51] In *Ideas sobre la incorporación de Cuba a los Estados Unidos* (1848) (Ideas about Incorporating Cuba into the United States), Saco argued that such a move would destroy Latin culture and replace it with one of Anglo-Saxon origin— that Cuba would lose its individuality and immortality.[52] This piece constituted a brilliant indictment of cultural imperialism, though Saco never used that expression.

He viewed annexation as a change in masters, and he disliked the concept of the "mother nation" and "daughter nation."[53]

He doubted the sincerity of the United States and thought that Cuba could best prosper in a position of equality within the Spanish empire. Saco proposed liberating Cuba from intellectual subordination to Spain before moving for political independence. He contended that the island's problems emanated primarily from an educational system that disregarded individual freedom and looked upon manual work as fit only for the dregs of society. He argued that in such a state political independence would not change the social situation, and that an uneducated independent Cuba would become subordinate to more progressive countries. He maintained that Cuba initially had to learn how to be free.[54] In theory, he took a step toward elevating the intellectual level of Cuba, thereby providing the genesis of more radical ideas to follow.

Saco wanted to unify Cuba and build its national identity into a political base for an independence movement. He stated that revolution was premature, physically impossible, and suicidal at the time but a grand ideal for the future.[55] He viewed the Ten Years War as a necessary preliminary step toward independence, which he believed would ultimately be granted under terms established by Spain.

Despite his realistic assessment of Cuban society, one cannot completely categorize Saco's thought, which political scientist Gordon Lewis characterizes as pervaded by a tone of "bourgeois class elitism and a vulgar social Darwinism."[56] Saco championed criollo aspirations for autonomy, independence, and justice for Cuba and vehemently opposed the ideas of the dominant *peninsulares* (ruling whites born in Spain). He made many radical departures in thought for his day. He opposed Scholasticism, as did Caballero and Varela, but in terms of his overall political and social philosophy he was at best a nineteenth-century liberal. He is clearly a precursor of Martí, with whom he shared humanistic concerns and a vision of a better

Cuba. Like Martí, he pointed out that the interests of Cuba had always been sacrificed in the quest for power and riches by individuals, classes, and businesses. In this vein ¿Hay en Cuba patriotismo? (Is There Patriotism in Cuba?), published in 1862, epitomized his defense of Cuban nationalism.[57]

Although fully aware of the power of the polemic, Saco also valued critical analysis. He represented a new level in political intensity among Cuban writers. He used historical forces and ideas to work toward an idealized set of circumstances for Cuba. He displayed great concern for community progress and the evolution of modern institutions within the context of Cuban culture. He understood, but did not derogate, Cuba's class system—one based on race. His work conveyed familiarity with, but no scientific analysis of, Cuba's relations of production— how they affected international commerce and how they led to conflict. He displayed interest in the plight of some white Cuban workers, and his writings constitute an informal history of labor on the island. In a unique fashion, he applied the Protestant work ethic to Cuba and adapted it to a Catholic society.[58]

While in his native land and also from exile, where he spent most of his life, he nurtured a revolution in Cuban customs and ideas, one based on education as the solution for social ills. Although many of his ideas are retrograde by late twentieth-century standards, his critiques of Cuban colonial society have been deemed by the revolutionary Castro government valuable enough to republish and use in its schools.

José de la Luz y Caballero (1800–1862)

As professor of philosophy at the College of San Francisco and founder and president of San Salvador College, José de la Luz y Caballero, the nephew of José Agustín Caballero, earned renown as a teacher, essayist, conference giver, and pensador.

The son of a military man, Luz was better known as Don Pepe. He initially studied for the priesthood, then relinquished that calling in favor of earning a law degree, which he received in Cuba. He subsequently continued his education in Europe and in the United States, where he was a student of the poet Henry Wadsworth Longfellow and the historian William H. Prescott, who wrote on the Spanish Conquest of Mexico and Peru.

Through his studies in Cuba and in Europe Luz was influenced, as were his predecessors Caballero and Varela, by the work of Bacon, Condillac, and Descartes. He also developed a fascination for the nominalism of John Locke—the denial of real existence to abstract entities or universal principles. Luz stressed that what is common to individuals and defined by a common term is often only their similarity to one another.

When he assumed Saco's chair of philosophy, Luz continued his predecessor's fight against Scholasticism and for social justice for Cubans. He introduced radical teaching methods in his classes, in particular inductive reasoning and empiricism—the theory that all beliefs are derived from experience.[59] His pedagogy and work on behalf of the Sociedad Económico de Amigos del País led Cuba's intelligentsia to consider him the inheritor of Varela's role as an apostle of thought, one who oriented teachers to train their students to methodically seek explanations for ideas, not merely accept facts.[60] Luz's teaching reflected Locke's nominalism, and in particular his sensualism. He urged students to conduct their inquiries and think with a great deal of critical skepticism.[61] He stressed that reality comes before ideology, that one must understand the natural sciences in order to apply their lessons to moral science. He explained that logic, too, was based on reality, that "man must observe before drawing conclusions, he must receive impressions before reflecting upon them, he must first walk before he can explain walking."[62]

Luz saw an inherent danger in directly imposing foreign doctrines on Cuba and therefore did not specifically talk to his students about such philosophers as Hegel, Kant, or Fichte, even though he accepted their idealism. He believed that ideas had to be adapted to social reality.[63] Thus he accepted some of Victor Cousin's eclecticism but rejected Hegel's idea that history had an "inevitable or determined evolutionary form," which he argued would make it intellectually impossible to think of revolution for Cuban independence.[64]

He considered harmful the notion that history was the visible government of God, from which came the attitude that all was as it should be and everything was in its place. He rejected the idea that what existed in government was an expression of divine desire and thus good, meaning that institutions such as slavery were acceptable.[65] He strove to get people to repudiate the popular sophisms of the day, to see liberty as the fundamental element in the human spirit and world morality, and to comprehend that moral principles and politics could not be separated.[66] To him the major obstacles to Cuban independence were ignorance, immorality, and lack of love between people, all of which permitted the degradation of humanity. He emphasized a lack of morality among business people and cited slavery, condoned by Cuba's commercial elites, as an example of the mentality that militated against independence.

Luz opposed violence and believed it was futile to expect revolutionary activity by the Cuban masses when the majority was ill prepared to understand, much less run, a government. Thus he dedicated the last years of his life to laying the groundwork that would enable some of the creole bourgeois to govern. He passed his ideas along to a generation of revolutionary philosophers who agitated for independence from Spain. His most prominent and eloquent disciple—and his biographer—Manuel Sanguily, defended and sustained Luz's thinking and, as is detailed in a subsequent chapter, carried it to a more radical plane. Among others trained by Luz was Rafael Mendive (1821–86) who served as a personal tutor to José Martí and imparted to him a love of the classics and an appetite for independence. Luz prepared his intellectual successors to search for causation in the past behavior of society and to draw historical comparisons. He represented a progressive tendency in Cuban thought, one opposed to ideological dogmatism. He endeavored to develop among fellow Cubans the consciousness needed to seek freedom.

As had Caballero, Varela, and Saco, Luz concentrated on freeing Cuba from Spain socially and intellectually. These precursors of Cuban radical thought strove to demolish false authority and construct a new awareness of reality. They disseminated a spirit of liberty and the desire for individual freedom and security from avaricious and ruthless foreigners. In varying degrees, they tried to prepare their students, the teachers they trained, the politicians they influenced, and the other Cuban citizens they reached to understand what social forces controlled capital accumulation and to recognize the dangers inherent in a society run by the wealthy. Caballero, Varela, Saco, and Luz constituted an intellectual vanguard that advocated a new order in Cuba. All, though sometimes for different individual reasons, wanted to rid their nation of a commercial base built on slavery, restricted international trade, Spanish economic, social, and political exploitation, and oppression by those who controlled the means of production.

The formation of a people is
begun by war, continued through
tyranny, renewed by revolution
and is secured by peace.

José Martí

CHAPTER 2

Independence Thinkers and the Proletarian Consciousness

Cuba's national identity grew rapidly between 1868 and 1898,
while the island remained part of the Spanish empire. For the
first time, the concepts of racial and social equality were talked
about publicly in the colony. The ideas of liberalism, free trade,
and abolition of slavery arrived from Europe, the United States,
and elsewhere in Latin America and gave rise to the Ten Years
War (1868–78).

Radical landowners from Oriente province coveted control
over their own economic destinies and expressed their nationalism by seeking to sever ties with Spain in 1868. From the area
around Yara, coffee growers, joined by other members of the
upper class—especially cattle ranchers who felt threatened by
the expansion of the sugar industry—declared independence
from Spain.[1] Carlos Manuel de Céspedes, a well-to-do lawyer
and sugar planter who had freed his slaves, read the *Grito de
Yara* (Shout of Yara) or call to freedom at the site of the initial
clash with Spanish troops. However, the class that initiated this
Ten Years' War was not united. Planters in other parts of the

island feared the movement's democratic tendencies and potential slave revolts and did not join the rebellion, which soon fell into the hands of leaders with greater mass support, such as Antonio Maceo and Máximo Gómez.

The Ten Years War failed to liberate Cuba, but it brought about substantial changes in the thinking of various elements on the island. Nevertheless, the conflict defies categorization. Some might see in the war aspects of a democratic-bourgeois revolution. But agreement did not exist between the classes allied in the struggle. The participants shared a desire for independence but generally disagreed on what they wanted in terms of government forms and economic and social relations after they achieved liberation.[2]

During the war Cuba underwent economic changes. Sugar dominated the island's economy, with the United States as the primary market.[3] The United States built more sugar refineries and centralized its capital on the island in one industry,[4] thus extending a system of monocultural dependence that Cuba could never break. While United States interests and influence in Cuba grew, Spain's industry and commerce declined and the Spanish empire deteriorated.

Social and cultural change also occurred in Cuba during the Ten Years War. The positivism of French philosopher Auguste Comte, a scientifically oriented form of empiricism with emphasis on order and progress, took hold among some of the island's intellectuals, who believed that political and social theory could be used to help solve social and political problems. Positivism also provided an elitist, potentially authoritarian philosophy, to which the more egalitarian members of Cuba's intelligentsia reacted negatively.

While some Cuban upper- and middle-class intellectuals were attracted to positivism, the island's working classes received inspiration from other European ideologies. Anarchosyndicalism—encompassing socialism, the minimization of government, and trade unionism as the instruments of working-class struggle and the fundamental vehicles for social transformation after revolution—appealed to members of the Association of Tobacco Workers of Havana. Unlike the situation elsewhere in Latin America, where anarchosyndicalism was led by immigrants from Europe, in Cuba natives for the most part ran the movement. Political consciousness grew among the tobacco workers who emigrated to Florida during the Ten Years War and those who remained in Cuba. Their leaders became acquainted with the ideas of Marx, Engels, Bakunin, and anarchosyndicalism. The rank and file, though not steeped in ideology, expressed sympathy for the ideas of anarchosyndicalism and its anticolonialism component and began to examine their social and economic problems as results of the capitalist system and Spain's role in it.

During the late 1860s and 1870s, the tobacco workers and other opponents of the Spanish presence in Cuba produced and distributed patriotic literature throughout the island. Pamphlets excoriating the mother country abounded. Polemical works, often devoid of historical perspective, preached the gospel of independence. At the same time, the writings of more profound thinkers gained an audience. For example, poet and essayist Pedro Santacilla (1826–1910) wrote *Lecciones orales sobre la historia de Cuba, pronunciadas en el Ateño Democrático cubano de Nueva York* (1859) (Lectures on the History of Cuba Read at the Democratic Club of New York), a passionate and virulent attack on Spain. It attracted readers in Cuba and the United States.[5] Saturino Martínez and his fellow reformers turned out a plethora of articles in *La Aurora* (The Dawn) and *La Razón* (The Reason), newspapers that circulated widely among workers. Their reformist tendencies were repudiated in print by Enrique Roig y San Martín, a well-known anarchosyndicalist who was influenced by the Paris Commune of 1871 and who pleaded for social revolution.

Throughout the Ten Years War, socialist, anarchosyndicalist, reformist, proindependence, antiracist, and anti-imperialist thought spread in Cuba and in the Cuban exile community in the United States and influenced both manual and intellectual laborers. Socialist lawyer Miguel A. Bravo served as an advisor to Vicente García, a Cuban general in the Ten Years War.[6] Non-intellectuals, such as Cuba's military hero Antonio Maceo (1845–96), were exposed to diverse new ideologies. The spoken ideas of Maceo, a Santiago-born mulatto of Haitian descent who led Cuba's forces in the Ten Years War, probably had more impact on his countryman than did the writings of other Cubans. The reflective "Bronze Titan," as he was called, opposed annex-ation and fought for racial equality, an end to slavery, and social justice. He dreamed of an independent democratic republic of Cuba with an honest government. Maceo understood that prop-erty caused exploitation and realized that Spain and Spaniards would not relinquish their property or control in Cuba peace-fully. He knew that compromise with the enemy was out of the question and that armed struggle was necessary. He told his fellow Cubans that they could not sacrifice their ideals if they wanted independence—that independence was not an end but a means leading to a new society. He spoke of violent rebellion and the destruction of property as justified, even to God, in the name of social justice. His liberal beliefs and radical morality served as a model for his people long after the Ten Years War failed to liberate Cuba and after his death in battle in the Span-ish-Cuban-American War.

The peace of El Zanjón, signed on 11 February 1878, ended a decade of conflict with neither Spain nor Cuba the victor. It provided a seventeen-year respite during which both sides pre-pared psychologically for the next war. With the Ten Years War over, the atmosphere in Cuba was again conducive to labor organizing. Factory employees demanded that the lector system of having someone read to them while at work be reestablished. Socialist and anarchosyndicalist thought became more popular among the cigar workers, and literature advocating independence gained favor among people in all sectors of Cuban society.

Briefly, after the war Krausism became the major philosophy among Cuba's intellectual establishment. German philosopher Karl Christian Friedrich Krause's (1781–1832) spiritualist and mystical panentheism suggested that God or Absolute Being is one with the world. He theorized that all humans were part of a spiritual whole and that the goal of history was to build an ideal "League of Humanity." Krausism's absolutism, internationalism, search for supreme harmony, and attempts to comprehend the dangers inherent in a historical process subject to the dialectics of nature had considerable appeal in Spain. This carried over to Cuba, where intellectuals whose thought reflected their Spanish heritage sought a philosophy upon which to build national political and social stability and international harmony.

But the mysticism and spiritualism of Krausism did not provide a solid philosophical foundation upon which to construct Cuba's future. Positivism, with its greater precision, had far more appeal than Krausism to Cuban intellectuals, who wanted to be a governing elite. The leaders of Cuba's middle and upper classes preferred to use positivist philosophy to help foster nationalism and as a valid rationale for independence. With its emphasis on reform within the existing system, positivism appeared to be the ideal philosophy for those acquisitive natives who wished to supplant the Spanish authorities. Positivism remained a force in Cuban thought into the twentieth century, though it continually came under attack by Cuba's socialists, to whom it represented the perpetuation of elite-dominated capitalism, which worked against the best interests of the masses.

In addition to Krausism and positivism, revolutionary romanticism, as exemplified by the thought of José Martí, and Hegelianism, popularized by Rafael Montoro (1852–1934), were explored by Cuba's intelligentsia after the Ten Years War. Montoro, a leader of the autonomist movement, eschewed revolution and worked for peaceful separation of Cuba from Spain. From Hegel he learned the theory that history pursues a path that cannot be altered by violence, that the dialectic moves on its own, and that change is inevitable. He feared Cuba would move precipitously toward revolution while it was weak and not ready for change and consequently would fall under the dominion of another state. Thus he advocated a period of training during which Cuba would rise above its colonial heritage and prepare itself for independence.[7]

New and diverse strains of thought permeated Cuba's intellectual circles during the 1880s, but most of them, such as Hegelianism, never reached the masses. Only anarchosyndicalism appealed both to intellectuals and to manual laborers. Mutual aid societies, most of them short-lived, emerged as enclaves of resistance to Spanish domination and pursued the struggle for individual and national emancipation. The cigar workers, guided by the periodicals *El Obrero* (The Worker) and *El Productor* (The Producer), spread anarchosyndicalist thought, aroused class consciousness, and supported trade unions and socialism, but they opposed political violence as a working-class weapon.[8] Radical changes took place in Cuba in 1886 as slavery was abolished, and a Workers' Center was established to spread anarchosyndicalist ideas. Simultaneously, antiannexationist sentiment grew in Cuba, which, though a Spanish colony, had become economically dependent on the United States as Yankee capital and technology built up the island's sugar plantations, tobacco industry, and railroads.[9]

The Second International Working Man's Association was founded in Paris in 1889 to further the laboring classes' struggle for economic and social improvement and political power. The socialist ideas of the Second International reached Cuba at a time when political and social thought on the island was in ferment. One of the Second International's leading exponents in France was Cuban-born Paul Lafargue (1842–1911). As a youth studying in France, Lafargue came into contact with the anarchosyndicalist thinking of Pierre Joseph Proudhon. Later, while attending medical school in London, he married Karl Marx's daughter Laura. Subsequently Lafargue worked as a publicist for socialism, an opponent of imperialism, and a supporter of women's rights and Cuban independence. He participated in the Paris Commune in 1871, and twenty years later he was the first socialist elected to France's parliament.

Most of Lafargue's political pamphlets were translated into Spanish and circulated in Cuba. In *Socialism and the Intellectuals* (1900) he examined the role of intellectuals in the capitalist world and showed how they were used by the church to support the desires of those who owned the means of production. He noted that intellectuals gave capitalism a "philosophical mask" behind which they hid their exploitation. He believed that when intellectuals recognized their social role they would accept socialism and be able to emancipate science and art from capitalism and free thought from the slavery of commercialism.[10] Lafargue's ideas were known to Cuba's small socialist community during the last quarter of the nineteenth century and were especially dear to radical thinker Diego Vicente Tejera, with whom he worked. After the Castro revolution, the thinking of Lafargue underwent a renewal in Cuba, where a collection of his works was edited and published.[11]

While Lafargue and Diego Vicente Tejera lived in Paris in 1892 and were consumed by the activities and thought of the Second International, some of their Cuban comrades helped found the Cuban Revolutionary party in Key West, Florida, to organize a new war of independence against Spain. Simultaneously, other colleagues formed the Congreso Obrero Regional (Regional Workers' Congress), which met in Havana to launch the struggle for socialism.

Cuba's war against Spain broke out on 24 February 1895. José Martí, Antonio Maceo, and Máximo Gómez led a three-year struggle for the island, which culminated in the entry of the United States in 1898 into the Spanish-Cuban-American War, which Lenin referred to as the first imperialist war of modern times,[12] initiating a period of accelerated Yankee expansion in the Caribbean. During the bloody struggle writers such as José Martí, José Enrique Varona, and Diego Vicente Tejera, as well as soldiers such as Máximo Gómez, wrote hundreds of patriotic pamphlets and position papers justifying their stance in defense of Cuban liberation. All classes in Cuba united against the Spanish during the war, and organized labor closed ranks. In 1896, in the midst of the conflict, the tobacco workers formed the Unión de Fabricantes de Tabacos y Cigarros de la Isla (Union of Island Tobacco and Cigarette Workers),[13] and its anarchosyndicalist leaders envisioned a march toward social-ism once the Spanish were defeated. On the other hand, the island's positivists dreamed of a free Cuba under their own control.

When the United States joined the hostilities in 1898, it endeavored to assume the physical and intellectual leadership on the island to the extent of calling the conflict the Spanish-American War, thereby excluding the Cubans from their own independence movement. This United States action did not go unmentioned in Cuba or in Latin America. The most famous response among intellectuals to the United States intervention in Cuba was the brilliant essay *Ariel* (1900), by Uruguayan José Enrique Rodó, which told Latin Americans to cultivate reason and sentiment, beauty and thought—the attributes of the Shake-spearean sprite Ariel rather than emulate the cannibal Caliban, who symbolized the materialism of the United States.[14]

While the United States occupied Cuba, Diego Vicente Tejera formed and promoted the Cuban Socialist party from exile in Florida. Cuba, which at one time or another had been a part of the imperial plans of Spain, Great Britain, and France, was to remain subordinate to the United States for over half a century. Ironically, formal Yankee dominion was established concurrently with the founding of the socialist movement that ultimately helped destroy United States–style capitalism in Cuba.

Enrique Roig y San Martín (1843–89)

Agitation designed to build sentiment for a socialist party began in Cuba during the 1880s. One of the leading agitators, Enrique Roig y San Martín is often considered Cuba's first Marxist of note. Born in Havana to a father who was a Cuban army physician and a Mexican mother, Roig was educated at the Colegio San Anacleto. By his early twenties he was writing poetry and investigating Cuba's agricultural system. His desire to learn more about the latter caused him to take a job in a sugar mill, where he worked first as a laborer and later as a manager.

A voracious reader, Roig was originally influenced by the Spanish anarchosyndicalist movement. He read Marx, Engels, Bakunin, Kropotkin, Proudhon, Zola, and Victor Hugo, became a student of political economy, and decided to dedicate his life to the interests of the working class. He took a position as a reader in a tobacco factory in order to educate the tobacco workers and unite them for the class struggle and social revolution.

The impulsive Roig affiliated briefly with the Autonomist party in 1881 but broke with it the next year to pursue more revolutionary goals.[15] He began to propagate socialist ideas in the newspaper *El Obrero* in 1882. That year he helped found in

Santiago de las Vegas the Centro de Instrucción y Recreo (Instruction and Recreation Center), devoted to initiating revolutionary struggle and furthering humanitarian virtues. In 1887 he launched the newspaper *El Productor*, using his talents as a journalist and polemicist to create a socialist ethos among the members of Havana's Círculo de Trabajadores (Workers' Club) and their friends. The following year he organized the Alianza Obrera (Workers' Alliance) composed of anarchists who instigated class clashes and inveighed against the exploitation of workers, despotism, shortages of food, lack of housing, and poor sanitary conditions.[16]

Through his articles in *El Productor* and in the bimonthly *Hijos del Mundo* (Children of the World), Roig linked politically the Cuban cigar workers in Havana and those in exile in Key West and Tampa, Florida. He carefully outlined the past so that the workers would understand how their situation had developed. He urged the workers to abandon Cuba's existing political parties, to forget about passive resistance, and to take part in productive strikes against the tobacco factory owners.[17] With an air of dignity, Roig's writing symbolized solidarity against injustice and equated socialism with the ultimate in democratic practices where everyone participates. He believed deeply in the power of the press and thought that *El Productor* could do more good for socialism in a day than socialism's apostles could accomplish individually in a year.[18]

Roig served more as a consciousness raiser or organizer of thought than as a theoretician. Through *El Productor* he disseminated the ideas of Europe's most profound thinkers. He spoke about scientific socialism, often cited Marx and Engels, and illustrated the basic differences they had with the anarchist Bakunin. Engels affirmed that proletarian revolution could solve class contradictions and that the proletariat had to take national political power and convert private property into state property.

The anarchists disagreed. They did not want the workers to build a national political party to instigate and lead a revolution. They preferred to see an international workers' movement override any national political movement. In this regard Roig and the anarchists did not support the tactics of most of Cuba's independence advocates, nor did they oppose them directly.

The anarchists rejected the concept of workers' affiliating with the independence-oriented political parties in Cuba. Roig and his associates opposed the liberal-democratic phase of the revolution, following Bakunin's idea that all state authority and formal political organizations had to be destroyed and Kropotkin's belief that fundamental human goodness could establish public order by voluntary cooperation of individuals and groups.[19] Roig cited Engels's contention that socialist thought illustrates the conflict between the forces of production and the form of production.[20] By so doing, he made his readers aware that the work of Marx and Engels primarily analyzed capitalism on a world scale, not socialism. Roig understood that considerable study was necessary to make socialists out of those brought up under capitalism. He maintained that only socialists could lead the revolution to free Cuba, which would begin by replacing capitalist institutions with socialist ones.[21] He admired the advances in socialist thought and action in Europe and the United States, deeply appreciated the forceful action the anarchists took in Chicago in the 1880s on behalf of trade unionism, and would have liked to duplicate the efforts of the Paris Communards in nineteenth-century Cuba.[22]

He encouraged solidarity with workers elsewhere and explained the universality of their problems. He stated that though work ought to free workers from feudal dependency, that does not occur under capitalism. He noted that the disappearance of the feudal order created wages and exploitation, whereas under socialism the concept of salaries would disappear and thus free the worker.[23]

In clear, concise, jargon-free Spanish, Roig got his message across to his readers. Without confusing rhetoric or the terminology often associated with ideology, he made simple points that opened the minds of unsophisticated workers to new ideas. He liked to stress the syllogistic thinking used by the ruling class to propagandize the masses, and occasionally, in jest, he used a syllogism of his own. He was fond of this one: "Capital is work, work is the exclusive property of the worker, therefore capital ought to be the worker's."[24] A devout believer in popular democracy, Roig viewed capital as the enemy of universal suffrage and believed that only when the notion of the supremacy of capital is destroyed will genuine democracy emerge. For example, he asserted that capital created the undemocratic institution of slavery in Cuba[25] and elsewhere in the world. On the other hand, he explained that capital invested in mechanization enhances the possibility of socialism, since advanced technology can free humans from slavery and exploitable toil.[26]

Roig wanted to recapture the spirit of ancient Sparta and combine it with utopian socialism. He envisioned everyone as a citizen-worker rather than a warrior. Each citizen could participate in decision making in Roig's ideal state, unlike Cuba, where most citizens were basically disfranchised and the Spanish crown, on rare occasions, met working-class needs because of its sense of noblesse oblige. He advocated replacing the state as it existed with worker control.

To him the state represented a part of the capitalist machine that had to be transferred to the proletariat, which could be done only by eliminating classes.[27] In a classless society the people constitute the state, and he claimed that one cannot be free without the other. Thus he repudiated the idea that the United States represented a classic example of liberty, contending that there the majority was exploited to satisfy the desires of the minority.[28] He warned readers not to accept the bourgeois vocabulary of "order and liberty," a positivist-elitist cliché of the day.[29] Roig enjoyed dispelling commonly held myths. He pointed out that constant references to "liberty" in the United States did not mean that it existed. He was one of the first to contradict the notion that bourgeois interests coincided with those of the workers when the former were closer to those of the upper class.

He differentiated between classes but drew no distinctions between the races. To him people existed as sisters or brothers, not blacks or whites, peninsulares or criollos, Spaniards or Cubans. He deplored the tendency of Cubans to categorize themselves according to race and sex, not class.[30] Roig attributed discrimination against women to the male ego, to their exploitation as inexpensive labor, and to the church's view of them. He cited prostitution as an example of what befalls women in an economic system based on exploitation.[31] Separation of church and state, he thought, would afford females greater equality. With the church out of politics, divorce might mitigate the brutality of some marriages and lessen the subjugation of women. He supported free love as a form of women's liberation and asserted that women as well as men should be emancipated and have freedom of choice, well-being, and the opportunity to follow their impulses. He opposed tyranny in marriage and believed that women should not be slaves to their husbands—that husbands should not own their wives' labor.[32]

Roig viewed many of the abuses in society as manifestations of capitalism, and he condemned and countered the thinking of the positivists who supported that repressive system. He began to pave the road to revolution in Cuba by increasing public awareness of the causes of inequality and the benefits of egalitarianism and by initiating a new era of conscious class struggle. His work was carried out and refined by close associates such as Carlos B. Baliño, whose political life extended from the origins of Cuba's socialist movement in the nineteenth century to the founding of Cuba's Communist party in 1925.

Roig did not live to see the formal organization of Cuban socialism. His spirited writings elicited an anticommunist response from Cuba's capitalist sector, which wanted to keep the workers disoriented. Cuba's ruling class branded him a subversive, unpatriotic Marxist propagator of alien beliefs.[33] He was imprisoned in 1889 on charges of distributing antigovernment tracts. Cuba's first major Marxist social critic died in a Havana jail at age forty-six.

Diego Vicente Tejera (1848–1903)

Diego Vicente Tejera succeeded Enrique Roig y San Martín at the forefront of socialist politics in Cuba. An indefatiguable political activist and writer, Tejera gained prominence as an essayist, translator, journalist, and poet with a keen sense of history. The son of a crown official, he was born in Santiago de Cuba and earned a bachelor's degree at San Basilio Seminary, where he was exposed to the writings of Luz y Caballero. While a teenager he traveled in Europe, and he began to study medicine in Paris in 1867 in the midst of political and social upheaval when democratic revolutionary ideas were gaining popularity there.

After absorbing the rebellious spirit of France, Tejera took part in an abortive attempt to overthrow the Spanish monarchy, then he left Spain and went to Puerto Rico, where he developed a deeper understanding of colonial systems. He visited the United States and eventually settled briefly in Venezuela. In Caracas in 1870 he was wounded in a rebellion against Venezuelan dictator Antonio Guzmán Blanco.

The Spanish interned Tejera during the Ten Years War then sent him into exile, where he studied literature and wrote poetry and pamphlets on class conflict and socialism. He developed an appreciation for the classics, especially Socrates and the Greek democrats, and for the heroic images in Goethe and

Cervantes. He saw analogies between the knight-errant Don Quixote's idealism and zeal to liberate and that of Cuban freedom fighter Antonio Maceo, whom he called a rare breed of successful black leader.[34]

Tejera's reputation as a poet began with the publication of his first collection of verses, *Consonancias* (1874) (Harmonies),[35] and reached its apogee with the much-acclaimed poem "En la hamaca" ("In the Hammock"), written during his stay in Venezuela. His love for poetry came from exposure to the work of Henry Wadsworth Longfellow. He felt a need to put into Spanish the best poetry written in English and French. In addition to his translations from those languages, Tejera produced novelas, sweet *trovas* (metrical compositions, often sung), and poems with themes running from eroticism to hope, liberty, and social justice. Throughout Cuba his poetry was better known than his political work, though the latter, with which we are chiefly concerned, was more biting.[36]

Tejera wrote and recited his poetry and worked for the independence movement while living in Cuba between 1879 and 1885. During that period he built a strong friendship with Spencerian positivist Enrique José Varona, a proponent of Cuban autonomy, from whom he learned a great deal about the value of systematic thinking. He then relocated in New York and established a close relationship with José Martí.

In 1888 Tejera went to France, where he remained for five years. He published the literary journal *América en Paris* and delved deeply into socialism. He was impressed by the French trade union movement and the Second International, especially the ideas of the utopian socialist Louis Blanc, the syndicalist proponent of direct action and strikes Georges Sorel, and the anarchists Proudhon and Kropotkin. While in France he formulated thoughts on a new social system for humanity.

Ideas excited Tejera, and he continuously sought knowledge. He learned best by researching and writing, so he studied and produced pieces on the numerous topics discussed in subsequent paragraphs. He wrote with clarity and precision but without the customary Latin American flourishes. His style included occasionally asking and answering rhetorical questions, but without using Marxist clichés. The originality of Tejera's poetry did not extend to his political and social works, which essentially reiterated the universal socialist ideas of Europeans. But among his Cuban contemporaries he stood out as a devotee of scientific rigor. He viewed the modernism of his age as poorly defined and the wrong vehicle to impart to Cubans moral and intellectual values in a context of equality.[37] He perceived inequality as a manifestation of individualism and believed that equality could be created by substituting state action for that of the individual. Though he was often accused of having unrealistic expectations, he never wavered from the belief that the state must ensure that work provide everyone with the beauty and comforts of civilization. In a way, he espoused secular spiritualism.

In Tejera's estimation, politics served as the instrument of human progress and deserved the same recognition and practice as religion. He examined the political components of Cuban society in order to project their implications for the future, and he concluded that only socialism could provide the revolutionary change necessary to improve the human condition and create participatory democracy. He attacked the false aristocratic pretensions under which Cuba's elitist leaders claimed to be bringing democracy and morality to the masses. Cubans needed a socialist spirit, one that could be developed only through education. Such a spirit could not be legislated from the top down but had to come from the bottom up, to be based on education, which originated with one's parents.[38]

Tejera believed that such teaching could enlighten the workers without destroying individuality. He saw the lessons of the French Revolution as the consecration of individuality by freeing the person and simultaneously advancing ideals and justice. Educated human beings could solve their earthly problems, eradicate hunger and suffering, and, through reason, prevail over natural adversities. But they could do so only by controlling the power of capital.[39] To move the workers from the stage of misery to a position of comfort, the means of production must be reordered to work for the common good. Tejera detailed how to accomplish this feat and how to foster Cuban development in a series of ten "conferences" or public lectures given in Key West, Florida, from 1897 through 1899.

1. The conference "Education in Democratic Societies" portrayed Cuban education as exclusivist and responsible for class antagonisms. Tejera expressed concern with educating people for public life, including political life. He talked about educating the popular classes and advocated making education through the secondary-school level available to everyone.[40]

2. The conference entitled "The Cuban Capacity" analyzed the Cuban intellect. Tejera characterized Cubans as not fanatically religious but influenced by a secular religion—positivism. He repudiated the myth that the Cuban peasant was naturally ignorant. He discerned considerable artistic capacity in Cuba, a tradition of scientific observation (natural science), and solid potential in the fields of prose and poetry. He suggested using scientific socialist, rather than positivist, methods to analyze social reality and capacity and urged Cubans to see that they possessed the tools necessary for such analyses.[41]

3. In "Autonomists and Annexationists" Tejera opposed Cuban autonomy within the Spanish parliamentary system, calling it unworkable and those who supported it opponents of genuine revolution. He asserted that proponents of annexation by the United States admired that country, but that Cuba could not be dependent on the United States and prosper. He called for a separatist insurrection for Cuba.[42]

4. The conference "The Cuban Woman" dealt with how females had historically been relegated to secondary roles and deemed too passive to engage in politics. Tejera expressed the belief that women should be educated to be the cultural influence in the home—the stabilizing factor and of noble character. He wanted to increase woman's prestige within what he considered her natural place in life. Unlike the European socialists, who demanded emancipation for women, Tejera wanted only to improve their education and to put them on a pedestal for female and motherly virtues.[43]

5. In "The Future of Party Politics in the Republic of Cuba," Tejera advocated diverse parties, not a dictatorship of the proletariat with a single-party vanguard. He predicted the development of two major parties in Cuba, one reactionary and the other progressive. He contended that both liberal and conservative parties would exploit the proletariat and that neither would resolve the problem of capital distribution, but that a democratic-socialist party would. He depicted politics as the art of patience and prudence. His political objective was to build a socialist party with a vigorous newspaper that would capture the support of industrial workers and peasants and represent the people traditionally excluded from the political process.[44]

6. "Cuban Indolence" characterized that condition as not physical and innate but mental and curable. In this conference Tejera noted the Cuban indifference to public life and ignorance of the value of solidarity and the potential for (collective) change. He urged Cubans to abandon the mentality of the colonized and to struggle for progress.[45]

7. To Tejera, Cuba's racial problems retarded progress. In the conference "Whites and Blacks," he acknowledged that Cuba had the essentials for racial coexistence without antagonism. Blacks, he said, had to be educated. He recommended that both races cultivate their individual traits as well as their com-

mon ones. He claimed that through educational regeneration of the nuclear family, especially in the wake of slavery, all people could be elevated to the same level. He saw United States intervention in Cuba as potentially harmful to race relations because the whites controlled the United States. He praised the example of the white Martí and the black Maceo, who worked together for the good of Cuba.[46]

8. In a conference on "Charlatanism and Fetishism" Tejera considered Cuban idyosyncrasies and indicated that one had to identify the charlatans or false patriots. He stated that Cubans commonly believed politicians were charlatans given to demagoguery and that one could not trust a criollo politician. Tejera then described fetishism as the cult of the *caudillo* (political boss) and politics conducted under the military or kings, practices traceable to Spanish origins. He noted that demagoguery and tyranny became a fetish—subject to the defects of the person in control—and that he preferred the collective way to govern found in true democracies where there exist natural leaders, not authoritarian pseudodemocrats. In essence, Tejera called for purity and honesty in government.[47]

9. The "Cuban Society" conference examined Cuba's social structures in terms of positivist influence. In Cuba, unlike Europe, there existed no formal social hierarchy. Class distinctions in Cuba were not a matter of noble birth, and no caste system prevailed on the island. Tejera stressed that educational, class, and cultural differences in Cuba could be altered. He wanted to start anew in Cuba after independence, when the ruling class would be eliminated. He expressed hope that no new pretentious class would emerge after independence and that the workers could develop socially and politically and build one cohesive class.[48]

10. During the last conference, "A Practical Socialist System," Tejera reiterated the ideas found in his pamphlet *Un sistema*

social práctico: Sus grandes lineas (A Practical Social System: Its Major Lines), published in Paris in 1884. He outlined his thesis on the organization of society for collective benefit and noted the abuses of the class system that resulted from social and economic inequality. He postulated a five-state theory of human existence including misery (no necessities), poverty (basic necessities), ease (two times the necessities), wealth (three times the necessities), and opulence (four or more times the necessities). He believed that these five parallel states existed and proposed moving the masses through them until more than a sufficiency existed for all.[49] He urged the poor to reject the five-state system and replace it with a classless state. He blamed human vanity for the odious system and believed that if vanity did not compel people to gain wealth at the expense of others, a more humane society would exist.[50]

While preparing and giving his series of conferences, Tejera joined Carlos Baliño and José Martí and actively worked for Cuban independence through the Revolutionary party. He opposed violence in general but approved of it in the form of a liberation struggle that would ultimately create a less violent Cuba.

After the hostilities leading to the defeat of Spain in 1898, when the United States began to occupy Cuba, Tejera warned that political independence was in jeopardy of being lost to the Yankees. During the occupation, when the United States relied on much of the old colonial bureaucracy to run Cuba, Tejera began to organize. He sought to balance the powers in national politics by forming a workers' party to try to eliminate the informal stratifications in Cuban society without initiating class warfare.[51] The Cuban government and its United States "guides" did not respond harshly to the classlessness that he advocated because they did not comprehend the full implications of his brand of radicalism.

Tejera took advantage of the working-class solidarity that had been building in Cuba since the nation held its first Workers' Congress in 1892, which resolved that "the Working Class will not be emancipated until it embraces the ideas of revolutionary socialism."[52] He and tobacco worker Ambrosio Borges founded the Socialist party in 1899, with visions of its directing the country toward allocating the laboring class a greater proportion of the wealth generated by the means of production.[53] Tejera strove for a transformation to socialism and advocated a sort of spiritual revolution to attain the social redemption of the masses. He took Martí's ideas one step beyond independence and sought liberation from capitalism. He wanted to tailor a practical socialist system to Cuba's specifications without rigidly applying European socialist doctrine. He took into account the predominantly rural and agricultural nature of Cuba and the technologically underdeveloped state of its major industries, tobacco and sugar. Although the countryside was not ready for European socialism, the concept of private property that prevailed, especially on the sugar and tobacco plantations, permitted surpluses for a few and not enough for most.

Tejera, the subtle idealist, hoped through the Socialist party to create justice without extremism. He supported a type of socialism that did not frighten Cuba's bourgeoise, whose talents he believed were needed to foster progress in the nation and who had to be made to feel comfortable with the Socialist party.

His influence can best be seen in the Manifesto of the Cuban Socialist party, which he helped draw up, and in the aspects of that Manifesto espoused by successor movements and enacted by the revolutionary government of Fidel Castro. The Manifesto provided for better working conditions, obligatory public education, an eight-hour working day, pension and retirement benefits, social security, children's and women's labor legislation, and the elimination of discrimination between Spaniards and

Cubans.[54] The Socialist party also advocated the separation of church and state, elimination of capital punishment, penal reform, diversification of industry, and freedom of conscience, thought, expression, and the press.[55]

The Socialist party was organized when the masses had little preparation for socialism and were overwhelmed by the problems created by the break with Spain. Few Cubans had the ability to link the objectives of the Socialist party to the needs of a newly independent Cuba. Most thought that to be free they just had to be rid of their old rulers, not of the prevailing system.[56] To them the attainment of national sovereignty was sufficient.

Tejera's optimism, and his desire to build a workers' movement in Cuba that would promote the transformation of the colonial social and economic structures into a democratic socialist state, never materialized during the next half-century. Under United States hegemony, Cuban politics took a different turn, and the Socialist party died. But the seeds of Tejera's socialism had been sown for future generations of radicals to reap.

José Martí (1853–95)

José Martí, who did not subscribe to socialism, is identified more than any of his countrymen with preparing the Cubans mentally for, and with organizing and launching, the struggle for liberation from Spain. A man of letters, not a warrior, Martí possessed the revolutionary's passion for victory and freedom. An intellectual who noted that "others go to bed with their mistresses, I with my ideas," through his brilliant oratory and writings in Spanish, English, and French, which fill twenty-five thick volumes, Martí shaped the thinking of modern Cuba. An agnostic who was excommunicated from the Catholic church, he placed his greatest faith in the eventual victory of good over evil, of the masses over a greedy and uncaring ruling elite.

Martí's interest in working actively to eliminate injustice began while he was studying at the Colegio de San Pablo under the revolutionary poet and journalist Rafael Mendive. The imprisonment of Mendive by the Spanish authorities for anti-crown activities left an indelible impression on young Martí, who in 1870 received a sentence of six years' hard labor for expressing revolutionary views during the Ten Years War. The Spanish commuted his sentence to exile on the Isle of Pines and then permitted him to go to Spain. In Madrid he campaigned for Cuban independence and wrote the pamphlet *The Spanish Republic Confronting the Cuban Question* (1873). Also while in Europe, he came under the influence of Victor Hugo, who sympathized with Cuba's revolutionary cause. Martí then earned a law degree from the University of Zaragoza. When the Spanish republic was overthrown in 1875, he was forced into exile again. He lived the rest of his life in Mexico, Guatemala, Cuba, France, Venezuela, and the United States. José Martí died in Cuba on 19 May 1895 in an encounter with Spanish forces and instantly became a martyr. He died without systematically explaining his revolutionary philosophy.

We know that Martí's ideas about independence and his nationalist fervor originated with his teacher Mendive, who derived many of his beliefs from Varela. Martí also received inspiration from the Cartesian reasoning and historical awareness of José de la Luz. He had a fair knowledge of classical Greece and Rome and was influenced by stoicism and Platonic idealism, which stimulated his search for a superior form of governance. He placed man above nature, but like Plato he accepted the "identification of God with the good and the conception of ideas as a superior intellectual synthesis of reality."[57]

While in Spain, Martí came to know the thought of Karl Christian Krause, especially the idea that God or conscience was an essence containing the universe. He shared Krause's organic conception of life but not his whole metaphysical scheme. Martí's idealism reflected that of Krause, Johann Fichte, and Friedrich Schelling.

In France Martí picked up the ideals of the French Revolution and the rights of man and a belief in people's responsibilities to each other. However, he rejected the elitism and racial and cultural determinism of the French positivists and resented the sense of social conservatism and political inferiority that positivism evoked in Latin America. But he liked the scientific nature of positivism and concurred with the aspects of it that stressed that political and social institutions were products of social process.

Martí's antipositivism is often explained in terms of his penchant for modernism—the international tendency that arose in the arts and literature in the last years of the nineteenth century and reached its peak just before World War I. Modernism merged diverse art forms, stimulated aesthetic cross-fertilization among countries, and endeavored to preserve the arts and literature from the social and historical forces that threatened them. Modernism made an antielitist plea for ideological pluralism—the acceptance of other modes of thought and the rejection of barbarism.

The pluralist spirit of modernism coalesced with Martí's love of humanity and the nonconformist traits he admired in the Scottish writer Thomas Carlyle and in the anti-imperialist Nicaraguan poet Rubén Darío, who referred to Martí as "maestro" (teacher). The thinking of Mexico's liberals Benito Juárez and Sebastián Lerdo de Tejada, who during the reform era of the 1860s tried to elevate the middle sectors in Mexican society, profoundly affected Martí. He also admired the Russian poet Alexander Pushkin, who he said "had extreme eloquence, a surprising literary fecundity, a precise intuition, a healthy love of truth, and the unalloyed sentiment of Nature."[58]

Martí read the works of a number of Yankee writers, including Ralph Waldo Emerson, Henry David Thoreau, Henry Wadsworth Longfellow, and Mark Twain. He was particularly taken by the sensitivity of Walt Whitman, who glorified the manual worker and believed that personal work affords one self-respect and liberty, and by Edward Bellamy's socialist novel *Looking Backward* (1888), which depicted United States capitalism in the late nineteenth century as inefficient, brutal, and undemocratic.

Martí endeavored to pass on his knowledge to the Cuban people, believing they would be free only when they were educated. He maintained that good governments serve their people best by educating them and insisted that education be conducted within the context of Cuba's national character. "There is no battle between civilization and barbarism, only between false erudition and nature," Martí said, meaning that contrary to the well-known (in Latin America) beliefs of Argentine thinker and statesman Domingo Sarmiento, there existed no homegrown barbarism, only a form of it derived by imitating foreign ways. He criticized as cultural imperialism Sarmiento's desire to replicate the United States educational system in Argentina.[59]

Martí stressed education that cultivated the intellect and taught one to think, not merely to memorize data. He emphasized the need for history and believed that to understand the present and prepare for life one had to look at the past. The church, in his estimation, should not control education, because of its tendency to accentuate dogma rather than reason and to analyze the past in terms of how it should have been rather than how it was. He carried on the fight, begun by Caballero, against Scholasticism with its stress on logic, rhetoric, and theology. Above all, he considered the church's doctrine of infallibility to be corrupt.

He viewed women as the intellectual equals of men and hoped to see them become better companions, rather than playthings, by being raised to the educational level of men. Like his friend Diego Vicente Tejera, he wanted equal intellectual partners but opted for wives to stay at home.[60] Perhaps his views on women were tempered by the fact that his nonintellectual wife opposed political activism.

Martí detested discrimination, which divided people, whether against women or those of another color. He considered all races equal—in fact he deplored the concept of race as divisive and "a sin against humanity."[61] His attitudes on race are strongly reflected in today's Cuba.

Martí had deep faith in all types of people; his highest mission was to solidify human bonds. His actions and writings were designed to serve truth, justice, and progress in politics as well as the arts. He was a universal man, devoted to knowledge and culture that analyzed and elevated humanity, and he could not resist probing into causation and significance in every discipline he studied, always with an eye toward educating himself and others. Martí's marvelously descriptive writings on politics, social questions, the plastic arts, theater, and music, as well as his literary works and children's stories, provoked thought throughout the Americas.

His ideas were to some degree predicated on the pluralistic American experience in addition to Cuban, primarily Afro–Latin American, nationalism. He thought in terms of universal and hemispheric problems that could be solved by reason. Although he realized that the American societies moved from one social state to another, he postulated no scientific theories regarding their economic or political development beyond restating Simón Bolívar's general belief that America could be a "regenerative force in world affairs."[62]

Unlike European-oriented political thinkers of his era, Martí did not regard America as an extension of Europe. To him American history began with the pre-Columbian Indian civilizations. He noted that many aspects of pre-Columbian America were superior to the Old World, that the conquerors deliberately destroyed the material culture of the Indians, and that the priests, the ideologues of the conquest, tried to obliterate the indigenous culture from the minds of the Indians. To liberate Latin America, Martí thought that there must be a belief in the greatness of the Indian civilizations.[63]

He continually referred to Latin America as "Our America" and to the United States as the "Other America." In "Our America," he maintained, the people needed to look to their own culture and understand themselves to progress, and would have to reject foreign solutions to native problems. Problems differed in the two Americas. In the United States Martí saw pervasive capitalism, with the entrepreneurs and the industrial proletariat engaged in the primary social conflict, whereas in Latin America the major struggle pitted the landed gentry against the peasants.[64]

He attributed the political ineptitude of Latin America to the dominant positivist ideas of the day, which came from Europe and were buttressed by the United States. He frequently noted that the interests of the United States differed from those of Latin America. At the first Pan-American Conference in 1889, which he attended as a Uruguayan delegate, he fought against United States attempts to control politics and commerce in the Americas. With regard to his homeland, he even opposed United States participation in the battle for freedom, stating, "Once the United States is in Cuba, who will get it out?"[65]

Martí understood the United States as no other nineteenth-century foreigner did except perhaps Alexis de Tocqueville. His astute observations appeared in dozens of articles on all facets of the economic, cultural, and political life of the United States. He maintained just enough distance from the United States to place it in good historical perspective and to envision the direction the nation was taking and how it could affect Cuba's independence. He understood how its tentacles enveloped Latin America and how its commercial relations created a situation of dominion and dependency. He was convinced that the United States wanted to impose a protectorate on Latin America, and in a two-part article in *La Nación* (The Nation) on 19 and 20 December 1889, he explored the imperialist motives behind United States secretary of state James Blaine's Pan-Americanism.[66]

Unlike Lenin, Martí did not see imperialism as the highest stage of capitalism, nor did he attribute the fundamental problems of society to capitalism. He thought that the injustices of capitalism could be rectified by eliminating the two inherent defects in that system: monopoly, which limited the free flow of goods in the national marketplace, and protectionism, which had the same effect internationally. He objected vociferously to the exploitation of labor and favored trade unionism, but he considered workers indispensable to the accumulation of capital, which was necessary for economic prosperity. His unsophisticated knowledge of economics led him to attribute the excess of production over needs in the United States to mechanization and to protective tariffs, which curtailed "free trade" states from dealing with the United States because of prohibitive costs. Thus United States supplies outstripped demand during the late nineteenth century, and prices dropped, as did profits and wages.[67]

Martí could never propagate hatred toward the United States; he believed Cuba's geographic and economic positions compelled it to pursue cordial relations, but without ties of political and economic servitude.[68] He opposed the United States robber barons but saw merit in the capitalist democracy's small farm sector and populism. He denounced the crass materialism of the United States, which led to the quest for excessive profits at the expense of the workers, who "fail to understand that they are merely cogs in the gears of society."[69]

Hoping that Cuba could learn from the shortcomings of the

United States, Martí pointed out that United States universities did not teach students to analyze the social and political dynamics of society. Most Yankees did not know how power worked.[70] He admired the industriousness of his neighbors to the north and the fact that most of them worked and read, but he noted that they did not always think. They were greedy, aggressive, authoritarian, scornful of other nations and cultures, and often undemocratic. He stated that the United States did not encourage sentiment or "find a condition worthy of higher esteem than wealth."[71] It is ironic that this cult of wealth was implanted in Cuba by the United States after Martí's death.

He deplored the racial arrogance of the United States, which viewed Latin America as primarily Indian and black and thus inferior. He feared that Yankee racism would succeed Cuban racism in his homeland after independence. Martí the *pensador* strove to provide lessons to benefit a free Cuba, while Martí the political activist worked to liberate Cuba. His studies led him to conclude that autonomy within the Spanish empire was not in Cuba's best interests and that only as an independent republic could Cuba flourish. In that spirit he organized the rebellion against Spain. His genius in handling fellow insurrectionists was exceeded only by his knack for enlisting newcomers in the cause. Martí understood the function of a political party as a unifying device in a revolutionary movement. He organized the Partido Revolucionario Cubano (Cuban Revolutionary party), which sought the absolute independence of Cuba, tried to organize and win a short war, and attempted to unify Cubans behind the war effort. To him national unity was essential to victory, and he persuaded all revolutionary groups to join the Revolutionary party.

He realized that although the middle-class creole leaders of independence in most of Latin America had given lip service to freedom for all, they primarily fought for, and attained, power for their own special interests.[72] Martí's ideal Cuba would guarantee freedom for all, recognize that economics was inseparable from politics, and be based on an economy primarily composed of small landowners.

He believed that after the independence era of 1810–30 the newly freed states of the hemisphere had fallen under the influence of the United States, which worked through national oligarchies to control the economies of the Latin nations. He desired a more genuine independence for Cuba, which would help maintain freedom in the rest of Latin America—a lesson subsequently incorporated into the thinking of Fidel Castro's revolutionary government.

History made Martí wary of the military, and he wanted to ensure that in Cuba, unlike the situation elsewhere in Latin America, after independence the victorious army would not become the arbiter of politics. He prophesied that popular civilian government inevitably would win out in Cuba. He was convinced that native and foreign despots would find out that the people, the suffering mass, constitute the true head of revolution.[73]

Martí believed in the masses, but he strove to maintain common cause with all classes. He noted the political and social injustices inherent in the uneven distribution of wealth to the various classes. He proposed achieving a better distribution of capital by parceling out government land to the peasants, not by taking land away from those who had it. He believed that free trade would also equalize capital distribution. He cited exclusive wealth as unfair and preferred a more equal distribution of private property. Political scientist Gordon Lewis has said that Martí exhibited the indignation of Rousseau, who opposed social injustice, more than the stance of Marx, who believed that the injustices perpetrated by the ruling class emanate from property and class relationships.[74]

Martí never accepted the philosophy of the Cuban anarcho-syndicalists he worked with in the United States. He agreed with Henry George that under industrial capitalism progress was accompanied by poverty. He criticized industrial capitalism as inhumane but offered few concrete alternatives beyond George's notion that society owned land, which created value, and that land reform and correct taxation could provide sufficient funds to end poverty.[75] He championed a vague form of societal organization that reflected Cuba's reality, was based on popular consent, equalized the political power of all classes, did not exploit the poor, gave land to the peasants, guaranteed the social rights of all ethnic and national groups, and set moral ethics above those based on wealth. He pursued human dignity rather than capital development[76] and sought to restructure social life in Cuba, to build a new ethical awareness, and to create a nineteenth-century version of the new Cuban man.[77]

Martí's political and social programs for Cuba lacked an economic base and scientific rigor. He rejected the concepts of historical materialism and class struggle. He saw no one class in Cuba as strong enough to rebel successfully, and he opposed government domination by a single class or party. He had some familiarity with, but not overall comprehension of, the writings of Marx, and he understood the value of the proletariat as a backbone of revolutionary change.[78] He admired Marx "for the way he puts himself at the side of the weak ones" and called him a "titanic interpreter of the anger of the European worker,"[79] but he contended that workers could attain their objectives without class conflict.

Martí became increasingly prolabor and sympathetic to his socialist friends as a result of living in the slums of New York and studying the role of organized labor in England and the United States. He vied with the anarchists for control over Cuban workers in exile and condemned the violence used by the anarchists, especially after the Haymarket Square riot in Chicago in 1886. He claimed that Marx went too fast and that his followers favored excessive violence.[80] He erroneously depicted Marx as a critic without a program for change, as one who pointed out the injury but had no remedy for it.[81] Although he wanted the individual subordinate to the state, Martí feared a socialist state. In *La América* of New York in 1884, Martí referred to socialism as a slavery of man serving the state.[82]

On the other hand, the socialists of his day respected Martí as a major collaborator in furthering the bourgeois-democratic revolution phase of societal development in Cuba, as a brother in struggle. Carlos Rafael Rodríguez, assessing the role of Martí in today's Cuban revolution, said:

One must not . . . attribute to Martí ideological bases that are alien to him and that distort his real significance. It is plausible, but it is artificial to probe the great man to extract from him a pretended socialist streak . . . in perspective we can see that no one was more the child of his times, more expressive of his class, more tied to the customs of his day, than José Martí. . . . The republic of Martí, therefore, is democratic in its political aspect, and bourgeois in its social content.[83]

Martí helped Cuba make the transition from colony to republic, though he would have detested the new neocolonial status of the country. His great revolutionary spirit sustained his successors, who struggled to fulfill his dream after the war with Spain. His political philosophy lacked cohesion, except for his analysis of the differences between the Americas, but his eloquent synthesis of the ideas of others and his ability to adapt them to conditions in Cuba endeared him to all future Cuban *pensadores*.

Cubans often refer to Martí's unsystematic thought as an *ideario* (a concept) rather than an ideology. He is looked upon as a people's philosopher rather than an academic because he never formulated a methodology through which to build an ideal world. He never devised a political or social theory, but he posited some ideas for a more perfect state. The love of humanity overrides all other factors in his work. He viewed politics as "the art of bringing humanity to justice."[84] To do so, and to foster progress, he believed in the need to unravel the mysteries of nature through science.

José Antonio Portuondo called him a man whose ideas made the transition between romanticism, positivism, materialism, and modernism.[85] Miguel Jorrín saw him as a critical idealist who reacted against positivism and its elitism.[86] Harold Davis said that he defies categorization but "is a precursor of the inquietude of Latin America that finds expression in many diverse ways in its twentieth century revolutionary movements."[87] Martí's efforts on behalf of independence, his literature, his tragic death just before the realization of one of his fondest dreams, and his ability to capture the poetic essence of Cuba elevated him beyond the stature of national hero to the position of "apostle of Cuba." His ideas have always been popular among Cuba's urban and rural laborers, and until the Castro revolution they formed the foundation of the thinking of a Cuban middle class bereft of the economic power of the upper class and United States interests and the political power traditionally held by a strongman. He is one of few non-Marxist Cuban leaders to escape being discredited after the Castro revolution. Roberto Fernández Retamar, director of revolutionary Cuba's Center for José Martí Studies, claims that Cuba does not try to make Martí a Marxist but tries to illuminate the ties between Martí's radical ideals and the ideology of the modern socialist revolution.[88]

Fidel Castro acknowledges the debt of the Twenty-sixth of July Movement to the political and social thinking of Martí but claims that the nineteenth-century freedom fighter did not understand the necessity of eliminating the nation's intolerable capitalism in order to achieve genuine social and political change.[89]

Martí also serves as a model for liberals and anti-imperialists outside Cuba. Three decades after his death his vision of the adverse effects of colonialism and his belief in the regeneration of Indianism as a means of making progress were confirmed by the grandfather of Marxist thought in Latin America, José Carlos Mariátegui (1894–1930). Pan-African Third World revolutionary thinker Frantz Fanon (1925–61) also substantiated Martí's negative image of the idyllic colony and the myth of common interests between the oppressor and the oppressed.[90]

The roots of radical thought planted earlier in Cuba by Caballero, Varela, Saco, and Luz were nourished during the late nineteenth century by new European ideological currents and by Martí, whose ideas stimulated nationalism and *Cubanidad* and guided the independence movement to success. The thinking of their compatriots Roig y San Marfin and Tejera added proletarian consciousness and other socialist dimensions to Cuban thought and helped launch the nation's labor movement, which served in the twentieth century as a foundation for building class struggle and social revolution. Their common belief in the idea of progress, and their collective wisdom, gave rise to a subsequent generation of radical *pensadores* who carried on the tradition of combining imaginative writing with political activism. Their democratic ideals and egalitarian philosophies remained an integral part of Cuba's intellectual life throughout six decades (1898–1958) of foreign domination and intermittent authoritarian rule.

The Bolivarian ideal ought
to be our aspiration; that
of Monroe is our death.

Julio Antonio Mella

CHAPTER 3

The Rise of the Left-Wing Intelligentsia, 1898–1934

After independence from Spain new ideological crosscurrents
entered Cuba, but the predominant thought of the first generation of the twentieth century was nationalist and liberal with
positivist overtones. Cuban social and political literature was
generally written by elitists who believed they had to guide the
new country, in which three-fifths of the population was illiterate.
A few embryonic social scientists applied neo-Darwinian social
evolutionary theory to Cuban society, believing that the "better"
people who moved closer to perfection would govern and the
"lesser" elements would gradually be rendered powerless.

Even though Cuba's Socialist party, established in 1899, lasted
only four months, Marxist ideas infiltrated the nation, mostly in
the guise of anti-imperialism, anticolonialism, and socialism-
humanism. While Cuba concentrated on rebuilding after three
years of war, anti-United States sentiment arose on the island in
response to Yankee control there. Nationalism often became
synonymous with Yankeephobia, expressed most forcefully by
Cuban university students and workers, who reiterated Martí's
fears of the United States.

United States influence, coupled with considerable immigration from Spain and *españolismo* (Spanishism), which guaranteed Spaniards' property rights, diluted Cuban nationalism.[1] United States military governors John Brooke and Leonard Wood controlled the island from January 1899 to May 1902, the United States marines under provisional governor Charles Magoon ruled from 1906 to 1909, the Platt Amendment sanctioning United States intervention limited Cuban sovereignty form 1902 to 1934, and the United States Federal Reserve Bank established Cuba's monetary policy for most of the first three decades of the twentieth century. Cubans began to rely upon the United States in political matters, and Cuban politics split into pro-United States and pro-Cuba factions. This destabilized Cuba's political party system and weakened its government. The United States concerned itself with all facets of internal rule on the island and made it difficult to distinguish between policy made in Washington and that made in Havana.[2]

Anti-United States attitudes in Cuba were buttressed by essayist José Enrique Rodó's rejection of United States utilitarianism and economic acquisitiveness. Rodó's work, especially his *Ariel* (1900), became very popular in Cuba, where the Uruguayan thinker symbolized the reaction against positivism and the idea that the answers to humanity's problems could be found in elitist scientific reasoning leading to material progress. Rodó's "New Idealism" and his enormous faith in the Latin American spirit cast doubt on both United States and Spanish traditions as means to progress in Cuba.[3]

United States political and social influence in Cuba grew during the first three decades of the twentieth century in proportion to its economic interests on the island. Distribution of Cuba's wealth did not keep pace with the nation's economic growth, nor did workers' wages. Workers who organized and struck for higher wages faced harsh repression. Those who tried to obtain some voice in politics met a similar fate. Although the Cuban government was theoretically autonomous from the private sector, it was not sufficiently free of it to enact legislation that would benefit labor at the expense of business.[4] Cuba's politicians never questioned the fundamentals of the private enterprise system or how it functioned in their country. Politics existed primarily to enrich the officeholders and their cohorts, not to improve social conditions and regulate the economy.[5] Political decisions frequently affected the masses adversely because politicians ignored their well-being.

Opposition to the government's attitude toward the social and political welfare of the masses occurred within the ranks of the Spanish anarchosyndicalists who found jobs in Cuba's factories between 1900 and 1910. These manual workers expressed an independent ideology and spread the strike concept and their belief in militant action to their Cuban colleagues.[6]

Simultaneously, dissension grew among Cuban intellectuals, who now had greater insights into the ramifications of imperialism and objected to the presence of the United States in their country. English theoretician J. A. Hobson's definition of imperialism as "the use of the machinery of government by private interests, mainly capitalists, to secure for them economic gains outside their country," fit the United States role in Cuba.[7] Like Hobson, some Cuban thinkers viewed worker exploitation as a manifestation of imperialism. Nationalists in the intellectual community inveighed against the United States, pursued scholarly studies to support their political views, and formed literary groups such as the one associated with the founding of Cuba's National Library in 1901.

Agitation by intellectuals induced worker action. The workers' party of Cuba, which emphasized the political independence of the working class as espoused by the Second International formed in 1904, allied with the Club de Propaganda Socialista (Socialist Propaganda Club) and became the

Partido Obrero Socialista (Socialist Workers party) in 1905 and the Socialist party of Cuba in 1907. El Círculo de Trabajadores "Carlos Marx" (The Karl Marx Workers Circle), composed mostly of cigar workers, was established in 1906 in Manzanillo in Oriente province as a forerunner of that area's Socialist party.[8] At the same time, anarchist novelist Carlos Loveira helped establish the Cuban League of Railway Workers and Employees, and a group of blacks, seeking political opportunities, organized the Agrupación Independiente de Color (Independent Colored People's Group) as a political party and participated in the 1908 elections. Cuba's Senate quickly passed a law prohibiting political parties organized on radical lines, numerous blacks rebelled in the mountains of Oriente, and the United States landed marines to help crush the revolt, in which about three thousand rebels died.[9]

United States military intervention elicited a negative response in Cuba, and in 1909 a group of Havana intellectuals established the Liga Antiplatista (the Anti-Platt League) to campaign for Cuban sovereignty. The following year the intellectual community organized the Academy of History to promote scholarly investigations. Led by Fernando Ortiz, the academy served as a pioneer in the areas of scientific historical analysis and revisionist interpretation, especially of the events that led to Cuba's separation from Spain.[10] Also in 1910, the Havana Conference Society started what became a tradition of scholarly presentations to the public on historical and political topics, and the National Academy of Arts and Letters began to edit and publish posthumously the papers of Cuba's outstanding literary figures.[11]

The radical, particularly anti–United States, anti-imperialist thought that existed among some members of Cuba's scholarly associations intensified during the second decade of the twentieth century. When the United States marines suppressed the last Afro-Cuban uprising in 1912, some black Cubans abandoned separatism and sought alliances with white radical activists both within and outside the scholarly community. Within a generation blacks and whites had joined forces, especially in the Communist party, to confront the United States and to work for the abolition of the Platt Amendment.

In a memorable meeting of the Economic Society in 1914, Fernando Ortiz, distinguished black lawyer and anthropologist, expert on Afro-Cuban culture, and editor of the *Revista Bimestre Cubana*, urged his fellow members to follow the lead of the nineteenth-century thinkers who had established journals and educational institutions, financed scholarships, imported professors, published books on Cuban problems, and "showed us how the work of a group of men with faith can carve a people and a nationality out of an exploited colony."[12]

United States investment in Cuba grew as corporations such as the United Fruit Company increased their holdings there, and the Cuban politicians and businessmen who profited most by it defended imperialist penetration as good for the country. The 1917 play *Tembladera* by José Antonio Remos depicted this phenomenon.[13] Other forms of Cuban literature used similar radical themes. Socialist poets José Z. Tallet, Rubén Martínez Villena, and Juan Marinello, encouraged by the Russian revolution, injected a spirit of revolutionary vanguardism into their works. But their subjects retained a Cuban character, since the Russian upheaval received little press space and Bolshevism had a very foreign ring in Cuba. On the other hand, the Mexican revolution, just entering its constitutional phase in 1917, received considerable attention among Cuban intellectuals.[14]

The Mexican and Russian revolutions, in conjunction with the University Reform Movement begun in 1918 in Argentina, caused Cuban students to seek new answers to political, social, and economic questions. These movements precipitated an outpouring of writing on Cuban nationalism, monoculture, and dependency. The University Reform Movement also produced some of the future leaders of the Ortódoxo party, the progenitor of the Castro revolution.

The Cuban government took its lead from the United States during this period. For instance, when Washington entered World War I, President Mario García Menocal (1913–21) immediately followed suit. On the other hand, Cuban intellectuals felt a need to assert their individuality and to view the world in nationalist terms. Despite the Platt Amendment, Cubans glorified their own traditions. They felt compelled to tell their history—to recount the deeds of the early moves toward independence, the Ten Years War, and the 1895 insurrection. Writers also expressed their disenchantment with Cuban leadership, United States business, and life under United States occupation.

The 1920s were crucial years in the development of radicalism in Cuba. The Workers' Federation of Havana was founded in 1920 by anarchosyndicalists who agitated for workers to receive a greater share of the fruits of their labor and rejected the neo-Darwinian racist interpretation of evolution that propagated the myth that blacks were inferior and thus deserved poorer jobs and pay.

Anarchist Carlos Loveira (1882–1928) awakened some of his countrymen to the plight of Cuba's proletariat in novels that stressed the class struggle. Much as Emile Zola did for France, Loveira in *Los immorales* (1919) (The Immoral Ones), *Generales y doctores* (1920) (Generals and Doctors), *Los Ciegos* (1923), (The Blind), *La última lección* (1924) (The Last Lesson), and *Juan Criollo* (1928) (John Doe) diagnosed Cuba's social and political ills, particularly during its last years as a colony and its early republican phase.[15]

The ideas of thinkers from other Latin American nations became popular among Cuba's intelligentsia during the 1920s.

The anti-imperialist themes of Uruguayan José Enrique Rodó and Nicaraguan poet Rubén Darío circulated, along with the ideas of Peru's José Carlos Mariátegui, who also opposed United States expansion in the Americas and espoused "open Marxism," the idea that Marxist thought should be revisable, undogmatic, and adaptable to Latin American situations. Mariátegui also advocated initiating the class struggle at the national level.[16]

Also popular in Cuba were the antidictatorship ideas of Mexican philosopher José Vasconcelos and the written works of Chilean socialist Luis Emilio Recabarren, who organized trade unions, urged worker control of industry and government, stressed nonviolent revolution, pushed for political education, and attacked the capitalist class for using religion as a political force to defend its privileges."[17]

The financial crisis of the 1920s intensified the criticism of Cuba's dependent position. The nation's sugar economy was controlled by United States and Canadian banks. Cuban traditions were being replaced, among the ruling class, by United States tastes. Money and the ostentation that accompanied it changed the character of Cuba's upper-class society, while the lower echelons suffered from all-around deprivation. The middle class aspired to upper-class elite status and sought access to it through politics.

Opposition to elitism originated at the University of Havana, where the Manicatos formed in 1922 as a broad-based athletic-oriented group. Led by crew and basketball star Julio Antonio Mella, the organization turned its efforts toward agitation for equality in politics. At almost the same time (1923), partially to combat racial elitism and separatism, poet Nicolás Guillén and Fernando Ortiz founded the Society for Afro-Cuban Studies.

The same year a major action, the Protesta de los Trece (Protest of the Thirteen), led by young radical writers, exposed the excessive corruption of the government of President Alfredo Zayas (1921–24). The protest began when Erasmo Reguiferos Boudet, Zayas's minister of justice, was seated at the head table at a meeting of the Academy of Science and poet Rubén Martínez Villena expressed his grievances against the government and left the hall with twelve others. Subsequently the grievances were published, and the incident touched off a period of militant idealism during which Cuban intellectuals invoked the names of Varona and Martí in voicing their opposition to the government's lack of interest in Cuba's social ills. Out of the Protesta emerged the Grupo Minorista (Minority Group), a literary vanguard whose mostly radical themes reflected political and social concerns.[18]

For five years (1923–27) the Grupo Minorista served as a voice of dissent for Cuban intellectuals, who for the first time expressed collective solidarity with the people of Latin America against dictatorship and United States imperialism and promoted agrarian and labor reform and popular government.[19] Calling its objective "ideological renovation," the Grupo also supported the elimination of false values, cultivation of diverse art forms, popularization of the latest artistic and scientific theories, reform of public teaching, secular education, university autonomy, and economic independence.[20]

The Grupo included most of the vital writers, artists, and journalists of the day, such luminaries as Juan Marinello, Jorge Mañach,[21] Francisco Ichaso, Félix Lizaso, Emilio Roig de Leuchsenring, José Antonio Fernández de Castro, José Tallet, Rubén Martínez Villena, and Alejo Carpentier. They believed that an intellectual minority could ably represent the sentiments of the majority of Cubans and build a hospitable political climate for them. Their thinking reflected the wisdom of their Cuban predecessors discussed earlier in addition to ideas taken from the Russian revolution and China's Sun Yat-sen (1866–1925), who, under the principles of nationalism, democracy, and socialism, overthrew the Manchu empire and founded the Republic of China. They also echoed the nonintervention sentiments of Nicaraguan Augusto César Sandino, whose guerrillas opposed the United States and whose tactics were to be studied by Fidel Castro three decades later.

The Grupo's activities centered on regular, and often emotionally charged, conferences and on the magazine *Social*, which published many of its works. Its members exchanged ideas and aspirations with colleagues throughout the Americas, whose revolutionary consciousness they helped raise. For example, the prolific American writer Carleton Beals was inspired by the Grupo Minorista to write *The Crime of Cuba* (1933), which examined the political treachery in the corruption-ridden nation.[22]

Students at the University of Havana, stimulated by the Grupo Minorista, the University Reform Movement, a resurgence of interest in the ideas of José Martí, and the Popular American Revolutionary Alliance (APRA or Aprista movement) of Peruvian political theorist Víctor Raúl Haya de la Torre, who spoke to them, demanded and received academic reforms in 1924. Encouraged by their success and by the Aprista program, which included Latin American unity, anti-imperialism, nationalization of land and industry, internationalization of the Panama Canal, and solidarity with all oppressed peoples and classes, the students then launched the José Martí Popular University as a center for revolutionary politics.

Intellectuals, students, and trade unionists increased their political activities. Rallies, conferences, and demonstrations were held frequently after Gerardo Machado assumed the presidency (1925–33); he immediately suppressed the more militant student and labor leaders. But Machado, known to some intellectuals as the "tropical Mussolini," could not curtail the growth of the labor and student movements.

The Comintern sent Mexico's Enrique Flores Magón, one of the ideological precursors of the Mexican Revolution, to Cuba to help organize a Communist party in 1925.[23] That year anarchists, Communists, and the Havana Federation of Labor formed the National Confederation of Cuban Labor (CNOC), which by the late 1920s contained thirty-five trade unions and was affiliated with the Profintern, Moscow's "Red Union" movement. However, the CNOC was not necessarily controlled by the Soviet Union.[24] Another central labor organization, the Federation of Cuban Workers, allied with the Pan-American Federation of Labor, was formed in 1927 by dictator Machado assisted by the United States State Department and socialist Juan Arévalo.[25]

Machado continued to crack down on left-wing organized labor and on the student movement. The Communist party was declared illegal in 1927 and driven underground, where it operated under the unofficial leadership of Rubén Martínez Villena. Students at the University of Havana organized the Directorio Estudiantil Universitario (University Student Directorate) in 1927, which mounted numerous protests against the government. When its leaders were jailed in 1931, a splinter group, Ala Izquierda Estudiantil (Student Left Wing) formed and allied with the urban and rural working classes, Martínez Villena, and the Communist party to oppose United States imperialism.[26]

Out of the Grupo Minorista and other dissenting factions, Alejo Carpentier, Juan Marinello, Jorge Mañach, Francisco Ichaso, Félix Lizaso, and Medardo Vitier created the leftist *Revista de Avance* (Forward Review) in 1927. The magazine lasted until 1930 and attempted to alleviate provincialism in Cuban culture and thought. Those affiliated with it believed they were an intellectual vanguard leading the struggle for social and political change.[27]

Supported by the student and labor movements, the primarily radical intellectuals who made up the *Revista de Avance* circle reacted vigorously against the mental and moral laxity of their nation. They based their essays on economic, social, and political themes, historical and dialectical materialism, and the ideas of some famous thinkers such as José Carlos Mariátegui and Maxim Gorky. The magazine became Cuba's major forum for new ideas, expressed in provocative articles and in the powerful poetry of proletarian writers such as Regino Pedroso and Nicolás Guillén.

In a short time the *Revista de Avance* had far-reaching impact. It helped launch a trend toward populism in the arts and culture.[28] It affirmed a sense of national conscience by focusing on cultural and political problems and by introducing Cubans to the leading literary, artistic, and political ideas of the era. It widened the spiritual bonds between the peoples of the hemisphere and showed Cubans how to relate to Marxist and radical Third World thought. It brought prestige to Cuba, and it stimulated the study of new doctrines and revitalized old ones.[29] For example, it inspired Ramiro Guerra's *Azúcar y población en las Antillas* (1927) (Sugar and Population in the Antilles), a very influential book by a nonradical, which examined the drawbacks of Cuban *latifundismo* (system of large landed estates) and the ways it affected society.[30]

The *Revista de Avance* reacted against romanticism and academic pedantry and led the way for a new generation of better-trained, more scientific writers and thinkers. It reflected hope for a purer political and social atmosphere, a universal order with which all Cubans could associate. In so doing, it elevated the protest against the tyrannies of Machado and the plight of Cuba's toiling masses.[31] The vanguardism that accompanied the *Revista de Avance* spilled over into all the arts. The Havana Philharmonic flourished, high culture received a broader audience, and the Office of the Historian of Havana undertook massive publishing projects designed to preserve the public record and popularize the writings of *pensadores* such as José Martí.[32]

The spirit of anarchism grew stronger among Cuban intellectuals, who complained that the Machado regime obstructed progress by continuing the nation's republican tradition of stealing from the treasury, political malfeasance, and selling natural resources to foreigners. Students, supported by urban workers, conducted some guerrilla actions against the dictator, who had himself reelected in 1928 for a six-year term.

Because of its close economic links with the United States, Cuba suffered enormously during the Great Depression. In 1931 a secret terrorist organization, ABC, composed of students and workers and mostly middle-class professionals, formed to combat the Machado government. ABC based its actions on a knowledge of Cuba's problems, the Aprista objectives, and the belief that violence was necessary to attain political and social freedom.[33] ABC's plan to eliminate Machado failed, but its actions, in conjunction with those of the Directorio and Ala Izquierda and protests by Cuba's intellectual community, led Washington to send Sumner Welles to Cuba to mediate between Machado and his opponents. Welles's presence in some ways exacerbated the situation. The Directorio denounced United States intervention, a general strike broke out, a few military units rebelled, and Machado resigned in August 1933. Radical alliances, merging thought with action, contributed significantly to his downfall and established, as we shall see, a foundation for future progressive political pursuits.

The Generation of 1930, which ousted Machado, looked to the thinking of José Martí for guidance and continued the struggle he had begun. Sentiment against the Platt Amendment spread as Cuba's students, workers, left-wing political groups, and radical intellectuals constantly contrasted Martí's humanism with United States greed. In the wake of the overthrow of

Machado, nationalism and optimism abounded. Ramón Grau San Martín assumed the provisional presidency in September 1933 and demanded abrogation of the Platt Amendment. Internecine warfare led to Grau's ouster in January 1934, and army commander Fulgencio Batista became Cuba's political power broker for the next quarter of a century, the one who negotiated the termination of the Platt Amendment and the one against whom Cuba's next revolution was directed.

Carlos B. Baliño (1848–1926)

Carlos Baliño never attained the popularity or stature of his friend José Martí as a journalist, freedom fighter, and *pensador*. But to socialists he is more of a precursor than Martí of the Castro revolution. Raised in a revolutionary tradition by his father Carlos J. Baliño, an architect and engineer who was deported from Cuba for his anti-Spanish activities, young Carlos became a political activist at an early age. At seventeen he wrote the article "El Alacrán" (The Scorpion), opposing slavery and the exploitation of workers. He worked with Cuba's laboring classes, particularly the tobacco workers, and that experience, together with the influence of Luz, books and articles on the French Revolution and the destruction of feudalism, European socialism, and the Ten Years War, turned him toward full-time political activities while in his early twenties. He then sought exile in the United States, where he met Martí, observed imperialism at first hand, and remained for over thirty years until Spain was dislodged from Cuba.[34]

While in the United States Baliño searched for a liberating philosophy, one that would enable him to plan for Cuba's independence. He was initially attracted to the anarchist thinking of Bakunin and of the Italian Giuseppi Fanelli. Subsequently he replaced their ideas with the thought of Marx and Engels, which he read while working in a factory in the United States between 1875 and 1881. In the United States he affiliated with Samuel Gompers and the workers' movement, organized cigar workers in Florida, lectured extensively, and wrote articles and poetry for various newspapers, including *La Tribuna del Trabajo* (The Workers' Tribune), and campaigned for Cuban liberation and the abolition of imperialism.[35]

He carried on the revolutionary activities of his friend Enrique Roig and collaborated with Martí to found the Cuban Revolutionary party in 1892. His brand of militance included scientific socialism and the belief that independence was not a political movement but a social one, made not in evolutionary fashion but by war.[36] Although he and Martí disagreed on the merits of socialism, they respected one another and shared what Baliño referred to as an uncompromising Christlike revolutionary attitude[37] and the belief that without economic liberty from the United States political liberty from Spain would be ineffective.[38] Martí called Baliño "a Cuban who has a beautiful soul and suffers the hardships of humanity," one "whose only sin might be his impatience to redeem it."[39]

Baliño returned home in 1903, where he worked on the newspapers *El Mundo* (The World) and *El Proletario* (The Proletarian) and tried to popularize the idea that breaking ties to Spain had not brought genuine independence to Cuba, since the United States dominated the island and Cuba's basic economic and social structures had not changed. He pointed out the need for economic freedom, without which the concept of liberty is diminished. He emphasized the need for economic diversification and production for the internal market as essential to Cuban economic independence.[40]

In 1903 he founded the Club de Propaganda Socialista (Socialist Propaganda Club), which was not a political party or a workers' union but an organization dedicated to propagating

Marxist ideas. He wrote article after article for the Club. When a group of workers formed a political party the following year, he criticized them for limiting themselves to reforms in the capitalist system.[41] In 1905 he organized the Socialist Workers party of Cuba,[42] based on the program of revolutionary socialism[43] articulated by the First Communist International.[44] The party hoped to achieve political power, convert individual and corporate property into collectives or common property, satisfy the needs of all people, emancipate the proletariat, abolish social classes, and let the workers own the fruits of their labor.[45]

Baliño gained a reputation for writing simple essays that the average worker could comprehend, for making socialism logical and the Socialist Workers party attractive. The same year that he founded the party he produced his most famous written work, a pamphlet *Verdades socialistas* (1905) (Socialist Truths), which displayed a sound knowledge of Marx and Engels. In it he stated that art and literature should be for all, not just the privileged, claimed that moral decay emanated from the system and could not be eliminated by reforms, condemned religion and the idea of social evolution as contributing to people's willingness to accept their fate, depicted socialism as a form of social planning and action and as an aspiration for justice, spoke about practical matters such as nationalized railroads and socialized medicine, asserted that equality of conditions and opportunity were not designed to deprive people of their individuality or to regulate their behavior,[46] and expressed a belief in the effectiveness of strikes in bringing justice to the exploited toilers.[47] *Verdades socialistas* represented the most articulate plea by a Cuban Marxist to that time, relating the plight of Cuba's workers to that of their brethren elsewhere.[48]

Baliño kept his finger on the pulse of the international socialist movement. He closely followed the numerous strikes in Russia in 1905, concluded that a strong workers' movement was developing there, and predicted that Russian intellectuals would organize a revolution. By 1918 he had become enamored of the Russian revolution and even wrote a poem identifying with it. The Soviet experience reinforced his confidence in the mission of the proletariat, whose cause he continued to champion in speeches and in print.[49]

He condemned the Platt Amendment and United States imperialism in the Caribbean as portrayed in Scott Nearing's *The American Empire*. In 1921, the year that book was published, he translated it into Spanish and added a prologue illustrating that United States capitalism had moved from a democratic spirit to one based on hegemony.[50] By this time the Communist International operated in fifty-three countries, and Baliño looked to Moscow for guidance. In 1922, under his direction the Socialist Group of Havana carried on the work of the International. When Lenin died in 1924 Baliño noted, "Lenin has died, but his work lives."[51]

In July 1925, soon after president Gerardo Machado assumed office, Baliño and Julio Antonio Mella, with whom he collaborated to produce the magazine *Juventud* (Youth), helped found the Cuban Section of the Anti-imperialist League.[52] The following month they participated in a congress that established Cuba's Communist party, affiliated with the Comintern. He and Mella worked through the Communist party to raise the consciousness of the Cuban people and put pressure on the government to abrogate the Platt Amendment.[53]

Besides indicting United States imperialism, Baliño blamed many of Cuba's problems on its native bourgeoisie, which he labeled hypocritical and accused of not caring about the nation's hungry, miserable, and ignorant citizens. He advocated an end to what he loosely referred to as "Cuban slavery," wherein the means of production were controlled by foreigners and their native accomplices. He agitated for socialism and advocated putting the means of production in the hands of the peasants, thereby elevating the ordinary citizen.[54]

He forcefully opposed discrimination against blacks, who he believed suffered the most under what he termed Cuba's slavery system. His writing did a great deal to make socialism appealing to Cuba's large black population, which henceforth played a vital role in the socialist movement. Baliño also expressed great concern for the welfare of children all over the world, whom he saw exploited by overwork and neglected, especially medically. He deplored poor pay for child labor, noted that millions of youngsters died of hunger, and felt that these situations were conducive to organizing young people into socialist groups.[55]

Baliño, whom Martí called "the Cuban that has a heart of gold," struggled for socialism until his death. He was not a profound or creative Marxist thinker, but he was an inspirational promoter of socialism—the first major twentieth-century Marxist in the minds of his countrymen.

Emilio Roig de Leuchsenring (1889–1964)

Cuba's twentieth-century radical intellectuals fit into two broad categories. Thinkers such as Carlos Baliño wrote primarily for popular consumption and disseminated the ideas of others, while *pensadores* such as Emilio Roig de Leuchsenring, whose works demonstrate greater originality and scholarly depth, generally wrote for limited academic as well as general audiences.

A graduate of the University of Havana, where he received a doctorate in civil law in 1917, Roig developed tremendous faith in the eclectic work of Enrique José Varona and regarded Félix Varela as Cuba's first teacher of revolutionaries in terms of adequately expressing Cuba's need for total independence.[56]

By the time he reached his middle twenties, Roig had earned a reputation for his articles on humor and the Cuban ethos. A frequent contributor to Havana's scholarly conferences, he served on various legal commissions, wrote newspaper articles, joined the Grupo Minorista, and affiliated with the Communist party to oppose Machado.

In 1927 Roig became historian of the city of Havana, a position he held until he was forced into exile by Machado in 1931. He resumed the historian's position in 1933 and held it until the Castro era. He expanded the Office of Historian of the City of Havana to become a rival of Cuba's Academy of History and established a precedent in Cuba for preserving the historical record. The office published over one hundred volumes under his direction,[57] including biographies, historical documents, and collections of the works of José Martí, Máximo Gómez, and Félix Varela.[58]

The author or editor of over thirty books, Roig served as an effective publicist for history. He led Cuba's revisionist school of history. In 1940 he formed the Sociedad Cubana de Estudios Históricos e Internacionales (Cuban Society for Historical and International Studies) to include scholars for whom the Academy of History was too conservative.[59] Under his guidance the society fought successfully to change the name of the 1898 conflict from the Spanish-American War to the Spanish-Cuban-American War, changed the name of the "Hispanic period" of Latin American history to "colonial period," led Cuban scholars in the struggle against United States involvement in Cuba's affairs, and formulated historical theories that subsequently influenced the Castro revolution.[60]

As a historian he specialized in the social and political history of Cuba. His best works dealt with nineteenth-century national and international politics. He edited numerous books, often to prove a particular theory, such as that the United States was

not the decisive element in the victory over the Spanish in 1898—
that Cuban forces, not the Rough Riders, made the difference
and that United States military forces at times deliberately
impeded Cuban military progress so that the United States
would get credit for the victory.[61]

Roig also wrote a history of Cuba's Thirty Years War, tracing
the development of nationalism in Cuba through the rise of the
independence movement and analyzing the latter's causes and
consequences.[62] He wrote on the nationalism and internationalism of Martí and the revolutionary ideology of Máximo Gómez
and tried to connect Maceo with the major anti-imperialist,
antiracist, anticlerical, antidespotic, anticolonial, and pro-free-
thinking themes in Cuba.[63] His works also included pieces on
law in the Americas, the League of Nations, United States intervention, José Agustín Caballero, and why the bloody sport of
bullfighting should be outlawed. He also wrote a book on the
evolution of the medical profession in Cuba.[64]

His fertile mind pondered numerous weighty questions and
explored new areas. For example, he concluded that Masonry
was a crucible for revolution and liberty in Cuba since it founded
schools and libraries and urged progress, equality, fraternity,
and democracy. He saw a parallel between the United States,
where most of the founding fathers were Masons, and Cuba,
where Máximo Gómez, Antonio Maceo, Calixto García, and
José Martí belonged to that secret fraternal organization.[65]

Like many of his erudite contemporaries, Roig viewed Martí
as the major Cuban thinker who confronted the nation's problems—who made people think and gave them a sense of
national pride and international recognition.[66] He shared Martí's
dislike of the racial discrimination encountered by black independence leader Antonio Maceo, attributing such behavior
to class distinctions based on skin color,[67] and he saw blacks
working for a society where color would be irrelevant.[68] He

76 √

concurred with Martí that after the ouster of Spain Cuba had to free itself from the North American empire.

Roig viewed Martí as a model for the liberation of all Spanish America, depicting him as an internationalist who saw the independence of Cuba and Puerto Rico as a major move toward achieving a desirable balance of power between the United States and Latin America.[69] Roig described Puerto Rico's great social philosopher Eugenio María de Hostos (1839–1903), who had a Cuban grandfather, as a transcendental figure of importance to Cuban independence, a "citizen of America" who shared Martí's ideology and strove for Spanish-American solidarity in the face of United States imperialism.[70] He lamented that Martí could not fully evaluate the modern phenomenon of imperialism because when he campaigned for Cuban and Puerto Rican independence imperialism had not become the "monopolist phase of capitalism" and the United States was not yet an imperialist in the twentieth-century sense.[71] Unlike Marx, who told the workers of the world to unite in the face of capitalism, Martí, according to Roig, merely urged the people of the world toward solidarity.[72]

In addition to his writings on Martí, Roig edited and analyzed the works of Manuel Sanguily (1848–1925) a gifted orator and contributor to Cuban anti-imperialist thought. Sanguily possibly merits a separate section in this book, but I have chosen merely to touch upon his ideas here. Sanguily analyzed the character of Cuban political life in novels, poems, and social and political critiques that were often more inspirational than profound. He was, in Roig's estimation, a literary defender of Cuban sovereignty with a historical approach, an ardent opponent of corruption in government, and a romantic who eloquently extolled the virtues of such Cuban heroes as Martí, Maceo, and Luz.

Though a general in the liberating army, Sanguily advocated civilian rather than military government. He concluded that independence with restrictions was preferable to military rule, and he subsequently voted for the Platt Amendment in order to secure the withdrawal of United States troops from Cuba. Also, after the victory over Spain in 1898 he was antagonized when Spanish citizens were permitted to remain in Cuba and retain their possessions. He served in Cuba's Constituent Assembly in 1900 and founded the Nationalist party.[73] He criticized monopoly and blamed foreigners for Cuba's system of latifundia, and in 1903 he introduced legislation in Cuba's Congress to prohibit the sale of land to foreigners.

Sanguily's essay "Official Teaching and Free Teaching" warned against excessive state interference in the universities.[74] He had little faith in the state and saw universal suffrage as a way to combat government domination over a people.[75] He also called religious influence on government farcical in Cuba, where irreligion was common and ignorance was rampant among the country's spiritual directors.[76] He viewed the church's thinking as "petrified" but believed that there existed true Christian humanists like José de la Luz, who cared for the oppressed, favored equality, and had the compassion of Christ and Socrates.[77] According to Roig, who shared his attitude toward the church, Sanguily argued for separation of church and state before Cuba's Constitutional Commission in 1901, using as historical evidence the church's antidemocratic practices, the fact that in France during the First Republic the church continually conspired against the state, and the fact that such practices did not occur in the United States, where separation existed. He said that Cuba's fear of the pope and of the clergy was caused by a church historically associated with oppression.[78]

Although not a socialist, Sanguily realized that a directing class rather than a popular class made the decisions that guided society and was primarily responsible for its problems. The people voted for whoever their directors chose after constitutionalism began in Cuba.[79]

Sanguily and Roig opposed the United States military presence in Cuba during the establishment of the new republic. Roig believed that as early as 1823, when the United States announced its unilateral Monroe Doctrine, Washington had been seeking to annex Cuba.[80] By 1881 Cuba had become an economic dependent of the United States, though still a political dependent of Spain. He asserted that United States business and government officials tried to prevent Cuba from becoming independent, from being incorporated by another European country, from joining with other young Spanish-American nations, and from affiliation with the United States as an equal state.[81]

Roig became obsessed with the Platt Amendment. His exhaustive two-volume *Historia de la enmienda Platt: Una interpretación de la realidad Cubana* (1935) (History of the Platt Amendment: An Interpretation of Cuban Reality) explained the continuous covert intervention of the United States in Cuba that existed from the moment that Tomás Estrada Palma, who headed Cuba's government in exile in New York and then served as the nation's first elected president (1902–6), permitted the amendment to go into effect in 1902.[82] In a way the Platt Amendment, which was affixed to the Cuban constitution and sanctioned United States intervention in Cuba, was tantamount to United States annexation of Cuba and a culmination of the 1853 Ostend Manifesto, under which the United States asserted its "self-proclaimed" right to acquire Cuba.

Roig demonstrated how the amendment permitted the United States, between 1902 and 1934, to dominate the Cuban economy.[83] He also contended that the amendment, and Presidents Calvin Coolidge and Herbert Hoover, helped create and maintain the tyranny of Gerardo Machado.[84] In addition, Roig claimed that although the 1933 upheaval against corruption and despotism for the most part failed, it contributed to the termination of the Platt Amendment; though it did not end United

States domination, it eliminated the instrument that made it official.[85] When the amendment was abrogated in 1934 and Franklin Roosevelt talked about abandoning intervention in the affairs of others in the Americas, Roig believed the myth of the Good Neighbor policy. In later years he realized that the Good Neighbor policy only changed the image of the United States by removing overt intervention or the facade of imperialism; the old substructure through which to channel covert intrusions remained intact.[86]

Roig's histories stressed the hypocrisy of the United States contention that it assisted humanity by involving itself in Cuba and Latin America. In *Males y vicios de Cuba republicana: Sus causas y sus remedios* (1959) (Faults and Defects in Republican Cuba: Their Causes and Remedies), he examined how Cuba was colonized and became the playground of the United States with multimillion-dollar hotels, casinos, and cabarets. Roig condemned the use of recreation to rob people and the decadent ambience of vice and corruption created in Cuba by United States capital.[87]

He called for an end to neocolonialism, which he noted had been cloaked in many guises. For example, he termed absurd Woodrow Wilson's reasons for entering World War I, which the American president called "a war of high and unselfish purposes." In 1918 Wilson guaranteed the rights of small nations to self-determination, but in 1916 he had sent the marines into the Dominican Republic, which they controlled until 1924, when they pulled out in favor of a United States–trained native police force under Rafael Trujillo, who then ruled the country in brutal fashion until 1961. Roig accused Wilson of attempting to conceal United States financial designs on the hemisphere under the rhetoric of universal democracy and international equality. He pointed out that after World War I and after interventions in Cuba, the Dominican Republic, Haiti, Nicaragua, Mexico, and

Panama during the second decade of the twentieth century, the United States had emerged as a creditor nation and a moneylender to Europe and Latin America.[88] As early as 1919, Roig explained how Washington used treaties, naval bases, loans, monopolies, and latifundia to make the Caribbean into a Yankee lake.[89] The United States continued to gain markets in Latin America, and into the 1930s it used Cuba as an example of what its foreign policy could achieve in the region.[90] Roig vehemently attacked United States policy in the Caribbean and in Puerto Rico in particular. He stated that Puerto Rico's 1950 rebellion for independence brought to power Luis Muñoz Marín, a United States puppet whom Washington sanctioned, along with "Operation Bootstrap" as the developmental model for Latin America. The island became a "free and associated" state but remained a colony.[91]

Roig labored for the Anti-imperialist League. He believed that an anti-imperialist tradition had existed in Cuba since the early independence activities took place. He saw anti-imperialism as a vital part of Cuban history, as noted in the works of Varela, Martí, and Varona, and called attention to the fact that it predated the scientific studies of Lenin.[92] He cited the 1954 United States overthrow of the democratically elected government of Jacobo Arbenz Guzmán in Guatemala as a continuation of United States imperialism and explained that the action was designed to destroy capitalist reforms,[93] which the United States attacked on the pretext of fighting Communism, what former Guatemalan president Juan José Arévalo defined as "Anti-Kommunism"—seeking to curtail any activity one opposes after labeling it "Communist inspired."

None of Roig's deeds had a greater impact upon future generations of Cuban intellectuals and students than his efforts on behalf of the Grupo Minorista. He and his Grupo cohorts inveighed against false values, strove for a renovation of Cuban ideals, and prodded a broad range of artists to apply their vision and talents to society's problems.[94] The Grupo's pleas for radical and progressive political and social change were heard by learned opponents of tyranny all over the Americas. Theoretically the freedom to write what one pleased existed in Cuba, but Roig said that a "sword of Damocles" hung continuously over the heads of Grupo Minorista members.[95] Although the organization had no official organ, its political tone was set by the magazine *Social*, directed by Roig with, in the words of Enrique José Varona, "Catalan tenacity, German systematization, and Cuban life."[96] Thanks in part to Roig, a special spirit surrounded the Grupo, an aura of individual subordination to a common purpose and belief that the individual will triumph only if the group does. Roig and his colleagues produced scholarly, provocative, and creative work without arrogance or academic ostentation.[97] In times of social and political stress the Grupo represented what Mexican philosopher José Vasconcelos called "the whole generous heart of Cuba, the best young Cubans, the most intelligent, the purest, most patriotic, the hope of Cuba."[98] Among those it inspired were Peru's Marxist thinker José Carlos Mariátegui, Argentine socialist thinkers Manuel Ugarte and Alfredo Palacios, and young Cuban intellectuals who would eventually help turn their country toward the socialist ideal and even revolution.

Emilio Roig de Leuchsenring pursued his work as a major scholar and political activist during the era of enormous growth in radical thought in Cuba when the efforts of the Anti-imperialist League, the student and trade union movements, the Grupo Minorista, the Communist party, the *Revista de Avance*, and the Twenty-sixth of July Movement coalesced. He helped prepare a new generation of radical *pensadores* who stressed the existence of classes and castes and broke down society into the exploiter class (the owners of the means of production) and the exploited class (the workers).[99]

82

Roig wrote old-fashioned narratives, not methodological Marxist works. He accumulated huge amounts of evidence to support his radical contentions. His urgent sense of nationalism, and his outrage at imperialism, encouraged him to do historical research to find new answers to old questions. He initiated a new wave of revisionist history based on facts and *Cubanidad*. He proved that the 1895 war had not freed Cuba, that foreign involvement in Cuba's domestic affairs had turned Cuban against Cuban, and that those in power had kowtowed to the United States to retain their positions. He ridiculed the Cuban church for maintaining superstition and prejudice and for never criticizing the domination of foreign capital for fear of jeopardizing its own wealth.[100] He argued for a more egalitarian society without privilege. He castigated racism in the workplace, which limited the possibilities of acquiring the necessities and also limited workers' access to recreational and cultural areas.[101]

To remedy the maladies of Cuba, Roig said, it was necessary not simply to change the leaders and institutions but to eliminate the economic and social conditions that had evolved since the colonial era.[102] Until the eve of the 1959 Castro victory, Roig repeatedly reiterated that the work of the nineteenth-century revolutionaries was incomplete. He saw the Castro revolution as the realization of most of his dreams. At the Thirteenth Historical Congress in February 1960 he rejoiced that the tyranny of Batista and the Cuban rulers supported by the United States had been banished.[103] To Roig the Castro revolution conquered the republic so that ultimately liberty could be forged.[104]

Julio Antonio Mella (1903–29)

Scholars tend to think of Julio Antonio Mella as a predecessor of Emilio Roig and a successor to Carlos Baliño, though they were all colleagues who worked together on various political and literary projects and reinforced each other's thinking. The son of a middle-class Irish mother and a father from the Dominican Republic, Mella began his education in a private Catholic school. During the 1920s he studied at the University of Havana, where he became acquainted with the Marxist works of Peruvian José Carlos Mariátegui and Argentine Aníbal Ponce and was influenced by the Aprista movement and by exiled Mexican poet Salvador Díaz Mirón, who taught him about the Mexican Revolution.

Mella thought that the ideas of the University Reform Movement were a step in the direction of radical, systematic change for Cuba.[105] He developed a strong belief in cooperation between intellectual and manual workers, and like Mariátegui, he supported university students' advancing the cause of the working classes. To attain that goal, in 1922 he organized Cuba's first revolutionary student movement, the Federation of University Students. That organization served as a forerunner of other university movements in Cuba, including the one that spawned Fidel Castro's revolution three decades later.[106]

Mella used his sharp mind and exceptional oratory to advocate the independence of teaching institutions from the state, a step that would democratize the universities and break the class monopoly on culture.[107] He opposed the authoritarian, diffident attitudes that prevailed among university professors and succeeded in obtaining the dismissal of over a hundred corrupt ones who received pay as political payoffs but never taught. He saw the University of Havana as medieval and colonial and demanded that students have the right to participate in its administration.[108] He said the university was a school of commerce where students went to learn how to make financial gains in life rather than an institution devoted to improving society.[109]

His dissatisfaction caused him in 1923 to help start the José Martí Popular University, modeled after Peruvian Víctor Raúl

Haya de la Torre's Popular University González Prada. Martí University's program, based on antidogmatic pedagogy, stressed the failure of Cuba's political system, intellectual treason, the dangers of United States capitalism, the struggle for legislation to benefit the working class, and the regeneration of Martí's ideas.[110] The university brought over five hundred workers together with students and professors in order to foster understanding. To Mella, it existed to encourage new ideas rather than to inculcate those of the prevailing system, as the University of Havana did. He used José Martí University as a vehicle to denounce the inhumane working conditions in Cuba, especially on the sugar plantations. Because of the school's politics and anti-imperialist posture directed against the United States, dictator Machado declared it illegal in 1927, and it ceased to function.[111]

At the University of Havana, and later through Martí University, Mella identified and tried to resolve the antagonisms between manual and intellectual laborers. He understood that physical workers had difficulty seeing the "value" produced by the fruits of cerebral labor and thus tended to identify intellectuals with the bourgeoisie and the prevailing social system. He urged manual laborers to relate better to the mental workers—to realize that both theory and practice were vital to the struggle for socialism.[112] He wrote that the intellectual is a worker who tries to bring about justice from tyranny, a concept he borrowed from Uruguay's José Enrique Rodó. Mella believed that intellectuals should take over the functions of priests, and he noted that those who worked for freedom were intellectuals but those who just talked about it were hypocrites.[113] Although he was an atheist he did not oppose religion for others. But he was anticlerical and found the clergy reactionary, opposed to scientific thought, and too influential in Cuba's schools. To combat this retrograde situation, in 1924 he started the Anticlerical Federation of Cuba.[114]

Mella was impressed by the Russian revolution, studied Soviet educational methods, and was enthusiastic about the effective use of cultural committees in Russian factories, which brought theater, music, art, and history to the workers. He claimed that workers had to be encouraged by intellectuals to further their education and to express themselves in the creative arts in order to enrich their lives—ideas he tried to popularize in Cuba. He said that he undertook such projects not as a utopian but as a realist who believed that he could contribute to social progress in his lifetime.[115]

Mella used his talent for writing stimulating, but not highly theoretical, essays and polemics to raise consciousness and promote socialism in a precise and inspirational fashion. He excelled at explaining in Marxist terms in *Juventud,* the journal he edited with Carlos Baliño, the contradictions inherent in post–World War I international, social, and economic conditions.[116] He understood the value of effective communication to the fight for socialism and wrote pieces on how to write articles, reach a wide audience, express a sense of the masses, and organize for collective action.[117] Mella also used his writing and organizational skills to propagate the idea that the Cuban people would be emancipated only when they understood their own society.[118] He claimed that art forms like Charlie Chaplin's and Sergei Eisenstein's films and John Reed's book *Ten Days That Shook the World* (1919) expressed reality and were extremely useful tools to make Cubans aware of how they were exploited and what they could do to engender change.[119]

Conversely, Mella viewed some types of popular culture as poor substitutes for work. For example, though he was an outstanding athlete, he believed that sports such as baseball, which became popular in Cuba during the Babe Ruth era, were promoted to make money, to hypnotize people or take their minds off their troubles, and to direct their energies away from solving social problems. The Olympic Games, he stated, primarily shifted the energies of middle-class youth away from work,[120] an opinion partially rejected by Fidel Castro, who feels that sports can build a sense of team or collective spirit as well as physical well-being and provide necessary heroes such as sprinter Alberto Juantorena and boxer Teófilo Stevenson, Olympic gold medalists who serve Cuban society as unifying forces.

Mella considered Cuba's social, political, and economic problems part of an international situation caused by capitalist imperialism. He advocated Latin American unity against the common enemy and believed radical change was particularly feasible in Argentina, Brazil, Chile, and Peru, where he thought it possible to impede the influence of the United States. He asserted that in the Caribbean, where the United States already had troops maintaining the status quo, change would be difficult to effect.[121]

To Mella, Wall Street represented the major oppressor of the Americas, operating under the Monroe Doctrine and in collusion with various Latin American native bourgeoisies.[122] He said that if the Monroe Doctrine did not exist, the United States would have to invent it to justify its expansionist policies. He viewed the Republican party as the one continuing to rape and pillage in Latin America on behalf of the Rockefellers and Fords. In his estimation the Democratic party also stood for imperialism but pursued it in a more frank and less deceptive way.[123] He feared a second world war provoked by capitalist avarice as an extension of class antagonisms. He used the word fascism to describe Mussolini's brand of state capitalism before the term became fashionable in the Americas.

Mella believed that internationalism—solidarity with the oppressed of the rest of the world—was the means to national liberation from the yoke of imperialism.[124] His ideas on imperialism were in part derived from Scott Nearing and Joseph Freeman's *Dollar Diplomacy* (1925). He agreed with them that the inevitable social revolution in Latin America had to be directed against United States capitalism, not the United States per se.[125]

He thought that such a revolution would be initiated by the Anti-imperialist League of the Americas, led by workers, students, peasants, and intellectuals. He and Baliño organized the Cuban section of the league in 1925 as a step toward building internationalism in the hemisphere. League members, including liberals and socialists, campaigned against Latin American dictators such as Augusto Leguía of Peru and Venezuela's Juan Vicente Gómez, whom they viewed as subservient to international capitalism.[126] The league criticized Cuba's United States controlled monoculture, castigated Yankee discrimination against blacks, and adhered to Emilio Roig's ideas on the Platt Amendment and his contention that the United States capitalism had always been Cuba's enemy.[127] Mella ascribed most of the blame for the wretched political and economic conditions in Cuba to the United States, in particular its influence on the first republican governors of the island, under whom dependency was extended.[128]

Mella edited the league's weekly *Lucha de Clases* (Class Struggle), communicated events in Cuba to the United States Communist party's newspaper the *Daily Worker* in New York,[129] and cooperated with the league's official organ *El Libertador* (The Liberator), published in Mexico.[130] Through the league and its publications Mella advocated Cuban control over the Guantánamo Naval Base occupied by the United States, independence for Puerto Rico and the Philippines, internationalization of the Panama Canal, and nationalization of basic industry.[131] He protested against United States military intervention and killings in Nicaragua and expressed solidarity with that nation's liberator Augusto Sandino.[132] Within the league Mella also established himself as Cuba's foremost expert on the Leninist concept of imperialism.

By the early 1920s revolutionary literature flowed into Cuba from Europe, Cuban socialists and anarchists were attracted to the idea of a more disciplined state party such as existed in Soviet Russia, and several small regional Communist groups formed in various cities on the island. These events led Mella and Baliño to organize the Constitutional Congress of the Communist Party of Cuba, held in August 1925 in Havana. Cuba's dictator Gerardo Machado responded to the formation of the Communist party by imprisoning Mella the following month on a trumped-up murder charge.[133] Mella immediately began a hunger strike, whereupon he was sent into exile, first to Honduras, then to Guatemala. Finally he settled in Mexico in 1926, where he worked with the Mexican Communist party.

In Mexico he spoke out loudly against the execution in the United States of anarchists Nicola Sacco and Bartolomeo Vanzetti, which he viewed as a manifestation of narrow-minded anticommunism.[134] He also wrote a thesis "El derecho y las clases sociales" (The Law and Social Classes), which examined political economy and the concept of work as the object of the science of economics. He analyzed Mexico's civil, penal, and work laws to find out how they were changed as a consequence of the bourgeois-democratic phase (1910–17) of the Mexican Revolution and demonstrated that the laws reflected the class divisions in society.[135]

In 1926 he wrote Glosas al pensamiento de José Martí (Commentaries on the Thinking of José Martí), exhorting Cubans to follow Martí's anti-imperialist, antifeudal, prointernational, and pro equal (black) rights positions. He showed how Martí's love for Cuba fit into the scheme of international solidarity for workers. In other words, Mella reconciled Cuban nationalism with internationalism.[136]

The following year Mella organized the National Association of Cuban Revolutionary Immigrants, a group with chapters in Bogotá, Madrid, Mexico City, New York, and Paris, dedicated to intensifying the struggle against, and warning the world about, the Machado dictatorship. In *Cuba Libre* (Free Cuba), the organization's journal, he wrote "¿Hacia dónde va Cuba?" (1928) (Where Is Cuba Going?), explaining that the nation's colonial position vis-à-vis the United States was analogous to that of Puerto Rico and that Cuba initially needed a liberal-national democratic revolution to rectify the situation.[137]

At the same time as he prescribed for the ills of Cuba, he criticized Peru's Aprista movement, which he formerly had supported but which he now believed denied the importance of the proletarian struggle in Latin America. He contended that the working classes had to unite the other classes and declared that *Aprismo* combated socialism by neutralizing the actions of the true revolutionaries[138] and by advocating a populist approach, including working with middle-class elements. Mella believed that ultimately the progressives in the Aprista movement would be devoured by its bourgeois elements and become reactionaries.[139] He criticized the Apristas as reformist-opportunists who approved of private property and opposed imperialism, but not on the grounds of class or as the final stage of capitalism.[140] Although the Apristas alluded to "intellectual laborers," Mella insisted they applied the expression not to workers but rather to petty bourgeois lawyers.[141] Moreover, he asserted that *Aprismo* was unscientific, a vehicle for rhetoric, and that no genuine *Aprista* method existed.[142] Mella's convictions about the Apristas were buttressed by political exiles from all over Latin America who belonged to the Anti-imperialist League, as did famous Mexicans such as artists Diego Rivera and David Alfaro Siqueiros and historian Isidro Fabela, who joined Mella in denouncing Cuba's Machado government in *El Machete*, the organ of Mexico's Communist party, and in *El Libertador*.[143]

Most scholars agree that agents of the tyrant Machado assassinated Mella in Mexico on 10 January 1929. Like his countryman José Martí, he became a martyr to the cause of Cuban liberation. To Martí's belief in international togetherness Mella added the dimension of a unified working class.[144] His standard interpretations of Marx and Lenin, couched in simple language, were instrumental in mobilizing thought in Cuba and in forming its revolutionary consciousness. In the tradition of Martí, but with a Marxist twist, Mella made an indelible imprint on his nation and became a hero to communists as well as to the non-Marxist left. He believed that the quest for social revolution was not an idealistic dream but a struggle to advance history.[145] His ideas were eventually translated into the reality of the Cuban revolution and its constitution, particularly aspects pertaining to limitations on property rights, marriage and divorce, anti-imperialism, agrarian reform, the elimination of illiteracy, and equal rights for citizens of both sexes and all colors.

Juan Marinello (1898–1977)

The last of this chapter's members of Cuba's left-wing intelligentsia, Juan Marinello, entered the University of Havana in 1916 and five years later, after earning a reputation as a student leader and fine orator, received the degree Doctor of Public Law. At the university he read the works of the major European and Latin American political philosophers and acquired a knowledge of the history and current politics of Latin America. He was particularly influenced by the thinking of Simón Bolívar and Mexican liberal president Benito Juárez, whom he saw as nineteenth-century practitioners of the Latin American tradition of liberty and democracy that he wished to pursue.[146]

Marinello participated in and gained national prominence from the 1923 Protesta de los trece against the corrupt government of Alfredo Zayas. He affiliated with the Grupo Minoristo, which emerged from the Protesta. In 1924 he edited the magazine *Venezuela Libre* (later called *América Libre* or Free America), and in 1927 he published *Liberación,* his first book of poems. The same year he helped found the *Revista de Avance.* Marinello's reputation grew among Latin America's intellectuals. He held professorships in Spanish and Ibero-American literature at the University of Havana and while in exile at the University of Mexico, and he gained acclaim for his academic and political conferences. His radical political activities and protests against the Machado government landed him in prison on the Isle of Pines, where he had plenty of time to familiarize himself with Marxist thought just as Fidel Castro did there a quarter of a century later.[147]

In 1931 at the First Congress of Revolutionary Writers and Artists of Mexico, Marinello befriended Aníbal Ponce, the guiding spirit of Argentine Marxism, whom he came to regard as one of Latin America's outstanding expositors of social conditions in the area. Ponce alerted him to the adverse affects of imperialism on Cuba.[148] They agreed that Peru's José Mariátegui was an advanced thinker who intelligently defended Latin America against an international economic system that would retard the region's overall development.

Marinello viewed Mariátegui as the master polemicist who argued eloquently against the prevailing system in the region and for its replacement by socialism.[149] He admired the humanism of Mariátegui, with whom he corresponded. He regarded him as the Latin American with the most thorough knowledge of Marxism[150] and applied his method of analyzing the Peruvian Indians to the Mayas of Guatemala, whose plight he attributed to imperialism and its search for cheap labor.[151]

Marinello praised highly Ponce's *Humanismo burgués y humanismo proletario* (1935) (Bourgeois Humanism and Proletarian Humanism). In that volume Ponce stated that humanism, characterized by a return to classical studies, had preceded the Renaissance, from which emerged an intellectual elite with too abstract a view of society. Ponce claimed that though Erasmus's bourgeois humanism declared the freedom of man, he was freed only to serve another master—one who owned the means of production. Ponce contrasted bourgeois humanism with Marxist humanism and concluded that humanity would flourish only if class distinctions were destroyed.[152] He believed this could be done by creating a love for literature, art, music, and the humanities and a classless culture with which everyone could identify equally. Ponce saw a correlation between transmitting the classics to the masses and eliminating human poverty, between opening up universities to all and permitting everyone to comprehend how exploitation works in order to eradicate it.[153]

Marinello also saw the influence of Mariátegui in Ponce's *Educación y lucha de clases* (1936) (Education and Class Struggle), which demonstrated how the rise of capitalism affected education in the Western world. Ponce saw in primitive education a social responsibility that reflected a collective sense of community.[154] But from classical times forward, he contended, education had become an arm of the ruling classes used by their state to maintain slavery and feudalism. The church, he believed, taught irrationality, passivity, fatalism, and faith in the supernatural. By the eleventh century and the founding of the first universities, the bourgeoisie, viewing education as the path to benefits formerly reserved for the nobility and the clergy, began to dominate intellectual life.[155] Ponce showed how the dominant class had directed the social organization of the state through education, which conveyed selected information but did not teach students to think for fear they might then question the system the education was designed to support. He lamented that children were being prepared to function as subordinates.[156]

The writings of Ponce contributed significantly to Cuba's revolutionary social planning and new educational system. Both of his books mentioned above were reissued by Castro's government, and his *Obras escogidas* (1975) (Selected Works) were published in Havana with an introduction by Marinello.[157]

In addition to his work on Ponce, Marinello wrote numerous articles and pamphlets on various topics, including politics and international economics, but specialized in literary criticism and the role of the writer in the revolution. His work included *Literatura hispanoamericana: Hombres, meditaciones* (Hispanic American Literature: Men, Meditations), which dealt with Cuban literary figures.[158]

Marinello was particularly interested in José Martí, whose works he reinterpreted[159] and whom he considered Cuba's premier writer. He believed that the literature of Martí was original, transcendental, and contagious and that the author was somewhat like El Cid in his quest for liberty. To Marinello, Martí answered the highest calling, the use of intelligence to free man. He saw a great deal of similarity in the humanism of Martí, Rodó, Darío, Ponce, and Mariátegui and in their attempts to dignify the worth of the individual.

To him, Martí took the initial step toward throwing off Cuba's chains of oppression by recognizing that imperialism causes economic deformation and by advocating the solidarity of the people of Latin America in opposition to imperialism. But Marinello pointed out that Martí did not think in materialist terms.[160] In Marinello's opinion, Marx and Martí sought equality and justice in a creative way, through both thought and action.[161] He said that Martí, without Marxism as a guide, worked like a doctor without X rays—lacking a valuable diagnostic tool for seeing societal problems more clearly. Martí operated without a methodology, without dialectical materialism and socialist objectives. Although Martí took the part of the exploited classes, he did not struggle to resolve the contradictions between social classes—he just tried to ease the pressures on those suffering.[162]

Marinello criticized those who used Martí like a bible, finding in his works whatever they wanted to express. At the time of Martí's centenary in 1953 he excoriated the clergy who referred to Martí in their sermons, on the grounds that attaching religious significance to Martí was "as disloyal as to wish to attribute Marxist thought to our man."[163] In *José Martí, escritor americano: Martí y el modernismo* (1958) (José Martí, American Writer: Martí and Modernism), Marinello displayed his own expertise on modernism and noted that the Cuban freedom fighter rejected modernists as artists.[164] He showed that to Martí modernism, which enjoyed considerable popularity in Cuba during the last years of the nineteenth century, attempted to preserve the aesthetic realm against the intellectual, historical, and social forces threatening it.

In another work, *Once ensayos Martianos* (1964) (Eleven Essays on Martí), Marinello demonstrated the liberal Cuban's indebtedness to Spanish classicists, his universality, and his anti–United States attitudes. Marinello declared that Martí defied categorization. He called him "the poet [who] expressing reality in an unaccustomed manner, transforms it within himself, makes it a part of his internal tumult, of his spiritual state, of his dominating emotion."[165]

Marinello claimed that some of the major middle-class Cuban intellectuals contributed to the barbarism of the pre-Castro era in Cuba.[166] He also maintained that a number of the nation's non-Marxist literary giants, in addition to Martí, opposed imperialism, advocated liberty of action for communists, and served as "men of transition" to socialism. However, he demonstrated that such thinkers as Enrique José Varona and Martí held different views of imperialism than did Lenin. To them it was a biological and social phenomenon, not one with an economic base.[167]

Marinello helped found Cuba's Communist party in 1925,

composed of humane intellectuals and workers who adhered to Cuba's anti-imperialist tradition. Simultaneously, he worked with the Anti-imperialist League. Within the Communist party he had a long career that included assuming responsibility between 1938 and 1961 for holding regular conferences. During the 1930s he attained national recognition as director of the magazine *Masas* (Masses), which he used to try to make Cubans aware of their position as pawns in an international game over which they had little or no control. In the magazine he portrayed Cuba as a dependent nation perpetually suffering from the reverberations of the conflicts within international capitalism.[168]

He served as a delegate to Cuba's 1940 constitutional convention, where the Communist party was instrumental in drafting provisions for collective bargaining, minimum-wage laws, the eight-hour day, the forty-eight-hour week, social security, and the requirement that workers be fourteen years of age.[169] In 1942 he was appointed minister without portfolio in the cabinet of Fulgencio Batista, in 1945 he served as vice-president of the Senate during the administration of Ramón Grau San Martín, and in 1948 he supported democratic elections and ran as the Communist party candidate for president, garnering 120,000 votes.[170]

Marinello the internationalist understood the causes of the tensions that resulted in excessive nationalist belligerence in Europe and predicted that a second world war would erupt as a consequence of competition for international markets. He feared that capitalist democracy would not be able to stem the tide of rising fascism, and he called the inability of France and England to defend democracy in the Spanish Civil War a sad portent.[171] He and his associates opposed Francisco Franco and Spanish fascism. He denounced wars predicated on imperialism but contended that just wars included those that opposed colonialism, imperialism, and class oppression. He considered it essential to fight for national and international liberty and to defeat such horrors as fascism.[172]

Marinello emphasized in 1940 that World War II would benefit the entrepreneurial class seeking new markets but would not help the masses. At that time he especially identified with the workers in the United States, who he felt did not want a war in which they could sustain the greatest casualties. After hostilities broke out in Europe, but before the Japanese attacked Pearl Harbor, he spoke of two types of democracy—the United States bourgeois type, which favored imperialism, and the Cuban Communist anti-imperialist form. He noted that World War II showed the contradiction between the two kinds of democracy and expressed the hope that the conflict would open the way for the type of democracy he desired—a people's democracy.[173]

His thinking approached that of the New Left and Castro's Cuba, which years later advocated "unitary democracy," distinguished from the "adversary democracy" of liberalism by its distrust of representative institutions and its preference for participation by all citizens in political deliberations and for decisions that require a consensus. "Unitary democracy" is inspired to some extent by Aristotle's idea of the polis as an association for the expression of civic friendship rather than the modern idea of the state as an instrument to serve private ends.[174]

Marinello believed that Cuba entered World War II on the side of the Allies to foster democracy and counter imperialism. Following the pre-1905 thinking of Lenin, he believed it necessary for Cuba to attain bourgeois democracy, such as existed in England and the United States, as a prelude to socialism. He hoped that the defeat of fascism would engender a wave of popular revulsion in Cuba against its own government excesses, stimulating a movement for democracy that would proceed against the imperialist aspects of bourgeois democracy and set in motion the next phase of the struggle for socialism.[175] He saw the termination of World War II as the beginning of a new era in United States imperialism. He realized that wartime exigencies had shifted a great deal of Latin America's economic dependence from Europe to the United States, a situation that the hemisphere's most powerful nation would strive to maintain and exploit.[176]

During the Cold War Marinello's personal actions repudiated the United States government's contention that all socialists were violence-prone agents of monolithic communism. He epitomized the rational intellectual striving for justice through peaceful radical means. He was both the dedicated *pensador* working at his craft with meticulous rigor and a revolutionary pursuing his ideals with facts and substance.[177]

He condemned the United States anticommunist crusade against the reformist governments that ran Guatemala from 1944 to 1954 and criticized Washington's poorly substantiated claim that the administration of Jacobo Arbenz Guzmán, which the CIA overthrew in 1954, was dominated by the Soviet Union. He found it ludicrous that the United States attacked the democratically elected Guatemalan government and solicited support for this stand in the United Nations and the Organization of American States from despots such as the Dominican Republic's Rafael Trujillo and Anastasio Somoza of Nicaragua. To Marinello, that Guatemala had the largest amount of multinational investment in Central America represented the key to United States policy. He was not surprised to see the United States keep a tight rein on Guatemala after 1954.[178]

He drew analogies between Guatemala and most of Central America, where the transnational corporations sought inexpensive labor and where the peasants were bound to the land as a result of archaic landholding systems perpetuated by the United Fruit Company and often supported by the conservative hierarchy of the Roman Catholic church.[179] In both Central

America and Cuba, where the United States presence was overwhelming, he saw social and political revolution and socialism as the logical response to centuries of capitalist exploitation and degradation.

Throughout his career Marinello simultaneously pursued revolution and cultural enrichment for the masses. His aesthetic orientation matched his political zeal. He explained that high culture, which he wanted to bring to the people, can flourish only when independence exists, when there is freedom to investigate fully and scientifically, when one can analyze societal development in terms of its historical context and thus understand the evolution of culture. Conversely, he thought that through the scientific examination of culture one can better comprehend society and its historical evolution.[180]

His writing reflected his belief that language is a vehicle for cultural expression. He advocated replacing the Spanish of Spain with noncolloquial American Spanish to uncover the dialectic between Old and New World culture. He incorporated into his language the sisterly and brotherly aspects of socialist expression[181] and was the first Cuban to use Marxist methods and a theoretical model in literary analyses that illustrated the contradictions in Cuba's culture.[182]

He believed that art was a wonderful place to make political statements. He wrote about art, especially opposing its pessimism, dehumanization, and subtle forms of colonialism.[183] He contended that one could discern Cuba's national character through its art. He respected the right of the artist to select his or her own aesthetic forms. Marinello believed that abstract art marvelously depicted the new revolutionary ideology and noted that art portrayed the dialectic well.[184]

He said that abstract art, like socialism, is often rejected because it does not conform to accepted norms. But in a true democracy both would be accepted. To him abstract art raised the discipline to another level, causing a new synthesis that dominant groups frequently reject because they do not understand it or fear that it will, if understood, undermine the status quo. He saw abstract art reaching out constantly, going ahead, synonymous with progress. It creates neither a live and let live attitude nor general acceptance, but it is universal, says something to everyone, and thus exists for the collective good.[185]

Marinello had a vision of the socialist-humanist enjoying all forms of art and culture and took pride in interpreting the works of others for the masses and also in presenting to them the fruits of his own labor. For instance, he wrote about the poignancy of the work of his comrade poet Nicolás Guillén, whom he admired because he practiced his craft with humility and whose works he depicted as the living integration of nature and culture.[186] At the same time, Marinello was equally comfortable producing lyrical metaphorical poems, delicately characterizing the melancholy and sadness in Cuba and touching the essence of *Cubanidad*, the problems of human destiny, of love and death.

Marinello's stature as a writer grew during the 1940s and 1950s, as did his role as a Communist party functionary. He worked diligently to maintain the visibility and legality of the party and remained prominent in Cuban politics. By 1956, when Fidel Castro began his battle against the Batista government from the Sierra Maestra, Marinello served as head of Cuba's Communist party.

After Castro's victory on 1 January 1959, Marinello played a role in reconciling the Communist party with Castro's revolutionary forces. This was no simple task given Castro's distrust of the party, which had for some years openly collaborated with the Batista regime and opposed armed struggle, while contending that only a broad united front and mass action could create conditions for the overthrow of Batista. Once Castro proved that other tactics, analyzed on subsequent pages, could succeed

and the Batista administration was ousted, and once a modicum
of accord was established between the Communist party and
Castro's Twenty-sixth of July Movement, Marinello was
appointed rector of the University of Havana. He subsequently
served as ambassador to UNESCO and in 1976 was elected
to Cuba's National Assembly of People's Power and to the
country's Council of State.

As rector, or head of the university, he endeavored to reach
the goals established by the University Reform Movement of
1918. He strove to terminate the elitism of the university and to
turn it into an institution providing a well-rounded education.
He also promoted democracy in the university, including self-
government by students and professors. He argued that students
should devote their full time to the university and should be free
of distractions that hindered their education. He maintained
that the university should permit all ideologies to be freely discussed, and that education, according to Marxist theory, was an
inalienable right, not a privilege. He vigorously supported
Cuba's literacy campaign, believing that society should not be
divided into an educated and an uneducated class, a situation
that had existed before the revolution and caused considerable
inequality.[187]

While rector of the university, Marinello spent a great deal of
time writing polemics, especially exhorting his Cuban comrades
in the various arts to channel their energies into projects illumi-
nating socialist realism.[188] He wanted his colleagues to promulgate a corpus of radical thought in the Americas that would
help explain the grand vision of revolution that had materialized
in Cuba.

He sought to eliminate secular distinctions between manual
and intellectual laborers by clarifying for the public what mental
workers did and how they contributed to the revolution. He saw
the novel as a wonderful device to transcend the gap between

manual and intellectual laborers. For example, he called Gabriel García Márquez's *Cien Años de Soledad* (1967) *(One* *Hundred Years of Solitude)* the best argument for the historical and socialist approach to literature, a splendid weapon in the Latin American fight for freedom, for the struggle against ignorance, superstition, imperialism, and tyranny.[189]

Like Carlos Baliño and Julio Antonio Mella, Marinello helped popularize standard Marxist-Leninist ideas in Cuba, but he did so in a more creative and innovative fashion. He acknowledged that Lenin could not have existed without Marx, but he saw Lenin as the thinker whose works enabled socialism to become a reality in the twentieth century, one who had the ability to integrate national culture into a cohesive international revolutionary whole.[190]

He learned flexibility from Lenin and adapted his ideas to fit new situations such as Castro's revolution, which he viewed as one of the major events of the century, a prelude to the triumph of Salvador Allende's Unidad Popular (Popular Unity Movement) in Chile in 1970, the growth of Peruvian nationalism during the late 1960s and 1970s, and the development of a populist pro-sovereignty movement in Panama under the government of Omar Torrijos (1968–78). The Cuban revolution, he asserted, brought a universal freedom to the Americas, exemplified by widespread opposition to the war in Vietnam and the black liberation struggle in the cities of the United States.[191]

Juan Marinello's career, like that of Emilio Roig, transcended all the major twentieth-century movements that helped develop radical thought in Cuba and that culminated in revolution. He was an integral part of the Protest of the Thirteen, the Grupo Minorista, the university student movement, the *Revista de Avance*, the Anti-imperialist League, the Communist party, organized labor, and the Generation of 1930 that ousted dictator Gerardo Machado and revitalized Cuban nationalism. More than any other member of Cuba's rising left-wing intelligentsia, Marinello served as a major link between the academic community, the liberals of the Martí ilk, the country's Communist old guard, and the insurrectionists who engineered the revolution.

The Cuban revolution does not
aim at the liberation of a class,
but at the liberation of humanity
from fears, prejudices, miseries,
shackles, shame, and dogmas.

Raúl Roa

CHAPTER 4

Revolutionary Thought, 1934–58

For more than half a century after Cuba's independence from
Spain, Cuban writers mounted attacks on their government,
public and private United States interests on the island, and the
socioeconomic system that bound the former to the latter. Most
who criticized without the luxury and protection of a university
appointment lived on the fringes of a disunited society, frequently with little means of support.

Before the 1959 revolution, Cuban society had little cohesion.
Institutions such as the military, the church, and the national
government were generally weak or ineffective. Although the
nation's economy grew considerably during the first half of the
twentieth century, there was little equity in the distribution of the
benefits of capital accumulation. All major social, economic,
and political groups shared access to government and tried to
eliminate each other to enhance their own positions.[1] Cuba's
middle class, which was not integrated in terms of organization,
used politics as a means of enlarging its portion of the national
income. Cuba's financially strong and politically weak entrepre-

neurial sector at times had little direct say in the island's governance under the successive dictatorships of businessman and
politician Gerardo Machado (1925–33) and professional soldier Fulgencio Batista (1933–44, 1952–58). Washington did not
object to the strongmen's policies, no matter how corrupt they
were or whom they hurt, as long as they did not adversely affect
the United States' enormous financial interests on the island.[2]

Opposition to the Machado regime took place among the
Generation of 1930, composed of students, intellectuals, and
young professionals who resorted to political action to terminate
the tenure of Cuba's repressive government and to institute
egalitarianism and political and social reforms. The Generation
of 1930 represented the numerous ideological currents present
in Cuba. Liberalism, socialism, Marxism, populism, nationalism,
corporatism, state capitalism, and syndicalism filled what had
formerly been an ideological vacuum. None of the new philosophies was conservative; all contained radical elements, and
all would eventually consolidate around the antidictator, anti-
imperialist Cuban revolution of the 1950s.[3]

From the 1930s on, Cuba's production of critical literature
increased considerably, especially works with historical themes
depicting the country's political inadequacies and dependent
status. The majority of Cuba's *pensadores* assumed left-of-center postures, opposed United States intervention in Latin America, and expressed sympathy for the working classes and trade
unions.

Working-class resistance to bad government increased continuously on the island, as did corruption in public office, government sinecures, and political dirty dealing. Cuba's organized
workers had played a major role in the ouster of Machado in
1933, and their ranks were swelling as social and working conditions failed to improve appreciably under Batista. Labor unrest
and strikes were manifestations of class struggle as workers

sought shorter working hours, a minimum wage, obligatory unionization, collective bargaining, maternity benefits, and

improved employment conditions.

The failure of the 1933 rebellion and of provisional president Ramón Grau San Martín (September 1933 to January 1934) to effect fundamental social changes left a deep feeling of frustration among the Generation of 1930 and its working-class allies, who increasingly equated the inability to progress with the prevailing socioeconomic system, predicated for the most part on the status quo. The socialist alternative now had greater appeal to Cuba's growing radical population, which began to articulate the need to change the nation's capitalist relations of production.

After Machado was driven from office, the Communist party successfully challenged the anarchosyndicalists for leadership of the labor movement and worked assiduously to unionize workers throughout Cuba. By January 1934, when the party held its Fourth National Labor Congress, its unions contained 400,000 to 500,000 members. Although not all were Communists, most were sympathetic to the Communist cause, and many were more radical than their Communist party counterparts.

Radicalism spread throughout Cuba in various ways. The Communist workers defended the rights of labor through the unions. Communist intellectuals wrote antigovernment and anti–United States tracts. The party called for the removal of Ramón Grau San Martín's "bourgeois landlord" government in January 1934. Peasants led by black Communist León Alvárez seized the land at Realengo 18 near Guantánamo and formed a "Red Guard" Soviet, which it maintained for well over a year before capitulating to Fulgencio Batista's army.[4]

Cuba's Aprista party issued a political manifesto in 1934, reiterating the principles laid down by Haya de la Torre a decade earlier. Its anti-imperialist thrust and its pitch for nationalization of land and industry and for solidarity with all oppressed classes particularly appealed to the Student Directorate at the University of Havana, which pursued revolutionary activities. The Apristas opposed United States finance capital and concessions in Cuba and strove to unite rural with urban labor to agitate for a democratic government and greater worker control over industry. The Apristas also wanted to place technology under state control, increase literacy, improve sanitation and public works, get small businesses away from the guardianship of foreign banks, protect and develop the economy, work for equal rights for women, and end discrimination against blacks.[5]

At the same time (1934) that the Communist party and the Apristas grew stronger, the Partido Revolucionario Cubano Auténtico (Cuban Revolutionary party) (PRC) or Auténtico party, led by Ramón Grau San Martín from exile and claiming to represent the thinking of José Martí, was founded on a platform of economic and political nationalism, social justice, and the breakup of foreign owned latifundia. Grau and his radical-reformer adviser Antonio Guiteras used the slogan "nationalism, socialism, and anti-imperialism."

During this period of political agitation and party organization civil war broke out in Spain, and the role of the communists, socialists, and anarchists in opposing General Francisco Franco stimulated communist and labor interest in opposing the Cuban caudillo (boss) Fulgencio Batista. Cuba's intelligentsia supported the Spanish republic in 1936. The following year Cuban Communists, socialists, anarchists, and radicals formed the Partido Unión Revolucionaria (Revolutionary Union party) (PUR) under the leadership of Juan Marinello and the Communist party. In 1938 the Communist party was legalized once again and initiated a tradition of continuous political activity and unity unequaled by any other party in Cuba. Since 1925 it had won the respect of the workers, and it continued to orient them to socialism. Since the days of Machado, the Communists had worked diligently not to incur the enmity of other political groups and the government, and they were included among the trusted friends and allies of diverse political constituencies for over three decades. This caused Jorge Mañach, a progressive turned conservative, to comment that "the greatest danger of Communism in Cuba is the honesty of their [its] leaders."[6]

Communist emphasis on inevitable progress provided comfort for a nation in distress, and balanced off the failures of the present against future successes. Under the guidance of exceedingly intelligent leaders such as Aníbal Escalante, Blas Roca, Carlos Rafael Rodríguez, and Juan Marinello, the party urged the government toward democracy and won many converts. It also controlled the nation's trade unions, which from 1938 to 1947 were oriented to the Communist-directed Confederación de Trabajadores de América Latina (Latin American Confederation of Workers) (CTAL). Unlike many workers in the United States, who built up a fear and distrust of communism, Cuban labor associated communism with judicious leadership and work-related improvements and benefits. Thus the Communist-led Confederación de Trabajadores de Cuba (Cuban Confederation of Labor) (CTC), founded in 1933, pursued its militant policies with considerable labor and popular support up to and during the World War II era.

Radical thought, especially that directed against the United States' financial and military incursions in Latin America, expanded in Cuba during the late 1930s, as did the cult of Martí. The ideas of Martí, together with those of anti-imperialist writers from other Latin American nations, such as Uruguayan José Enrique Rodó and Chilean Communist poet Pablo Neruda, provided Cubans with a flight into a fantasy world contrasting Yankee greed with Cuban spirituality.[7] Radical essays and verse became popular, as did the journal *Archivo José Martí*, established in 1940, whose articles expressed Martí's optimism and desire for political and social progress and sovereignty.[8] Raúl Lorenzo's book *Sentido nacionalista del pensamiento de Saco* (1942) (Nationalism in the Thinking of Saco) concluded that Varela, Saco, and Martí exemplified the successive stages in Cuban nationalism.

In the midst of this wave of nationalism the Japanese attacked United States installations at Pearl Harbor, which the Havana government considered a declaration of war on Cuba. Cuba froze Italian, German, and Japanese assets and interned over four thousand Germans and Italians. Cuba established diplomatic relations with the Soviet Union, and the United States was given a virtual carte blanche to post troops and operate military bases on the island.

The new wave of nationalism, begun in the 1930s, continued during World War II. It was led by the Generación de Entrerevoluciones (Between Revolutions Generation)—those who had opposed Machado a decade earlier and were now mature political activists. Activist *pensadores* such as Blas Roca, Raúl Roa, and Carlos Rafael Rodríguez blossomed. The Communist party, which changed its name in 1944 from the Revolutionary Communist Union to the Popular Socialist party (PSP), gained stature as the Soviet Union was a trusted World War II ally. The party controlled most of Cuba's labor movement, and its newspaper *Hoy* had one of the largest circulations in Havana. During the war Communist leaders Juan Marinello and Carlos Rafael Rodríguez served in Batista's cabinet—the first Communists in Latin America to hold such positions.

By the end of World War II one-quarter of Cuba's organized labor force was pro-Communist. More and more the nation's intellectuals criticized and disassociated themselves from the leadership of the urban middle class, which lost almost all of its

fervor for reforms and for the most part reinforced the existing
social and economic structure.[9] After the war much of Cuba's
economic policy continued to be made in the private sector,
without regard for the interests of the masses. No cohesion
existed between political parties and interest groups. Even class
interests were not unified in a formal way. But the Batista government was somewhat more responsive to the needs and
desires of the people as it enacted reforms, made concessions
to labor, built schools, generally left the press uncensored, and
governed better than had its predecessors. Conditions deteriorated under Batista's successors Ramón Grau San Martín (1944–
48) and Carlos Prío Socarrás (1948–52) as corruption and graft
grew, reform legislation stagnated, and public services broke
down.

The Cuban government drew closer to the United States during the Cold War. To appease the United States, Batista, who
returned to power in 1952, severed relations with the Soviet
Union in 1953 and established the Bureau for the Suppression
of Communist Activities, which functioned without enthusiasm.
Washington rewarded the anticommunism of Batista with military assistance and honors, while the United States–controlled
Mafia used the Caribbean island as a prime investment site.
Gambling, prostitution, and drug running increased under the
watchful eyes of the mob's henchmen and their Cuban
protectors.

The Korean War deepened Cuba's economic and military
dependence on the United States. Washington disregarded
Batista's abuses of power, preferring to number him among its
loyal circle of anticommunist Caribbean friends, including such
notable tyrants as the Somozas in Nicaragua, Rafael Trujillo
in the Dominican Republic, François Duvalier in Haiti, and Mar-
cos Pérez Jiménez in Venezuela.

Revolutionary currents and radical thoughts persisted among

Cuba's intellectuals, workers, and students, many of whom saw their nation being increasingly drawn into a global ideological battle on the side of the United States and big business, two sectors that historically had worked against the interests of the Cuban majority.

While the nation languished under a facade of prosperity that brought the island new luxury hotels, casinos, and tourist resorts, radical intellectuals continued to oppose Batista. Socialist professor Rafael García Bárcena, who founded the National Revolutionary Movement advocating armed action against the despot, and the Cuban Society of Philosophy and its organ the *Revista Cubana de Filosofía* (Cuban Magazine of Philosophy) led the struggle for democracy and against dictatorship and foreign imperialism. García Bárcena and his colleagues shared a "revolutionary ideology," which sociologist and historian Nelson Valdés defined as a "unified and systematic set of beliefs about society and politics."[10] This ideology tries to explain the organization of a social system—its objectives and methods—and is associated with the political, economic, social, and cultural roles of specific classes.[11] The radical opponents of Batista, according to Valdés, did not have a "revolutionary theory" or a scientific appraisal of society and its strengths, weaknesses, socioeconomic and political structures, and internal contradictions. In fact, they had no systematic or theoretical studies of Cuban society.[12]

However, Cuba's radicals knew that by the mid-1950s United States companies owned or controlled 40 percent of Cuba's sugar industry, 90 percent of its utilities, mines, and cattle ranches, 50 percent of public railways, and 25 percent of all bank deposits on the island.[13] They understood the degree to which Cuban entrepreneurs had abandoned political responsibility to the United States. Among Cuba's significant radical political entities, only the Communist party talked about the need for systematic analysis of Cuba's problems and scientific planning for their alleviation. However, the program of the Popular Socialist Party during the 1950s included coexistence with the United States. Anti-imperialism in the eyes of the Communists was, according to Carlos Rafael Rodríguez, a proscribed word, a set of ideas that the majority of his *compañeros* considered temporarily harmful to the existence of their party.[14] Any useful study of Cuba's problems would have to include analyses of the effects of United States involvement in all facets of Cuban life. Penetrating examinations of this type were for the moment deemed by the Communists antagonistic to and incompatible with coexistence.

While the Communist party endeavored to maintain a modicum of accord with the Batista government and not disrupt relations with the United States, Fidel Castro, without a theoretical program, began to fight against the state apparatus and its Yankee connections. At the time of his abortive attack on the Moncada army barracks in Oriente province on 26 July 1953, during his subsequent imprisonment in Cuba and his exile in Mexico, after his return to Cuba in 1956, and throughout the lengendary guerrilla struggle in the Sierra Maestra, Castro sought support from the middle class and labor unions.

Public outrage after the murder of many of Castro's compatriots who were captured at Moncada and increased repression by the Batista forces enhanced Castro's stock as a potential liberator. While his stature as a humane and dynamic opponent to Batista grew, the Communists criticized the Moncada fiasco, calling it putschism and adventurism guided by bourgeois misconceptions. At the same time the Communist party, which had been outlawed in November 1953 at the urging of the United States, condemned the brutality meted out by Batista's forces. The Communists also deplored the lack of theoretical cohesion and ideology in the Twenty-sixth of July Movement. But Castro and his rebel band gained popularity and support throughout Cuba.

Castro knew that rebellion was a component of his nation's character and history. While in prison on the Isle of Pines from 1953 to 1955, he read omnivorously, searching for solutions to Cuba's social, economic, and political problems, which he concluded had to be dealt with by radical actions. He expressed his hopes and his program for the future in the *History Will Absolve Me* speech and pamphlet (1954), which was smuggled out of the island prison; its statistics appear to be based on *Los fundamentos del socialismo en Cuba* (1943) (The Fundamentals of Socialism in Cuba) by Cuban Communist party secretary-general Blas Roca.[15]

Considerably before the last months of the guerrilla struggle in 1958, when the Communist party worked diligently to establish a working relationship with the Twenty-sixth of July Movement, Castro understood the strengths as well as the weaknesses of the Communists and their potential for assisting his embryonic revolution. By the fall of 1958 Castro had the support of pro-communist and noncommunist labor unions as well as many middle-class intellectuals. Fidel's cohorts searched for a plan or model. While none came forth immediately, Cuba's existing corpus of radical thought, including a somewhat ill-defined socialism stressing anti-imperialism, agrarian reform, and a better way of life for rural and urban workers, served as a guide to revolution and as an option to positivist thought that still flourished in the country.

Antonio Guiteras (1906–35)

Revolutionary folk hero "Tony" Guiteras's contributions to the Cuban revolution and to the thinking of Fidel Castro are discussed in chapter 5, but his thoughts, as well as his actions during the 1930s, merit elaboration here. Tony lived in the Philadelphia, Pennsylvania, suburb of Bala Cynwyd from birth until the age of seven, when he moved with his father, a Cuban schoolteacher, and his mother, who was of Puritan stock, to Pinar del Río, Cuba. While in secondary school, history and politics caught his interest. In 1924 he entered the University of Havana, where he was exposed to social science and philosophy, developed a deep desire to combat social injustice, and wrote two stories on that theme.

Guiteras read the literature of William Shakespeare, Edgar Allan Poe, and Oscar Wilde, but he preferred the political and social analyses of Rodó, Saint-Simon, Rousseau, Montesquieu, Voltaire, Barbusse, Jaurès, Marx, and Engels. John Reed's *Ten Days That Shook the World* (1919) and Lenin's *State and Revolution* (1917) impressed him, as did the Russian revolution in general. He also developed an interest in the activities of revolutionary leaders Sun Yat-sen of China and Mustafa Kemal Pasha of Turkey.[16]

While at the university, he joined the 1927 Student Directorate and helped draw up its well-publicized manifesto denouncing President Machado and United States imperialism. Under the influence of his friend Julio Antonio Mella, Guiteras became an astute politician who viewed the university as a microcosm of a society that existed for the benefit of elites. He envisioned a more perfect university, one that would serve as the nation's social and physical science laboratory and would help forge a state that operated for the good of the majority.

Guiteras's associates found him to be amiable, humble, humorous, energetic, and nonmaterialistic and sometimes referred to him as "the man with only one suit." Enemies viewed him as inflexible and implacable. His close friend leftist writer Carleton Beals saw him as the John Brown and the Augusto Sandino of Cuba.[17] Friends and foes alike respected him as a pragmatic man, a fighter who put ideas into action.

Antonio Guiteras differs from most of the Cuban radical thinkers discussed in this book. He did not conceive of himself as a *pensador*, nor did he seek immortality by having his thoughts ensconced in print. His ideas are found primarily in public manifestos, government decrees, interviews, private correspondence, letters to editors, and the pamphlet *Joven Cuba* (1934), composed by a committee. Although he wrote no books and few articles, his thinking represents an important link in Cuba's revolutionary chain. Cuba's new Communist party frequently points out his political and social contributions, and in 1974 the Cuban government reproduced the documents containing his revolutionary thoughts.[18]

Those thoughts matured after he completed a degree in pharmacy and returned to Pinar del Río to work as a traveling representative for a drug company. He strengthened his political contacts as he moved about the country, and he continued his antigovernment activities, which landed him in jail in 1931.[19] After being released from prison through a declaration of amnesty, in 1932 he went to Oriente province and built strong revolutionary opposition to the Machado government.

In April 1933 Guiteras and his followers, hoping to initiate an uprising against the Machado regime, attacked and captured a military barracks at San Luis adjacent to the Sierra Maestra and close to Santiago de Cuba. They then fled to the nearby hills, where they managed, through guerrilla tactics, to hold off Machado's forces for a few weeks before being captured and imprisoned. These events established a precedent for Fidel Castro's assault on the Moncada barracks twenty years later and enhanced Guiteras's reputation as a champion of the masses.

Guiteras then served the short-lived, more progressive administration of Grau San Martín as minister of interior, war, and the navy. He led the government's radical wing and proved an incorruptible sponsor of social legislation, including the eight-hour working day, the minimum wage, workers' compensation, social security and retirement pay, and the legalization of trade unions.[20] The enfant terrible of the Grau cabinet was governed by the philosophy that "No movement in Cuba can be revolutionary unless it is anti-imperialist. One can either serve imperialism or the people; their interests are incompatible."[21] He placed the American-owned Compañía Cubana de Electricidad (Cuban Electric Company) under Cuban control, thereby lowering rates to consumers, and he urged passage of a law requiring that 50 percent of workers for foreign companies be Cuban citizens. While a cabinet member, he also aided Dominican insurrectionists working against dictator Rafael Trujillo.

He understood that a revolutionary administration, in order to implement lasting change, had to control the military. He spoke about balancing off the army with an equally vital force, perhaps by arming the workers, but he never achieved that end. After the Grau administration fell to the military, Guiteras blamed its failure on its inability to move far enough to the left. He cited the downfall of Grau as proof of the duplicitous nature of Cuban representative democracy and concluded that the nation needed a benevolent revolutionary dictatorship to prepare it for genuine democracy.[22]

After the ouster of Grau in 1934, Guiteras went underground and founded TNT, a secret insurrectionary and terrorist organization designed to create support for revolution in the nation by demonstrating that the government was unable to maintain stability. Later the same year, he formed Joven Cuba (Young Cuba), a populist-oriented militant political group with nationalist social-democratic tendencies.

Joven Cuba, made up of relatively well educated members and supported by students and labor, extracted the anti-imperialist component, but not internationalism, from Marxism and blamed most of Cuba's problems on foreign control of the island's economic and political processes. Joven Cuba stood for liberation of the oppressed classes, not single-class rule. It also opposed *caudillismo* (bossism) of the Fulgencio Batista type. The organization presented a socialist and revolutionary alternative to the Communist party, which regarded Guiteras as a socialist demagogue.

Approximately six hundred ideologically aligned members of Joven Cuba organized for armed struggle with the objective of installing a revolutionary government that would restructure Cuban society. The program of Joven Cuba, based on the elimination of foreign economic domination, reflected the ideas of Guiteras and contained some extrapolations from Lenin's *Imperialism: The Highest Stage of Capitalism* (1916).[23]

Joven Cuba predicated its program on the belief that Cuba possessed the elements for nationhood but had not yet become a nation. It implied that nationhood would be achieved when political unity against colonialism existed and when Cubans controlled their foreign and domestic policies and the means of production—conditions that could not exist under the international capitalist system.

Among the more innovative and radical features of the Joven Cuba program were plans to convert Cuban diplomacy from a class-oriented cortesan operation to one reflecting the cultural interests of the masses and a proposal to create an American parliament composed of representatives of all progressive Latin American organizations united to nurture common spiritual and cultural values and to oppose tyranny and European and United States imperialism. The Joven Cuba agenda included measures for political, constitutional, social, electoral, juridical, educational, and fiscal reform. It advocated equal rights for women; confiscation of property acquired through corruption; nationalization or municipalization of subsoil resources, public services, and large landholdings; the abolition of monopolies; increased workers' rights; spreading culture and revolutionary ideas among the masses; and abrogation of the Platt Amendment.[24]

Through Joven Cuba, Guiteras fought for economic independence and social progress and opposed the inequalities in capitalism that enabled the wealthy to prosper at the expense of the poor. He wanted the state to reconquer the national assets that had historically been taken over by avaricious foreigners and natives. He maintained that once the state regained its property it should not let it fall back into private hands,[25] that government should not let the majority suffer the consequences of rapacious corporate interests.

Guiteras believed Cuba needed social revolution and noted in his 1934 article "Septembrismo" that the first step toward that goal was to initiate a campaign against economic imperialism and the managerial class.[26] He reasoned that social revolution meant political revolution and that it entailed building a popular, not an elite, vanguard to strip power from foreign imperialists and their bourgeois Cuban allies.[27]

Guiteras viewed work as the highest calling, the most important part of life, and asserted that once a popular vanguard obtained power it would move to provide full employment in Cuba. This would be accomplished in part by the state's assuming control over the nation's basic resources, developing new industries in Havana, and making that city the primary distribution point for goods and materials—possibly a free trade zone that would enable the country to become a major commercial hub in the Americas.[28]

Guiteras allied Joven Cuba with other radical organizations to try to overthrow the Batista government and seize power on behalf of the Cuban people. Joven Cuba and its confederates called a general strike that resulted in increased repression by the dictator's army. On 8 May 1935, while attempting to flee into exile, Guiteras was shot and killed by Batista's police, and the Joven Cuba movement disintegrated.

Although Antonio Guiteras never attained most of his political, social and economic objectives, his spirit *(Guiterismo)* and that of Joven Cuba lived on, especially among students and workers. His ideas influenced Eduardo Chibás, who in 1947 founded the Ortodoxo party, in which Fidel Castro received early political training. Guiteras contributed significantly to Cuba's nationalist revolutionary tradition by providing the concept of a small, well-organized force engaging in armed struggle to attain political ends and by inculcating the belief among some Cuban intellectuals that genuine change was possible and that violence could be a viable way of achieving that goal.

Raúl Roa García (1908–82)

In this age of specialization, universal men have ceased to exist in powerful industrialized societies. But they occasionally appear in the underdeveloped world. Raúl Roa might be the most universal of Cuba's revolutionary *pensadores.* Born to an educated middle-class family, he was both inspired and bedeviled by José Martí, whose works he considered profound, but who had cast aspersions on the Roa name by criticizing Raúl's grandfather for writing a book discouraging Cubans from fighting against colonial rule. Young Roa developed a desire to contribute to society, perhaps to atone for his grandfather's regressive stance. At age fifteen he heard Julio Mella deliver a fiery speech castigating the University of Havana for its corruption and its links to United States imperialism.[29] He soon followed in the footsteps of student leaders Mella and Rubén

Martínez Villena, supported the University Reform Movement, and developed a deep appreciation of the goals of the radicals who wrote for the *Revista de Avance*.

While completing a law degree at the University of Havana, Roa delved into intellectual history and searched for philosophical models. He adopted a variant of Spanish humanism predicated on acceptance, humaneness, and spirituality.[30] He joined the Cuban Communist party in 1927, withdrew from it because of doctrinal differences, and spent the next three decades as an independent Marxist. He built a solid reputation as a left-wing student leader, directed the radical Directorio Estudiantil Universitario (University Student Directorate) in 1930, and led the Marxist-oriented Ala Izquierda Estudiantil (Student Left Wing) that broke off from the Directorio in 1931.

Roa participated in a 30 September 1930 march on the presidential palace to demand the resignation of Gerardo Machado. His efforts landed him in jail.[31] Henceforth he was known as part of the Generation of 1930, one who "never lost his bearing."[32] His antigovernment activities elicited retribution, and he entered exile in the United States, where in 1935 he founded Izquierda Revolucionaria (Revolutionary Left), the only political party he belonged to until he became a member of the Central Committee of the Communist party of Cuba in 1964.[33]

Roa returned to Cuba and by competitive examination won the position of professor of history of social doctrines and social philosophy at the University of Havana, where he devoted more of his time to literary and scholarly pursuits and academic infighting than to active participation in national and international politics. He spent 1944 and 1945 in New York on a Guggenheim fellowship, working on the New Deal,[34] and developed enormous respect for Franklin Roosevelt, whom he believed created legislation to ameliorate conflicts between labor and those who owned the means of production.[35] In 1950 he was

named cultural director of Cuba's Ministry of Education. He
later became dean of the School of Social Sciences and Public
Law at the University of Havana, a position he held until 1959.
While at the university he opposed Stalin's socialist totalitarianism and claimed that the Soviet Union had assumed aspects of
capitalism. In 1956 he caused a stir among Cuba's Communists
by writing "El ejemplo de Hungría" (The Example of Hungary)
denouncing the Soviet invasion of Hungary.[36] Nevertheless, he
held hope for socialist democracy.

Roa disappointed many of his middle-class colleagues and
friends when he chose to remain in Cuba after Castro's takeover.
The revolutionary government appointed him ambassador to
the Organization of American States (OAS) in February 1959,
and he gained renown for his colorful oratory, a reputation he
expanded during the seventeen years he served as Cuba's foreign minister beginning in May 1959. His battles at the United
Nations, including his use of profanity in public—such as telling
a verbal assailant "fuck your mother"[37]—became legendary.
His volatile style was best illustrated by an incident in April 1961
when United States United Nations ambassador Adalai Stevenson denied, in a Security Council session, the true origin of B26
bombers that had attacked Havana airport. Roa exposed Stevenson as a liar. Stevenson sent a New York Times reporter to
see Roa and request that he not make the attack personal. The
Cuban diplomat responded: "Tell Mr. Stevenson that Cubans
are being killed by United States—sent mercenaries, that I consider him an enemy and will deal with him implacably, both
personally and officially."[38]

Roa's political, diplomatic, and speaking skills were equaled
or surpassed by his abilities as a writer. He wrote numerous
newspaper and scholarly articles on political and social themes,
stinging polemics, some verse, historical works, and literary
criticism. Reading through the huge collection of his articles in

Quince años después (1950) (Fifteen Years Later), one would categorize him as a renaissance man and social commentator with a political orientation. He wrote easily understood prose, at times with an acid pen, and eschewed social science jargon. He combined highly descriptive metaphors with incisive expression and a sharp wit.

Roa spent his adult life associating with politically active, talented leftist writers such as Juan Marinello, Rubén Martínez Villena, and Julio Mella, and much of his writing, like theirs, was designed to stimulate critical historical analysis and raise consciousness. Roa thought of himself as a "Marxist-Leninist sniper," a revolutionary rather than a scholar,[39] though he was both.

He examined revolutionary thought from its earliest origins to the present. He saw socialist and anarchist tendencies in the prophets of the Bible, who passionately defended the poor, pleaded for social justice, and espoused human fraternity.[40] He admired Socratic introspection and exhibited honesty toward himself and the world. But he saw a lack of scientific rigor in the works of most Greek thinkers. Roa viewed ancient Greek and Roman social and legal institutions in light of their contributions to contemporary situations.[41] He agreed with Hegel that the Greeks demonstrated the first universal spirit in Europe and endeavored to export it, thus practicing an early form of cultural imperialism.[42] He saw the Greek imprint in most Western thinking. Like Marx, he believed that the Greek contribution was not in the magic of their gods but in the realization that the development of humanity was a dialectical process.[43] He thought that Aristotle continued Socrates' idea of approaching social reality analytically by conducting historical and empirical investigations. Those Greek thinkers, he maintained, initiated the history of ideas or humanistic thought.[44] He saw Plato as a forerunner of modern utopianism as well as an early contributor to the theoretical foundations of the juridical state, whereas the sophists were early opponents of slavery and human exploitation.[45] He connected Plato to Thomas More's *Utopia* as well as to Rousseau, Kant, Fichte, and Hegel, all of whom helped develop orderly social and political thought and clarify the concept of the state, with its role in society and its disputes.[46]

Roa knew the thinking of most prominent eighteenth-, nineteenth-, and twentieth-century philosophers. He especially appreciated the work of French neo-Thomist Jacques Maritain, a creator of Christian democratic doctrine who believed that man was subordinate to his society and defended ordered democracy against the divisive excesses of liberalism and totalitarian denials of individuality. Roa also agreed with Thomas More, who believed in the sovereignty of the spirit, and he projected More's ideas to the point of the ultimate development of a utopia in America.[47]

Roa found a bit of Machiavelli's approach in most institutions, including democratic nations, the church, political parties, and international relations. He saw aspects of the Italian philosopher-statesman's rigidity, tenacity, and ego in a broad range of individuals such as Lenin, Trotsky, Mussolini, Hitler, Franco, Churchill, Franklin Roosevelt, Truman, and various popes.[48] He was impressed by the neo-Hegelian Benedetto Croce's contention that the study of history dominated all other intellectual activity by relating the past to the present and the present to the future.[49] From Henri Barbusse he got the idea that politics is the effective work of social thought—that politics is life.[50]

Roa developed a strong interest in the politics of the British Labour party and in Fabian socialism, which repudiates some of the major canons of socialist revolution by advocating tactics of infiltration and working within the system to transform it.[51] He also liked British economist Harold Laski's brand of democratic socialism and concluded from it that only social and economic engineers, not free-enterprise advocates, could solve Cuba's crises.[52]

Arnold Toynbee's critical analyses of societal dynamics, with emphasis on culture and humanistic development, appealed to Roa,[53] as did Marx's worldview. He credited Marx with being the first to identify political struggle in terms of ideology and the first to systematically study capitalism.[54] To him, Marx subtly illuminated the economic substrata of social life, and Toynbee affirmed Marx by showing how he exemplified elemental historical unity.[55]

Roa read many of the works of Lenin, especially those pertaining to the state, revolution, and imperialism—areas of vital interest to the future of Cuba. He called Leninism a dialectical adaptation from Marxism, one that came forth in the era of imperialism and proletarian revolt. He also noted that Marxism-Leninism became deformed in the Soviet Union under Stalin.[56] Roa felt a sense of kinship with the spirit of the Russian revolution but believed the ideas of his Generation of 1930 owed more to the liberating objectives of the Spanish Generation of 1898. He particularly appreciated the thoughts of Spanish professor Fernando de los Rios, a Socialist Workers party militant and a member of the Generation of 1898. Fernando de los Rios, once rector of Madrid's Central University and Spain's minister of education and minister of state, reflected socialist humanism along with German abstruseness and Spanish generalities. Roa met de los Rios in Cuba in 1926 and later, when the Spaniard taught in New York City,[57] concurred with some of his ideas and commented, "Humanistic socialism hopes to go beyond the achievement of present day statism by humanizing the economy. . . . Socialism thus conceived is a means of refreshing and spiritualizing the soul."[58] Roa connected de los Rios's humanistic socialism to Spanish philosopher José Ortega y Gasset's demand for spiritual renovation, viewing the latter as consistent with the quest for radical social change.

Although Roa reflected European thought, he took his lead from Latin American thinkers. He believed in the Hispanic America of Simón Bolívar. He was impressed by Argentine José Ingenieros's depiction of Latins as idealistic, creative people. He identified with the anti-imperialism of poets José Rodó, Rubén Darío, and Pablo Neruda. From the Mexicans, philosopher José Vasconcelos and statesman Benito Juárez, he learned to understand the thinking of mestizos (those of mixed Spanish and Indian blood) and to respect the values of some middle-class liberals.[59]

Roa befriended Venezuelan novelist Rómulo Gallegos, whose work he claimed contained the elements of conflict between culture and barbarism—the violence and justice of Latin America. He asserted that Gallegos captured the universal spirit of workers and peasants.[60] He appreciated Gallegos's quasi–social democratic stance. He admired Venezuelan president (1959–64) Rómulo Betancourt's revolutionary nationalism, his early proworker, anti-imperialist stances, and his ability to replace dictatorship with electoral democracy in Venezuela.[61]

From the writings of Peruvian Marxist José Carlos Mariátegui, Roa learned about the role of the intellectual in the revolution, lessons the Peruvian derived in part from Italian Communist Antonio Gramsci. But the Latin American who served as Roa's major model was Jesús Silva Herzog, the sagacious Mexican socialist writer, teacher, and government advisor, who taught his Cuban friend that it is the obligation of governments and thinkers to try to eliminate hunger, disease, illiteracy, and ignorance. From Silva Herzog he adopted the idea that the academy is a bulwark against tyranny and for freedom—an instrument of national conscience.[62]

Roa also heeded the teaching of his countrymen. He paid tribute to Cuba's first internationally known socialist Paul Lafargue in *Evocación de Pablo Lafargue* (1973) (Evocation of Paul Lafargue), a work that provided a solid account of early socialist workers' activities and described how Lafargue's writings on class struggle helped develop French and Russian

worker consciousness, how he influenced Lenin, and how he clarified Marx's work on the mechanics of the reciprocal relations between the structure and the superstructure.[63]

Roa was impressed by Enrique Varona's call for greater empiricism in teaching, by his warning to Cubans not to become culturally or economically indebted to the United States.[64] He praised the social science methods and historical perspective of Varona, whom he referred to as an intellectual force, praise Roa hoped one day to share with his countryman. He adored José Martí, whom he called "the essence of pure and progressive democratic thought."[65]

Roa learned from, and maintained ties to, many of Latin America's outstanding intellectuals. He knew all the major anti-imperialists, social democrats, academic liberals, and radical *pensadores* in the region as well as some in the United States. Until 1959, he appeared to fit more into left-of-center academia than with Marxist political activists.

His scholarly pursuits included examining Cuban national questions. In so doing, he repeatedly invoked the name of Martí, whom he believed epitomized the collective spirit of national liberation. The "Caesarism" of the Machado era caused him to dwell on Cuban events. He contended that history shows that revolution is always a possible road to freedom. He referred to the rebellion against Machado that began in 1930 as a continuation of what Martí had started.[66] Roa considered the 1895 insurrection inconclusive in that it did not seek to alter Cuba's economic and social structures. But in his opinion, the 1930 protest demonstrations[67] and the successful anti-Machado uprising of 1933 sought to transform the colonial basis of the country's economy and the social conditions of its people.[68]

In 1947 he claimed that Cuba was on the threshold of European-style fascism under the influence of finance capital and an antidemocratic ruling class—fascism that used political violence to maintain itself.[69] He inveighed against the falangist mentality that he found in Batista's approach to government.[70] When the "little sergeant" seized the presidency again in 1952, Roa characterized the nation as "the mummified democracy" and "the piece of the big stick," referring to the votes of the dead counted in elections and connections with the United States master. He said in print that Batista's megalomania led the dictator to think of himself as the Cuban counterpart of Mexico's successful reformer President Lázaro Cárdenas (1934–40).[71]

Roa feared for his life and sought peace in Mexico in 1952, an exile that lasted three years. Like Martí, he felt himself a citizen of "Our America" and kept abreast of the political and social situation everywhere in Latin America. He feared a neo-fascist trend in the Caribbean and South America in the 1950s, with dictatorships led by Batista in Cuba, Somoza in Nicaragua, Trujillo in the Dominican Republic, Pérez Jiménez in Venezuela, Juan Perón in Argentina, Gustavo Rojas Pinilla in Colombia, Alfredo Stroessner in Paraguay, and Manuel Odría in Peru.[72] He wanted the OAS to take action against the dictatorships, to galvanize the region's democracies into an Inter-American Conference for Democracy and Liberty. At the same time, he deplored the idea of a Cold War ballet, with music by the Cominform and the show staged by the State Department.[73]

The University of Havana frequently provided Roa with refuge from political recriminations while he researched and wrote on national and international politics. He loved the university, which he believed represented the scientific and technological renaissance of the twentieth century—a place where logic and reflection abounded, an institution with a humanistic heart—[74] an attitude directly descended from Luz and Varela. To him the university existed for the collective and progressive interests of the nation, not for private functions or individual professors.[75] He advocated a strong, action-oriented, but peaceful university where energy was directed toward concrete programs.[76] He perceived the University of Havana as a beneficiary of the University Reform Movement of 1918, which identified the crises caused by semicolonial economic domination in the Americas and led to the liberalization and radicalization of future generations.[77] He saw the transformation in the academy from rhetoric to scientific analysis as a major step toward progress.[78]

Roa's elegant, yet earthy and irreverent classroom style attracted young Cubans, whose idealism and restlessness he stirred up. His course on the history of social doctrines inspired his students to put ideas into action, to work for peaceful social change in the best radical traditions of the university and Cuba. In his classes Roa stressed that there existed two types of utopian thought—one the unrealizable myths of dreamers, the other the realizable ideology of scientific socialism. He noted that a utopian situation could be attained or approximated through scientific reasoning that takes the notion of progress out of the realm of the spiritual and makes it real and ideological. He claimed that the scientific reason of the community (the people) could supplant the prevailing, but generally unscientific and often mythical, reason of the state.[79] He maintained that myths, such as the immutability of private property, become entrenched and must be broken down by social analysis.[80]

He pointed out in his *Historia de las doctrinas sociales* (1949) (History of Social Doctrines) that social science investigations must be based on historical foundations—that to comprehend society's problems one must know their origins and causal relations. To him empirical study devoid of historical method was as superficial as were studies done by scholars who dismissed the importance of class relations and economic determinants in their analyses of society. Roa asserted that modern capitalism brought major social and spiritual changes that could be understood only by examining them systematically.[81] He believed it was the function of social science to "reconcile the aims in the democratic conception of society, still haunted by its past, with the means afforded by socialism."[82] He concluded that modern capitalism contained elements of the Protestant work ethic directed toward individual gain, as opposed to the collective and utopian goals of socialism. He believed that dehumanization occurred under capitalism as man became a slave to technology, detracting from his ability to achieve democratic distributive justice. Yet he discerned in human nature an inherent desire for equality and justice, one contradicted by the materialistic nature of capitalism.[83]

His dream of a socialist revolution in Cuba came closer to reality when Castro landed in Cuba in 1956 and declared his intention to oust Batista. Roa joined the civic resistance movement composed of university teachers and professional people who procured supplies and provided refuge for Castro's rebels.[84] From his position at the University of Havana, he helped consolidate clandestine support for the revolution.

Roa then served the Cuban revolution at the OAS, where he agitated for independence, self-determination, and sovereignty for all American nations and Puerto Rico. Then, as foreign minister, he defended Cuba's revolution, especially against the United States onslaught. When the United States condemned Cuba for aggression in 1960, Roa declared it was guilty of the same charge for its long history of contributing to Cuban underdevelopment, and he asked how Washington, which supported Batista and the Dominican tyrant Trujillo, could criticize humanistic Cuba.[85] He also joined in the censure of Trujillo by the OAS in 1960. He valiantly, but unsuccessfully, tried to get the United Nations to stop the United States economic blockade of Cuba, and as early as 1960 he exposed the attempts of the Central Intelligence Agency (CIA) to topple the Castro government. He displayed great vituperative spirit in denouncing, at the United Nations, the invasion of Cuba's Bay of Pigs in 1961 by United States sponsored and trained Cuban exiles. He also worked among nonaligned and Third World states to counter the overwhelming power and competing ambitions of the dominant countries in the United Nations and fought for the inclusion of the People's Republic of China in that body.

During the first two years of the revolution Cuba's Communist party attacked foreign minister Roa for his anti-Soviet postures. In October 1959 he had republished some of his articles, including the one critical of the Soviet invasion of Hungary. By 1963, after Cuba was declared Marxist-Leninist, in an attempt to indicate that Cuba did not hope to replicate the Soviet experience, he warned about excessive bureaucratic control and rigid interpretation of Marxist dogma.[86]

Roa also planned, organized, and ran the Ministry of Foreign Relations, supervised Cuba's diplomatic missions and consular offices, and gained respect for Cuban diplomats. He established diplomatic procedures, standards, and precedents that would endure. He devised a methodology for Cuban use in international organizations, which consisted of fostering economic and political alliances with underdeveloped, oppressed Third World and nonaligned nations, building Cuba's prestige, and undermining the world standing of the capitalist superpowers. He helped elevate the political and cultural consciousness of Cuban workers. Finally, he coordinated international activities with domestic planning and helped acquire the foreign technology necessary to eventually develop Cuba and free it from dependence.[87]

Raúl Roa's work as a writer and political activist constitutes a primary source or living history of Cuba's struggle for independence and social justice. His articles and essays, which often

mirror his political actions, are mildly imaginative, at times a
bit contrived, but always those of the antidogmatic radical, what
C. Wright Mills called a "plain Marxist." Basically Roa was a
disseminator of information, a teacher who was aware of the
philosophies of the Western world and the power of ideas, one
who stimulated others to use those ideas critically and apply
them practically to current conditions.

Years before the public emergence of Fidel Castro, Roa
stated that revolution in Cuba would not be that of France,
Mexico, Russia, or Spain but would be one in keeping with
Cuba's character and historical tradition. It would be nationalist,
anti-imperialist, antifascist, and pragmatic and would insist on
agrarian change, emphasize industrialization, believe in solidarity with all workers and oppressed people, and stress social
democratic ideology.[88] He believed "contradiction to be the
mother of all progress"; thus paradoxically he saw the need in
the post–World War II era to get the major capitalist and
socialist powers to agree intellectually on their individual sovereignty and the collective need to work together to maintain
peace.[89]

Before the revolution Roa was generally a quiet, controlled
revolutionary who deeply felt the need for radical change. Most
of the liberal intellectuals and government functionaries, with
whom he got along splendidly, never saw him as an independent
Marxist but rather considered him a little to their left but as
sharing a majority of their beliefs. They refused to understand
that philosophically he belonged to the socialist, not the liberal-
capitalist world. He became more open and assertive after
1959—freer, more willing to take a stand. His first book published after the revolution *En pie, 1953–1958* (1959) (On Foot,
1953–1958) is like a huge sigh of relief, at last an opportunity to
let out what was repressed for so long, the chance to reveal
his disdain for the patrician sector in Cuba.[90]

As early as 1953 Roa saw Castro as a dedicated advocate of liberty, a romantic following in the footsteps of Máximo Gómez and Antonio Maceo, a more radical José Martí[91] who might attain the goals of 1895. *Fidelismo* embraced most of Roa's aspirations. He categorized it as part of the Third World revolution, and it deepened his identification of Cuba and Latin America with Asia and Africa.[92] He appreciated the uniqueness as well as the traditional radical *Cubanidad* he found in *Fidelismo*, and he moved quite easily from the university campus and the facade of social democracy to the revolutionary front. He stated in 1963 that the Cuban revolution was theoretically socialist and used the Marxist-Leninist method but was subject to creative change as a result of vigorous study and learning.[93]

He continued to examine all currents of thought for useful ideas, believing that nothing except change is constant within the dialectic.[94] For Cubans to whom faith was important, he noted that the revolution was a religious phenomenon and that without its religious and mystical elements it would not have survived.[95] Until his death, Roa believed that all in Cuba are free to express themselves but that creative work should be judged through a prism of revolutionary glass.[96]

Blas Roca (1908–)

Francisco Calderío, better known by his pseudonym Blas Roca (Blas the Rock), followed a somewhat different road to revolution than Raúl Roa. The great-grandson of an African slave, Roca, a militant member of the shoemaker's union in Manzanillo, joined the Communist party in 1930. Within four years he became its secretary-general, a position he held until 1965.

A clear-headed practical thinker, respected journalist, storyteller, author of children's tales, accomplished polemicist, and party theroetician, Roca was primarily influenced by the political writings of José Martí and the socialism of Carlos Baliño.[97] During his long political career Roca became well known in Cuba for his numerous articles in the Communist newspaper *Hoy* (Today) and the magazine *Fundamentos* (Fundamentals).

Roca journeyed to the Soviet Union in 1934, took a firsthand look at socialism at work, and subsequently dedicated his life to the Communist party of Cuba and the teachings of Marx, Engels, and Lenin. To him the strength of the Cuban Communist party lay in its internal democracy, the right of the membership to discuss every question fully, to express individual opinions about all problems, and to criticize any measure. To Roca the party represented a living body—one in Cuba, not controlled from afar.[98] Within the party he strove to illuminate Moscow's positions for his sometimes skeptical Cuban comrades. For example, during the late 1930s he explained the Soviet Union's opposition to Franco in the Spanish Civil War, and Russia's Popular Front policy of allying with other socialist and capitalist left-of-center groups.

Roca became well known in Cuban political and literary circles after the publication of *Los fundamentos del socialismo en Cuba* (1943) (The Fundamentals of Socialism in Cuba), a volume important enough that the Cuban government updated and republished it in 1962. In that book he cited as a primary objective of socialist revolution the elimination of Cuba's semicolonialism by developing production, especially in agriculture, and creating an independent economy—acts that would raise the standard of living.[99]

In the book he attacked the early atrocities committed by the Spanish under the pretext of preserving Christian humanism in Cuba. He deplored the fact that the church sanctioned malevolent despots such as Spain's Franco, Portugal's Salazar, the Dominican Republic's Trujillo, Nicaragua's Somoza, and Cuba's Batista.[100] He also depicted the church as historically a major

defender of private property. He noted that using private property as a basic means of production exploits workers. He then
134   linked Cuba's Catholic-dominated Congress to private property and its abuses and maintained that if property belonged to the state a form of exploitation would disappear.[101]

He looked to Europe, particularly the Catholic countries, for ideas that could benefit his people. He found that France's worker-priest movement contributed to organizing the masses for action and inadvertently united the left for the struggle against exploitation. Liberation theology, which emerged in Latin America in the late 1960s, sustained his belief that the church, as one of the region's cultural institutions, could help foster social change. Although he believed that material is not a product of the spirit but the spirit is a product of material, he emphasized that Cuba's Marxists had always defended the freedom of religion and opposed persecution of the church.[102] He made a plea for Communist-Catholic unity and stated that those who believe in God should not be excluded from Communist party membership.[103] He subsequently said that the Cuban revolution, while not a religious movement, followed the lines of the Papal encyclical *Rerum novarum* and the doctrine of social Catholicism.[104]

The earlier edition of *Los fundamentos del socialismo en Cuba*, written when the Communist party worked with Batista, advocated coexistence with the United States and indicated a need for working-class and middle-class collaboration in order to achieve progress. The newer edition altered the stance on class alliances, since Roca concluded that only some strata of the petty and national bourgeoisie would swing to the left as a result of intense capitalist oppression and the growing influence of the left.[105] Also, the final chapter of the 1943 version was "National Liberation and Socialism"; in the new edition it was entitled "Socialism," implying that national liberation had been attained.[106]

Roca's historically oriented primer on Cuba's problems examined how the Spanish turned Cuba's Indian community into a slave society. According to him, after the abolition of slavery Cuba entered the feudal stage of development, which preceded the establishment of capitalism, under which some elements of feudalism remained. He provided a full analysis of the class structure in neocolonial Cuba. He viewed the nation as languishing under the control of the landed gentry, including United States landowners, the sugar bourgeoisie directed by United States firms, and Cuban middle-class importers and merchants. Lower on the social ladder in Cuba, he said, were the industrial bourgeoisie not related to the sugar industry, followed by the urban and rural proletariat.[107]

Roca viewed Cuba before the revolution as a quasi-colonial dependency and blamed the Platt Amendment for violating the principle of national independence.[108] To him, Cuba fit the situation Lenin called "unequal capitalist development," wherein the imperialist capitalist countries determine how quickly the underdeveloped nations develop, or not, especially in a semi-feudal *latifundista* state with an agrarian and monocultural (one-crop) orientation. He contended that liberation from United States domination was a prerequisite for Cuban development[109] and attributed Cuba's periodic severe economic crises to capitalism and to the fact that the dependent island suffered considerably when the dominant nation experienced hard times or even mild recessions. Under independent socialism, he predicted that Cuba would not be subject to the fallout from changes in economic conditions in the capitalist world.[110] He concluded from Cuba's long plight under United States hegemony that a component of internationalism is national liberation. He also came to abhor the element of imperialism that made nations try to enhance their own positions at the expense of others.[111]

Roca has always maintained a deep interest in the attempts of various Latin American states to break the bonds of imperialism and dependence and engender social reform. The Mexican Revolution intrigued him, and at a time when Mexico's president Lázaro Cárdenas (1934–40) was referred to as a "socialist" in many quarters in the Americas, Roca analyzed *Cardenismo* and found it to be a form of state capitalism that advanced Mexico's national independence but did not move the country closer to socialism.[112] He averred that the Mexican revolution was dead—taken over by foreign enemies, primarily the United States. Roca concluded that the Mexican revolution had influenced Cuba's liberal constitution of 1940, but from Mexico's experience he learned that to build a genuine revolution Cuba had to free itself from United States political and economic hegemony.[113]

Roca also traced the history of discrimination against blacks in Cuba to economic origins, the need for a labor base for the colonial plantations.[114] His ideas on the pervasiveness of anti-black sentiment and the need to eradicate it had considerable impact on Castro's revolutionary government, one of whose greatest successes has been providing equal opportunity to blacks. Simultaneously, Roca's writing has displayed compassion for the plight of women and peasants, other groups that he correctly predicted would benefit from a classless society.

In addition to analyzing internal Cuban social and political problems, Roca also examined his country's role in international politics. He stated that in 1933, after the overthrow of Machado, there came to power "not a revolutionary government, but a government formed through North American mediation."[115] Cuba's policies continued to be shaped in the United States, and after World War II they fell in line with Washington's rampant anticommunism. He condemned the United States, which took literally Marx's idea about the inevitable clash between socialism and capitalism. Roca advocated peace and coexistence between the Soviet Union and the United States and dismissed as absurd the Cold War concept of an inevitable conflict.[116] To him the dominant international conflict was between peaceful coexistence and nuclear world war, and he saw socialist states as advocating the former and capitalist nations the latter.[117]

With regard to the Americas, Roca viewed the OAS as Washington's colonial department, perpetuating the fable of continental solidarity through Pan-Americanism and imaginary Soviet intervention. He cited the United States–supported 1954 overthrow of the democratic-reformist Guatemalan government of Jacobo Arbenz Guzmán as an example of contrived anticommunism—an action undertaken against a nonexistent threat in order to protect United States hegemony in Latin America.[118]

He exhibited great disdain for Latin America's liberal statesmen such as Venezuela's Rómulo Betancourt, who he said turned the OAS into a "Continental Digepol" on an anticommunist, anti-Soviet crusade.[119] He criticized liberals such as Betancourt and Costa Rica's José Figueres for believing that Latin America could not develop without the aid of the United States and, to obtain it, adopting United States Cold War postures. To him such positions hindered social progress.[120] He also noted that United States use of the OAS as an anticommunist instrument protected tyrants such as the Dominican Republic's Rafael Trujillo.[121]

Roca explained that the United States conjured a vision of monolithic communism opposing democratic elections, whereas true socialism strives for genuine participatory democracy with elections in which the people have a say, not just a vote. He later noted that Poder Popular (Popular Power), revolutionary Cuba's form of grassroots participation in the decision-making process whereby the will of the people, not that of the politicians, is heard and heeded by the government, is a form of democracy that the United States does not understand. He pointed out that United States anticommunism is blind to the true democratic teachings of Karl Marx.[122]

According to Roca, the major sentiment in Latin America is anti-imperialist, and United States aid is not conducive to progress in the region, since it sustains despotic right-wing military governments and transnational companies such as United Fruit, Standard Oil, and Bethlehem Steel, which have no interest in social change.[123] He suggested increased Latin American trade with socialist nations in order to escape subordination to the United States.[124] To him the Cuban revolution represents the final step in the implementation of the doctrines of self-determination and nonintervention—the expulsion of the United States.[125]

Communist leader and onetime Stalinist Blas Roca has devoted a lifetime to fighting imperialism, to building a socialist community in Cuba, and to integrating workers and peasants into a viable Marxist-Leninist party. For years he and his comrades planned, often clandestinely, and waited for the propitious moment to topple capitalism in Cuba. They cooperated with the Batista regime in order to maintain legality for their party and provide safety for its members. They justified the alliance with Batista on the grounds that it enabled them to mobilize the masses, build a constituent assembly, foster the 1940 constitution, and initiate revolutionary procedures in the university and in the labor sector.

Roca contended that the July 1953 attack at Moncada was designed not to capture the government, but to plant the seeds of revolution. He believed that the action created a new "center of political attraction for the urban petty bourgeoisie, for various workers, farmers," and others. Above all, it brought about a leadership different from that of the Ortodoxo party to which

Castro belonged. The Twenty-sixth of July Movement, with Castro at its head, replaced the anticommunist Ortodoxo party on the political scene and thus furthered the revolution.[126] As the Batista regime began to crumble, the Communists, who previously had opposed armed struggle, threw their support to Castro's liberal and radical insurgents, who in turn started what Roca called the first socialist revolution made without the Communist party.[127]

In his report to the Eighth National Congress of the Popular Socialist party of Cuba in 1961, Roca generally lauded Castro, but he also gently criticized him for neglecting "other aspects" of the revolution in the early days of the struggle, implying that he did not use Marxist ideas or a Marxist model.[128] Roca, however, believed that the Marxist-Leninist party eventually provided the cohesion necessary for the triumph of the revolution, that the Communist party served as the coordinating element that unified the rebel army with radical labor, student, and political organizations and brought the races together.[129]

After Castro's victory, as the revolution turned sharply to the left, Roca, the secretary-general of the Communist party, stressed the transitory nature of the dictatorship and envisioned eventual passage to socialism.[130] He viewed the quasi-socialist agrarian reform laws of 1959 as a major step toward socialism. The laws moved to eliminate the system of latifundia and revealed the true economic and social nature of the movement that changed Cuba's class character,[131] afforded workers more human dignity, and eliminated hunger, unemployment, and considerable misery. Roca drew an analogy between Cuba's agricultural advances of 1959 and those made in China in 1949.[132]

When Cuba's Politburo was reorganized in 1975, Roca and Carlos Rafael Rodríguez were the only two members who remained from before 1961. Roca became president of the Cuban revolution's first elected National Assembly in 1976. He has tried to explain the revolution to the Cuban people. He has striven to create a socialist mentality, to clarify how people's power works, and to counter anti-Marxist thinking.[133]

Since the Communists reconciled their differences with the *Fidelistas*, Roca has portrayed the revolution as a humanist extension of the October Revolution, a social upheaval in the best tradition of José Martí. To him, it destroyed the Plattist, anarchist, reformist, and Trotskyist tendencies in Cuba.[134] It set a precedent whereby a small Latin American nation could initiate a guerrilla war and win it against a professional army, destroy the machinery of the neocolonial state, terminate the power of the bourgeoisie, establish an independent progressive people's state with new institutions,[135] and refute the myth that progress was impossible in Latin America. Roca asserted: "The people of Latin America see in the Cuban revolution the realization of their aspirations, their hopes, ideals and dreams, they regard the people of Cuba as brothers who have arisen against the common enemy and the common misery."[136] He concluded that progressives in Latin America could learn from the Cuban revolution about the effectiveness of international socialist and national liberation movements and that the petty bourgeoisie and workers' and peasants' movements could be significant in building a revolution.[137]

Since 1959 Roca has addressed many of his writings to other Latin American states that he believes need radical change. He has been a major figure in Cuba's shift away from producing literature stressing the need to defeat tyrants such as Batista and Somoza, and toward emphasis on eradicating their primary source of sustenance—foreign, especially United States, imperialism.

The Cuban revolution altered Roca's orthodox Communist beliefs about the viable strategies for successful social change, but many of his standard interpretations of Marxism-Leninism stand in contrast to the thinking of other radical Cuban *pensa-*

dores who have, as subsequent pages relate, adapted more creative and varied types of socialist thought to conditions peculiar to Cuba.

Carlos Rafael Rodríguez (1913–)

Cuban Communist or People's Socialist party leader Carlos Rafael Rodríguez claimed that he was politicized in 1930 when University of Havana students demonstrated in favor of Enrique José Varona, a critic of the dictator Machado, and police killed a law student, Rafael Trejo, touching off national protests.[138] That year Rodríguez became part of the Directorio Estudiantil (Student Directorate) in Cienfuegos, formed to oppose Machado.[139] After being imprisoned in 1931, Rodríguez renewed his political activities at the University of Havana, where while studying law he immersed himself in the written works of Martí, Ingenieros, and Rodó.[140] He participated in the 1933 rebellion against Machado, which involved Cuba's workers in the anti-capitalist, anti-imperialist cause and began to socialize the working class on a mass basis. Rodríguez read Scott Nearing's *The American Empire* (1921), *Dollar Diplomacy* (1925) by Nearing and Joseph Freeman, and Leland Jenks's *Our Cuban Colony: A Study in Sugar* (1928), which taught him about imperialism and led him to the works of Lenin and Marx. The forbidden fruits of communism increasingly tempted the young revolutionary in search of a philosophy.[141]

The Spanish Civil War forced him to probe deeply for insights into the origins of that violent struggle. His studies led him to understand how Spanish feudalism carried over to the colonies, how agricultural feudalism retarded the development of industrialization, how the French Revolution helped abolish situations analagous to those existing in Spain and Cuba during the 1930s, and how the Spanish Civil War was essentially a class conflict.[142]

Rodríguez codirected the magazine *El Comunista* between 1930 and 1940 and became a sort of unofficial historian of Cuba's Communist party, always reminding his countrymen of their nation's radical tradition. By 1939, the year he graduated from the university, he had become a member of the Communist party's Central Committee and Politburo. His comrades regarded him as the intellectual with the greatest theoretical knowledge of Marxism.

During the era of the Communist party–Batista alliance he served in the dictator's cabinet (1940–44). Unlike his colleague Blas Roca, he tried to avoid leftist sectarianism as much as possible while in public office[143] and worked actively, and through his writing, to develop harmony among socialist factions in Cuba.

Throughout his career Rodríguez has maintained ties to leftist intellectuals, politicians, and labor leaders in the United States and Latin America. During the late 1940s he saw hope for socialism growing out of the Confederación de Trabajadores de América Latina (Latin American Confederation of Workers) (CTAL) a hemispherewide labor organization led by Mexico's Vicente Lombardo Toledano. He worked with radical intellectuals and labor leaders and urged them to unify against common problems through CTAL. He also encouraged America's Communist parties to coordinate their efforts and to take advantage of the post–World War II democratic spirit in the hemisphere.

During the Cold War, Rodríguez criticized the United States' program for Latin America, which included making the area a permanent reserve for primary materials, controlling imports and competition, locating inexpensive labor, and guaranteeing enormous benefits to those who promoted United States investments.[144] In later years he condemned the post–World War II expansion of United States business interests into the parts of

Africa, Asia, and Latin America formerly colonized by European empires.[145]

During the 1950s Rodríguez became an auxiliary or adjunct professor of social science at the University of Havana, where he taught a course in political economy. He also wrote some expository pieces for the journal *Fundamentos*. He understood the value of the pen to the political battle and constantly strove to improve his writing skills and his mental processes so he might fit into the third category of writers, described by Arthur Schopenhauer as those who write without thinking, those who think in order to write, and those who write because they have thought.[146]

Rodríguez's pioneering work, *El marxismo y la historia de Cuba* (1944) (Marxism and the History of Cuba), criticized most historians of Cuba for focusing on the bourgeoisie. To him most Cuban historians had been idealists and positivists who had not understood Marxist methods.[147] He viewed most historians of Cuba as apologists who, in order to legitimize the condition of Cuba after Independence and to impart prestige to the nation and build patriotism, wrote about the struggle against colonialism but stressed the role of heroes or individuals instead of the people. They neglected class analysis and economic determinism and did not place Cuba's problems in a world context.[148]

He illustrated the differences in the way capitalist and socialist historians function and articulated the need for scientific, well-documented analyses of Cuban history. He emphasized that Marxism is not entirely an economic interpretation—that historical materialism is much more, that it studies social relations. Unlike Leopold von Ranke and T. B. Macaulay, who explained history in terms of diplomatic struggles, treaties, and parliamentary debates; Thomas Carlyle, who dealt with history in terms of heroes of given epochs; Hegel, who saw history as the march of a universal spirit or ideal of liberty; or Comte (influenced by Darwin), who viewed the example of the struggle of individuals and groups in a process of rigorous selection— Rodríguez stated that Marxism does not exclude any or all of these factors. He found all the elements noted above subject to forces and relations of production that determine the ideas of each epoch.[149]

Rodríguez credited Marx with finding the laws that govern capitalism. In the work of Engels he found analogies between the potential for revolution in Asia and that in Cuba and Latin America. Basing his analysis of Cuban history on the thinking of Engels, he located the genesis of the country's struggle for independence from Spain in the political and property relations between Spain the metropolis and Cuba the satellite. From the first third of the nineteenth century, he argued, the colonial relations of Spain with the island did not contribute to the development of Cuba's economic forces or even the development of Cuba's bourgeoisie, who wanted to control their own destiny and nation. He believed that during the middle of the nineteenth century the Cuban middle class assumed a revolutionary posture in opposition to Spanish control in order to defend Cuban wealth. Thus the conflict with Spain was part of the larger capitalist struggle.[150]

In the essay "El movimiento reformista" (The Reformist Movement) Rodríguez alluded to the period 1862–67, when a spirit of liberty grew among some professionals and middle- and working-class Cubans. According to him these people banded together to seek political change. Their failure to secure reforms led to more violent action in 1868.[151] Rodríguez's contentions are borne out by Marxist historian Sergio Aguirre, with whom he worked and who agreed that the 1868 rebellion began as a bourgeois movement for national liberation, whereas the violent upheaval of 1895 was an attempt to protect the national liberation of the democratic bourgeoisie.[152]

In *Cuba en el tránsito al socialismo (1953–1963)* (1978) (Cuba
in the Transition to Socialism), a sequel to *El marxismo*, Rodríguez's scholarship faltered somewhat as he occasionally lapsed
into unsubstantiated rhetoric. In this history of the transformation of Cuba into a socialist society he used the word communism to refer to the higher stage of society that follows socialism
as well as to designate the period when the means of production
are initially converted to common property,[153] leading me to
speculate that he advocated building socialism and communism
simultaneously in Cuba. He referred to Cuba as one of the first
nations in the world for which the term neocolonialism was
appropriate, explaining that though the country formally gained
independence in 1902, the 1901 Platt Amendment put Cuba
under the guardianship of United States monopoly capital until
1934.[154]

Rodríguez held no false illusions that United States dominion
ended with the termination of the Platt Amendment in 1934. He
knew that when United States ambassador Sumner Welles
helped negotiate the ouster of Machado in 1933, he did so
because he attributed the poor economic conditions on the
island to the dictator's ineptitude and inaction and believed that
this damaged United States interests.

The removal of Machado opened the way for Batista, through
whom the United States solidified its ties to Cuba for the next
quarter of a century. During the Batista years Cuba functioned
in neocolonial fashion under its commercial, sugar, and industrial bourgeoisie, which operated at the mercy of United States
interests that determined the country's relations of production
and government actions.[155]

Rodríguez viewed Cuba in the post–World War II era as part
of a global movement toward socialism, which grew concurrently with the demise of worldwide colonialism. More specifically, he initially thought of Castro's 1953 attack on the Moncada

barracks as a putsch, not a revolution, as the initiation of the final phase of the struggle for national liberation that began in the 1860s. He depicted Cuba, from the time Castro toppled Batista in 1959 until 1963, as in transition, going through an atypical democratic-bourgeois phase where private capital still formed, where limited agrarian reform took place,[156] and where the radical nationalization of foreign property was an anti-imperialist move.

According to Rodríguez, Castro changed the direction of the bourgeois-democratic, anti-imperialist movement from the type advocated by José Martí to socialist revolution because he knew that, historically, reform processes ousted the dominant political powers only temporarily. Castro's knowledge of the history of the short-lived reform movements in Guatemala (1944–54), Bolivia (1952–64), and Colombia (1948), enabled him to understand that Cuba needed positive and permanent societal restructuring.[157]

Rodríguez noted that by the last days of the fight against the Batista government, Castro was almost obsessed with destroying the dominant political class in Cuba,[158] a feat that the *Fidelistas* accomplished rather quickly once in power. He also claimed that representatives of Cuba's Communist party met with Castro within weeks after the *Granma* landed on 2 December 1956 and Castro launched the crusade against Batista.[159] He noted that by 1958 Castro understood and respected the Communists and felt the need to ally with them but was not an ideological comrade, since he still harbored prejudices built upon a lifetime of exposure to anticommunism.[160]

In June 1958 the Popular Socialist Party sent Rodríguez into the Sierra Maestra to meet Castro's guerrillas, and he, like his *compañero* Blas Roca, eventually gained the trust of the *Fidelistas*. At that time, Castro told Rodríguez that it would be tactically unsound to alert the enemy by defining his revolutionary

goals too clearly.[161] By April 1961 Castro told a group of workers, "Long live our socialist revolution."[162] But according to Rodríguez, not until the fall of 1963, with the advent of the second
agrarian reform, did Cuba leave the transition (or reform)
phase, at least insofar as agriculture was concerned, and start
on the road to socialist revolution.[163]

Once Cuba's revolution was secured, Carlos Rafael, as he is
commonly called, became increasingly important as a liaison
between the liberal revolutionaries, the Communist party, and
the radical socialists. He demonstrated considerable doctrinal
flexibility while encouraging members of Cuba's disparate left
to minimize their differences and to coordinate their efforts
in order to build socialism and a better quality of life. He took
time, after the fighting ended in 1959, to assess conditions in
Cuba and to help plan for the transformation to socialism. He
also served as editor of Hoy when the Communist party was
rehabilitated and its organ resumed publication in 1959.

Rodríguez noted four major changes in Cuba after the military phase of the revolution. Plattism ended in 1959, the old
mercenary forces were replaced by the rebel army, a national
leader (Castro) enjoyed the support of the majority, and genuine
agrarian reform measures were a first step toward restructuring
the economy.[164] Also, the nationalization of the sugar industry
destroyed the power of Cuba's creole elite and its controlling
Yankee partners and opened the way for agrarian revolution.

According to Rodríguez, the Communist party began to
organize Cuba's agricultural workers as early as 1931, and by
the 1940s they constituted a somewhat politically advanced
group compared with their counterparts elsewhere in Latin
America. Most of the sugar and tobacco workers had made
some social gains before the revolution, and they came to see
the solution to their problems not in reforms that would permit
them to own a small plot of land and be small producers but in

a revolution that would provide steady work and a higher standard of living.[165]

To continue the work the Communist party had begun in the agricultural sector and to implement the 1959 agrarian reform laws, Carlos Rafael took over as president of Cuba's National Institute of Agrarian Reform in 1963. He administered a system that differed considerably from that fostered by Russia's revolution, where after 1917 nearly 90 percent of the land was in small landholdings. In Cuba the state held most of the land. Cuban peasants who owned small plots, Rodríguez stated, would not engender capitalism, as Lenin feared their Russian counterparts would do, because the Cuban state controlled them by fixing prices and regulating the distribution of machinery.[166] He asserted that Cuba's workers preferred state-owned lands because they come with social services, housing, recreational facilities, and day-care centers, which private farmers cannot afford. He predicted a trend toward publicly owned estates, or private cooperatives regulated by the state, and believed that the peasants would choose their forms of agricultural operation within the framework of the transition to communism.[167]

Just as he felt compelled to distinguish between agricultural systems under the Cuban and Russian revolutions, so has he, for decades, been defending socialism against those who equate it with the political system of the Soviet Union. Until the Cuban revolution, Rodríguez repeatedly tried to demonstrate the weaknesses of capitalism in contrast to the mythical, somewhat utopian, strengths of socialism. After the revolution began to progress, he defended socialism against its critics with greater certitude.

Despite his long affiliation with the Communist party, he has taken note of the defects in Soviet socialism. He called bureaucracy "one of the permanent dangers of socialism," since it substitutes for the masses in the decision-making process and imposes an administrative or political apparatus on the workers without taking them or their organizations into account.[168] He has deplored the attitude of the bureaucrat who is separated from the production process and believes that his office is the center of the universe. Like Lenin, Rodríguez has opposed "bureaucratic degeneration" in the revolutionary state.[169]

Rodríguez has viewed Cuba's close links to the Soviet Union as temporary, believing they will diminish as Cuba develops. He has anticipated less economic subordination to Russia in the future, an idea corroborated by the fact that the Soviet Union finds Cuba a political asset but a financial liability and is urging it to become more economically self-sufficient.[170] He also has contended that Cuba makes its own policies and admits that it disagrees with the Soviets on some substantial questions such as the USSR's actions in Poland and Afghanistan.[171] He has denied that Cuba imitates Soviet international postures in return for protection.[172]

To Rodríguez the Cuban revolution derives from Marx and Engels, Enrique Roig y San Martín, Lenin, Martí, Baliño, Mella, Mariátegui, Castro, and Guevara, who discovered the laws of society and organized a workers' revolutionary movement— men who understood the necessity of combining theory and praxis.[173]

He has acknowledged that Marx's written references to Latin America were not always factually or theoretically sound but avers that they came from a viable global conception of history from which today's thinkers can extrapolate.[174] Rodríguez prefers Lenin's approach to the study of social reality, particularly his belief in abandoning old schemes for new ones more compatible with contemporary life.[175] He applied Lenin's theories on colonialism to Latin America, especially the idea of a crisis in capitalism arising out of the imperialist stage. He noted that by analyzing the peculiarities of the social composition of the Orient, Lenin came close to comprehending the Latin American situation, particularly the plight of the peasants. By following Lenin's method of examining social reality and devising a plan for action, Rodríguez claimed that Castro threw off the old—the soldiers and the priests—and replaced them with the new—worker and peasant power—thereby bringing about Latin America's first socialist revolution.[176]

Carlos Rafael has spent considerable time since the revolution trying to raise the cultural, political, and ideological levels of fellow Cubans, to accomplish Lenin's dream of creating a socialist country where the simplest cook would know how to handle state problems. He has tried to educate his people, to enable them to comprehend and participate in socialist democracy.

He explained that democracy connotes the desire to innovate continuously, to introduce into society new forms of genuine popular participation that will increasingly give people's power its full significance.[177] He illustrated that no incongruity exists between the idea of democracy and the concept of dictatorship in the scientific sense. Dictatorship, he stated, should not be used in the vulgar way some employ the term in reference to the Soviet Union. It does not mean one-person rule or oppression; in Cuba, as to Marx and Engels, it means extraordinary power, a working class that is the majority and therefore the state—a viable dictatorship of the proletariat. To him, as to Lenin, a dictatorship of the proletariat is a hundred times more democratic than a bourgeois democracy with its class stratifications and conflicts.[178]

Rodríguez has portrayed Cuba as part of a Third World revolutionary movement that has increasingly turned underdeveloped countries to socialism. His views on how socialism will be attained have changed as a result of the Cuban experience. Before the Castro era he believed that capitalism would be diminished by its inherent corruption and failures and, within a given country, could be replaced peacefully by socialism.[179] In recent years he has come to believe that ideological and class antagonisms and imperialism generally cannot be eliminated peacefully and that they cause fights for national liberation or civil wars such as those that occurred in the late 1970s in Nicaragua and El Salvador. Out of these struggles, rather than from world war, socialism will emerge.[180] He declared that Cuba follows the policy that "armed struggle is the fundamental instrument for the advancement of the revolutionary process in the majority of the Latin American countries," but that does not mean that "armed struggle is indispensable in each and every country."[181] At the same time, he has insisted that accords on peaceful coexistence between capitalist and socialist nations can prevent global war.[182]

Carlos Rafael Rodríguez has served the Cuban revolution as a member of the Central Committee of the Communist party, as an elected deputy from Cienfuegos to the National Assembly, as vice-president of the Council of State, and in various capacities relating to foreign policy. Most of all, he has been a major ideological mentor of the revolution, a living link between it and the radicalism of the Generation of 1930, one who, with his compañeros Raúl Roa and Blas Roca, has guided Cuba toward collective action and socialism, toward a greater comprehension of revolutionary events in Russia, China, Vietnam, and Cuba and how they have affected the course of world history.

So many theories, doctrines and beliefs,
now out of date, that long ago were
like bibles of science. Man has to pay
dearly for human progress! Yet I never
stopped wondering if it was worthwhile
spending my time on such studies, if
they would help me combat existing
evils. Still, one can only feel a deep
reverence for those men who gave their
whole lives to thinking and finding new
ways to leave a legacy to humanity.

Fidel Castro

CHAPTER 5

The Socialist Revolution, 1959–

Fidel Castro spoke the words above from prison in 1954. He
could pay no greater tribute to the tradition of radical thought,
and the role of Cubans in it, than to pursue the struggle he
believed started militarily in 1868,[1] reached a critical turning
point in the revolution of 1933,[2] and was continued by the
Twenty-sixth of July Movement.

Once the military phase of the struggle ended with the victory
of the Twenty-sixth of July Movement in 1959, Castro realized
that to implement a revolution he would have to rely upon those
with innovative and organizational skills, people who shared
his radical perspective and had political experience. Among
Cuba's active political groups, only the Communist party, toward
whom Castro was probably temporarily bitter, had a developed
worldview, including an anti-imperialist stance.[3] Revolutionary
groups, including the Communist party and the Twenty-sixth
of July Movement, coalesced into the *Organizaciones Revolucionarias Integradas* (Integrated Revolutionary Organization)
(ORI), directed by Communist leader Aníbal Escalante. After

Escalante was accused of personalism and despotism and relieved of his position, ORI continued to unite Cuba's progressive elements. Communist and radical intellectuals soon became a sort of vanguard of the vanguard and were charged by the new Cuban government to study and compare the problems of underdeveloped and nonaligned nations, which Cuba hoped to serve to some extent as a model. Intellectuals also were entrusted with the job of explaining the revolution to the Cuban people, preparing them to deal with its vicissitudes and to make the transition to a different way of life.

From a socialist point of view, the fact that so many middle- and upper-class Cubans chose to leave the country after the Castro takeover proved fortuitous. Strong middle- and upper-class institutions no longer existed on the island, nor did the independent economic base necessary for a counterrevolution.[4] Most of those who remained in Cuba had been raised in an atmosphere where radical intellectuals and socialist labor unionists were accepted by those who understood their positions and were not feared by those who did not understand.

Cuba's counterrevolutionaries, mostly exiles, misread the character of the early revolution. Many of them thought of it as basically a peasant movement. But the long-term struggle in Cuba had been primarily conducted by the urban proletariat. Although urban labor played a limited role in Castro's armed conflict, it nevertheless constituted the sector most cognizant of its own class interests as a result of years of organization and education by the Communist party, anarchosyndicalists, and the writers noted prominently throughout this book. The urban workers, not the *campesinos* (peasants), had the tradition and experience to play a leading part in transforming Cuba from an underdeveloped state with a weak national capitalist class, rampant inequality, and political and economic instability[5] into a more socially and economically progressive nation.

Cuba's progressive elements—urban workers, the peasants who assisted in the guerrilla war, the approximately seventeen thousand members of the Communist party,[6] fellow travelers, and radical students and intellectuals gradually cohered in pursuit of the revolution. The revolutionary administration stressed the importance of intellectuals in building a new society. Radical thinkers Raúl Roa and Juan Marinello assumed major government positions. Other radical intellectuals were placed in charge of various government agencies.

In 1959 the Casa de las Américas publishing firm was founded to encourage and promote the dissemination of the writings of some of Latin America's outstanding socialist and nonsocialist scholars and literary figures and to build closer cultural ties to sister nations in the hemisphere. The National Printing Agency (Imprenta Nacional), directed by world-famous novelist Alejo Carpentier, produced volumes of the works of Voltaire, Marx, Lenin, Castro, and Blas Roca, anti-imperialist tracts by others, and a variety of literature including works by Cervantes and Tolstoy.[7]

The National Union of Cuban Artists and Writers was launched in 1961. Under the aegis of its president Nicolás Guillén, renowned poet and longtime Communist party member, the Union stimulated creative endeavors and tried to ensure that the artistic and literary works produced by its members defended *Cubanidad*, reflected the revolution, and fostered solid relations with other socialist countries. Those elected to the Union received jobs as teachers, translators, and editors, which included free time for creative work. Their salaries helped subsidize their ongoing scholarly, artistic, and literary efforts. Royalties to writers, considered a vestige of the capitalist past, were for the most part abolished. Henceforth the fruits of artistic labor were generally to benefit the masses rather than individual artists, writers, or consumers.

The government established the Cuban National Publishing Company in 1962. Revolution Publications was formed in 1965. The two merged in 1967 to create the Cuban Book Institute, which supervised the production of volumes to stock the two hundred bookshops and countless bookstalls the government set up near or inside workplaces throughout the island.

From the inception of the new regime in 1959, culture and education played a significant role in revolutionary planning. Army barracks became schools. Education was deemed vital to the country's economic and political development programs. To build an egalitarian society all people need access to educational institutions and diverse means of developing their minds. A massive literacy campaign began in 1961 and eventually raised Cuba's literacy rate from approximately 76 to 96 percent, the highest in Latin America. Education through the university level was open and free to all.

Revolutionary education emphasized nationalism, Third World internationalism, and Marxism. It was primarily geared to produce engineers and technologists, not social scientists or political philosophers. By the middle of 1961, after the CIA-sponsored invasion of the Bay of Pigs by Cuban exiles failed, and after Castro pronounced Cuba a Marxist-Leninist state, Cuba's progressive sectors began to integrate more rapidly. The nation's established radical *pensadores* were quickly thrust into the mainstream of the struggle to create a homegrown variety of socialism.

Thinkers representing the three major groups mentioned repeatedly on previous pages—Communist party theoreticians, nonsectarian Marxists, most of whom had participated in the revolution of 1933 and retained links to international socialist cultural traditions, and younger and less sophisticated Twenty-sixth of July Movement leaders—eventually became integral parts of Cuba's revolutionary intelligentsia. Many of their social and political ideas and tendencies, and those produced by earlier generations of Cuban radical intellectuals, are reflected in the thoughts and deeds of Ernesto "Che" Guevara and Fidel Castro as documented on the following pages.

Ernesto "Che" Guevara (1927–67)

Ernesto "Che"[8] Guevara, international folk hero of the Cuban revolution, guerrilla fighter, Renaissance man, and prolific writer, was born and raised in Argentina, where numerous *pensadores* and political and labor organizations had gone beyond positivism. He began to study Marxism seriously after he completed his medical education. Under the tutelege of Hilda Gadea (who became his first wife) in Guatemala in 1954, the year a CIA-sponsored coup overthrew that country's social-reformist government, Guevara delved into Marxism and found ideas consistent with some of his own beliefs. For instance, he disagreed with the Freudian psychoanalysts he worked with in Buenos Aires, who accepted the existing social order as a norm. Che believed, as Marx did, that much of what exists is learned.

Like Marx, he had a passion for books and ideas and understood the value of cultivating the mind as a vital instrument in the revolutionary battle. Guevara put theory into action, spoke with candor, felt compelled to put his ideas on paper, and wrote well, despite a penchant for obtuse abstractions. Close examination of his works shows the influence of Antonio Gramsci, Jesús Silva Herzog, Immanuel Kant, Karl Marx, V. I. Lenin, Leon Trotsky, Joseph Stalin, Vo Nguyen Giap, Frantz Fanon, Milovan Djilas, Ernest Mandel, José Carlos Mariátegui, and Paul Baran. Legend tells that Che always carried a copy of Chilean poet Pablo Neruda's *Canto general*. In the midst of courageous struggle he found time for poetry.[9]

Guevara learned a great deal from the thinking of Gramsci about the vital role of the intellectual in building a new cultural consensus by fostering historical awareness and interpreting it for others. The Italian thinker's works taught him that one does not have to wait for the inevitable revolution; one can use the party to build a revolutionary consciousness among the masses. Che liked Gramsci's eclectic approach, his willingness to keep theoretical discussion open to all new contributors and to continually verify ideas in relation to historical circumstances. As we shall subsequently see, in some ways Guevara's ideas on the new socialist person reflect the thinking of Gramsci.

One scholar noted that Guevara probably had read Frantz Fanon's Les damnés de la terre (1961) (The Wretched of the Earth), since it was available in Cuba and he read French. From it he might have concluded that many of Latin America's revolutionaries, especially those in its various Communist parties, would drag their feet forever waiting for the propitious moment for revolution.[10] Fanon, like Gramsci, felt an urgent need to get on with the revolution, to create the correct conditions if they did not exist. Che also adopted Mariátegui's Marxist ethics, which advocated building proletarian humanism from the class struggle. He most likely had read the Peruvian pensador's Defensa del marxismo (1934) (Defense of Marxism), which was republished in Castro's Cuba.

Guevara dug deeply into political and social theory after Castro's victory. He asserted that the scientific principles of Marxism were present in the events of the Cuban revolution, operating independent of what the movement's leaders knew about Marxist theory. Once the Twenty-sixth of July Movement controlled Cuba, Che turned to Marxist thought for more formal revolutionary guidance. He followed Marx's dictum that man can cease being a slave to his environment and, by making qualitative changes in historical thought, can take charge of his own destiny.[11]

In justifying the violence used to liberate Cuba, Guevara agreed with Lenin, who stated: "Social-Democracy has never taken a sentimental view of war. It unreservedly condemns war as a bestial means of settling conflicts in human society. But Social-Democracy knows that so long as society is divided into classes, so long as there is exploitation of man by man, wars are inevitable. This exploitation cannot be destroyed without war, and war is always and everywhere begun by the exploiters, by the ruling and oppressing classes."[12]

Like Marx and Lenin, Guevara concentrated on the idea that "the emancipation of the working people will be the task of the working people themselves,"[13] and he realized this had to begin with a mass education program. He did not consider study the patrimony of a privileged class but believed it was the right of everyone. He personally taught literature classes to groups of Cubans and issued them copies of *Don Quixote*,[14] which enabled them to build confidence and think in terms of progress, since they saw Guevara as a modern knight-errant who had defeated the previously unconquerable foe.

In conjunction with the massive literacy campaign he engineered, Che stressed the role of art in the revolution. He thought that intellectuals should provide ideology through political theory as well as through artistic works. To him, culture and art had traditionally been used to free people (temporarily) from alienation after long workdays. Before the revolution Cubans had sought relief from alienation by communing with their environment—an escape that differed from the concept of art as a weapon of protest and change. He claimed that art too often combined aspects of the socialist present and the dead past. He attacked socialist realism, which he believed arose on the foundations of nineteenth-century class-oriented art, as fundamentally capitalist and not truly expressing freedom. He sought a society that breeds the true artistic freedom that comes with communism, and he contended that art forms must not represent nature as basically "positive" social reality, as an ideal society almost without the contradictions and conflict that the revolution seeks to illuminate.[15] Simultaneously, he believed that art could shift people away from the crass materialism of capitalism and get them to create aesthetic satisfactions to replace material ones.[16]

Although Guevara put considerable emphasis on the cultural aspects of the revolution, his world renown came primarily from his exploits as a guerrilla fighter, tactician, and theorist. To implement the revolution he turned to guerrilla warfare, which had existed in Cuba since 1511 when Indian chief Hatuey battled the Spanish. Che's ideas on guerrilla warfare came from Mao Zedong, Ho Chi Minh, and Alberto Bayo, author of *Ciento cincuenta preguntas a un guerrillero* (1959) (A Hundred and Fifty Questions to a Guerrilla) and veteran of the Spanish Republican Army, who trained Guevara and Castro in Mexico before their departure for Cuba in 1956. Che also used as precedent for his guerrilla actions Augusto Sandino's heroic stand against United States expeditionary forces in Nicaragua in the 1920s and 1930s.[17]

Guevara's concept of the catalytic role of the guerrilla departed from conventional Marxist thinking and revised the thought of Lenin. Marx approved of guerrilla warfare as a popular form of struggle but, unlike Che, did not link it to proletarian tactics for gaining power. Lenin taught that one could move only when the objective and subjective conditions for revolution matured, a situation that was almost nonexistent in Latin America in the 1960s. Guevara believed that by using a catalyst one could prepare the Latin American countries for the revolution.[18]

With regard to Cuba's revolution, Che is credited with two innovations. First, he viewed the guerrilla as an unyielding social revolutionary who battled against the institutions that permit poverty and misery[19] and was capable of winning a total victory. To some extent he disagreed with China's Mao Zedong and Vietnam's Vo Nguyen Giap, major Marxist guerrilla warfare theoreticians who believed that guerrilla warfare had some limitations. Second, he proved, at least in Cuba, that Mao and Lin Piao were wrong when they contended that one had to prepare the rural people to await the right conditions for armed revolution.[20] To him, Cuba built its own road to socialism, one that included using guerrillas as catalysts, along with numerous other improvisations.

Inspired by success in Cuba and by Bakunin's theories that a social revolution could begin before a political one because even the finest army could not overcome irregular troops supported by the masses and that deeds provide the most encouragement to revolution, Che advocated starting insurrections independently in the countryside to serve as catalysts for the spread of the revolution to the cities.[21] He understood that Latin Americans saw the objective conditions for revolution—hunger, oppression, poverty—and believed that the subjective conditions, including cognizance of the possibility of victory, could emerge only by engaging in armed struggle.[22] In contrast to most of Cuba's radical thinkers, Guevara dismissed the possibility of peaceful transformation to socialism in Latin America.

Marx and Lenin saw the urban proletariat as the most effective revolutionary force and believed that the cities were the place to launch the battle, but Che modified their ideas on revolution to fit the countryside. He concluded that the peasants wanted control over the means of production and could be the vehicle for liberation.[23] He believed that the peasantry might not lead the revolution but would participate in it, cooperate with the guerrillas, and play a key role in rural areas where it dominated numerically.

He maintained that in underdeveloped Latin America rural guerrilla action was preferable because the most repressive forces of the incumbent regimes operated in the cities. Like Giap and Mao, Guevara advocated alliances between guerrillas and the peasantry, which could be mobilized by implementing agrarian reform. He believed that the peasants would fight to obtain land, and this constituted the mainspring of Third World revolution.[24] But his ideas on peasant revolution could not be fully adapted to all parts of Latin America, as was subsequently proved by the diverse experiences of insurrectionaries in Bolivia, Colombia, El Salvador, and Nicaragua.

Che contradicted the theory supported by Latin America's Communist parties that they had to win political victories at the polls before launching a conflict with the power elites. He realized that the essence of Marxism does not always come from books but can be derived from the revolutionary process—that the active struggle in Cuba enabled the proletariat to attain self-consciousness,[25] with which it became the agent to resolve, through socialism, the problems caused by society's contradictions. To Guevara the human mind, not ideology per se, was the essential element in building a revolution.[26] He disputed Lenin's dictum that "without a revolutionary theory there can be no revolution,"[27] but he did not dismiss the importance of theory.[28] He understood that the upheaval in Cuba during the 1950s had little theoretical base and realized that the revolutionary leaders were not theoreticians. But he asserted that they were not totally ignorant of the laws governing social phenomena and that with such knowledge and an understanding of reality they were able to create a revolution.[29] To Che, "the revolutionary makes the revolution and the revolution makes the revolutionary."[30] He disregarded Lenin's admonition to "never play with insurrection" and Mao's plea to "engage in no battle you are not sure of winning."[31]

Guevara rejected coexistence, preferring confrontation as the best method of conducting relations between the growing socialist alliance and the capitalist states in the process of losing

their empires.[32] For instance, he held that the United States invasion of the Dominican Republic in 1965 stirred up nationalism
and stimulated socialist opposition to capitalist intervention. He
hoped that guerrilla actions throughout Latin America would
cause new United States interventions and force confrontations
leading to a continental war that would end with Yankee capitalism's losing to Latin American socialism.

When given the task of building socialism by organizing the
economy of revolutionary Cuba, Guevara became an advocate
of planning as a creative device for overcoming what he termed
wrong development rather than underdevelopment.[33] He
believed that the United States had imposed "democratic" capitalism on Latin American and Third World nations, that they
had become the colonial estate of the United States.[34] He knew
that political domination accompanied economic control, and
thus he preferred the Chinese position that it is better to advance
economically on one's own than to rely upon more developed
states. He asserted that all socialist nations had the duty to assist
one another,[35] but he disliked the idea of Cuba's relying too
heavily on the Soviet Union.[36]

Fidel Castro became increasingly oriented to the Soviet
Union and wanted to concentrate on building Cuban communism, whereas Guevara moved toward Trotskyism and the belief
that socialism and communism in Cuba could be constructed
and maintained only by opening new revolutionary fronts in the
Third World. Che concurred with Trotsky's views on permanent
revolution in the colonial countries and believed in proletarian
internationalism. He originally agreed with Lenin, who claimed
that a proletarian party, serving as a vanguard, was necessary
to help create conditions needed to seize power, and who
pointed to the failure of the Paris Commune of 1871 as an
example of a premature, ill-prepared revolution not led by a
party. Guevara subsequently rejected Lenin's and Trotsky's view

that a vanguard is necessary to participate in the daily struggle of the masses in order to win them to socialism. He favored the idea that the masses are already mentally committed to socialism.[37] Guevara concurred with Lenin that imperialism represented the highest stage of capitalism. He argued for a grand strategy to defeat imperialism, a Third World unity that would take advantage of the contradictions of capitalism that he believed were leading to a global explosion. He agreed with Marx's prediction that capitalism would disappear and make way for a new socialist order and with Lenin's conclusion that the transition to socialism could be accelerated by human actions.[38]

To initiate action, he backed the *foco* theory. By *foco* he meant a center or nucleus of guerrilla operations rather than a base. A *foco* consisted of a unit fighting in a specific province, not stationed in one place. The *foco* could be seen as a force rather than a center or, to use the Cuban expression, "the one small motor that sparked the big motor" of the revolution, providing the leadership, subjective conditions, and revolutionary drive that led to the creation of a people's army.[39]

French intellectual Régis Debray, who observed Guevara in Cuba and Bolivia, called the *foco* theory more than a strategy. To Debray it represented an ethical philosophy recognizing that a person's life-style gradually determines his or her activities and demanding that revolutionaries be activists who impress others by what they do, not what they say.[40] *Foco* theorists claim that orthodox Communist organization benefits only urbanites and ignores the peasantry. They also believe that the *foco* philosophy combines Marxism with existentialism by using existing circumstances to start the revolution. *Foco* advocates diverge from more traditional Marxists because they believe that the rural guerrilla movement need not be led by a party and that a party will emerge once the guerrilla force is established and after it has won liberation. They claim that the next phase of the revolution will be guarded by a Marxist-Leninist party that functions to develop production and raise consciousness.[41] On the other hand, Communists, Maoists, and Trotskyists argue that guerrilla warfare needs years of careful political and ideological preparation, and they view *foco* theorists as unscientific adventurers who avoid historical analysis.[42]

After the death of Guevara and the failure of *foquismo* elsewhere in Latin America, *foco* theory advocates came under attack for failing to comprehend the economic and political aspects of mounting a revolution and for not building the consciousness of the urban working classes. It became clear that the peasantry could not be organized in isolation, that local communities had to be educated and made aware of national and international problems, and that vanguard parties were necessary to perform organizing and educative functions.[43] Even Debray changed his position and concluded that urban workers are the ones who, in the final analysis, make the revolution. Debray may have been premature in dismissing the importance of the rural sector, which time might prove is an integral part of the revolutionary process along with the urban proletariat.

Che's advocacy of the *foco* theory must not be misinterpreted as small-scale thinking. He was a man of considerable vision who predicted widespread insurrection in the form of multinational, coordinated people's wars around *focos*. He believed that the *foco* theory could best be applied to dictatorships of the kind perpetuated by Cuba's Batista, the Dominican Republic's Trujillo, and Nicaragua's Somoza. He also realized that where a government has come to power through any form of popular consultation, fraudulent or not, and maintained at least a facade of constitutionality, it is exceedingly difficult to precipitate a guerrilla war, since the possibilities of civil struggle have not been exhausted. Nevertheless, Guevara believed that in countries under the ideological domination of the United States—such as Venezuela—where insufficient social progress occurred, it might be worthwhile to create revolutionary focos.[44]

The foco that Guevara tried to create in Bolivia was thwarted by conflicts among left-wing groups and by Bolivian nationalists who resented a foreign interloper in their country. After he was murdered while trying to ignite a revolution there in 1967, the foco theory lost supporters. New revolutionary theories emerged, particularly ones stressing urban guerrilla warfare. But Che's foco concept and writings on guerrilla warfare continued to be analyzed and influenced revolutionaries everywhere. Their close studies of his works revealed that he understood that the struggle would eventually have to be conducted in the cities and that he believed that urban revolutionaries would grow in proportion to the successes of rural insurrections such as that in Cuba.

Guevara taught that one ignorant of ideology may become a guerrilla but cannot survive combat without acquiring some theoretical knowledge. He believed that the revolutionary's social conscience grows with his military skill but that the latter could not carry one through the hardships of battle. To him, the best fighter was the most politically aware person, one fit to lead after the victory. That individual was also more realistic and revolutionary than anyone who had not fought.[45]

No leader of the Cuban revolution possessed greater political awareness or realism than Che. He knew that after seizing power the "revolution becomes speeches, military reviews, parades, committees, political parties, and intrigue," but he also recognized the need to establish order and to administer collectively.[46] He understood that a new class had taken power in Cuba and that new cadres had to be trained to lead the movement, especially at the intermediate level. To him the ideal cadre type, because of political awareness, could interpret directives from the central power and convey them to the masses while understanding the desires of the people. Such a person must also understand collective decision making, and be able to make his or her own creative decisions.[47] Guevara envisioned cadres as the "major part of the ideological motor which is the United Party of the Revolution."[48]

Once victory had been attained in Cuba, Guevara tried to build an ideology that would accelerate the transformation to socialism. Marx and Lenin envisaged socialist revolution in societies where the capitalist material base would be fully developed and where the proletariat had a high degree of consciousness. After the Russian's revolution it became obvious that the material base the Soviet leaders expected did not exist; thus they could not stress moral incentives as Marx had believed possible. Instead they had to pay more attention to developing the material base. Che knew that the Cuban revolutionary government inherited many potentially corrupting capitalist ways alien to the revolution, including material incentives. In utopian fashion he defined *value* according to moral and social or human worth, not supply and demand. To him work was more valuable in human terms than in terms of economic efficiency. He construed economic man as a monster created by capitalism and believed that the economic system should serve society— that money was worth no part of human life.[49]

Che disagreed with classical Marxists who maintained that one must establish a socialist economy before there exists the foundation for building a revolutionary mentality. He concurred with Mao's contention that one immediately constructs a revolutionary conscience or else runs the risk of holding on to capitalist incentives, as he thought had occurred in the Soviet Union.[50] Guevara believed that moral incentives made people community oriented, willing to volunteer to cut cane for the good of society rather than having to be compelled to do so by social pressures. He felt that under socialism, equality of treatment drove people to productivity, whereas in capitalist society fear of being left behind drove them to produce. He sought to develop in Cubans an inner desire to contribute to society without seeking society's approval or receiving remuneration.[51]

His moral incentives concept, which derived from "from each according to his ability, to each according to his need," implied the elimination of the market wage system of labor allocation. He understood that a policy of moral rather than material incentives could hinder the production so desperately needed for Cuba's development. He also knew that, politically, opting for moral over material incentives could enhance mobilization and give the people a greater sense of participation in decision making. Socially, moral over material incentives could help eliminate class stratification, advance income equalization, reduce alienation, and strengthen solidarity.[52]

Che did not deny the objective need for material incentives, but he was unwilling to use them as a basic driving force. According to social democrat Michael Harrington, Guevara erroneously assumed that the "Marxian vision of what man can become under conditions of democratically planned and socialized abundance, can be operative in a society of scarcity." Harrington thought that Guevara was too idealistic and that moral incentives could not work in Cuba, that for people to be able to love each other there has to be material sufficiency, and that Che miscalculated in believing that people will sacrifice and accept shortages while building a material base.[53]

Guevara apparently did not pay much attention to the need and right of workers to make their own decisions regarding material versus moral incentives. Only after he left Cuba did the idea of workers' initiatives appear.[54] By the 1970s Cuba, following the prescription of Carlos Rafael Rodríguez, moved

toward a balance of moral and material incentives. In keeping
with Marx's *Critique of the Gotha Program*, Cuba found itself in
168 the initial stages of socialism adhering to the premise "from
each according to his ability, to each according to his work."
Cuba accepted a more traditional interpretation of postcapital-
ist development based on the material base, followed by abundance, and then the creation of the new socialist person. While
loyal supporters of the moral incentive idea claimed that the
change in policy would create competition and hostility instead
of promoting production, others rationalized the change as
"collective incentives." Cuba's leaders found that even moral
incentives could be motivated by ego, that people could compete
for them on a material basis. This raised the question to what
extent there exists psychological or spiritual materialism.[55]

Besides introducing the concept of moral incentives into
Cuban society, Che sought two other major goals after the military successes of the revolution—the creation of a new, more
utopian socialist person for the twenty-first century, and the
development of technology appropriate for life in the new Cuba.
He believed that socialism could be constructed in a former
colonial dependency of the monocultural type only by simultaneously developing technology and a new value system. Taking
his lead from Karl Marx and Argentine Marxist Aníbal Ponce's
Humanismo burgués y humanismo proletario (1935) (Bourgeois
Humanism and Proletarian Humanism), Guevara noted: "Man
still needs to undergo a complete spiritual rebirth in his attitude
toward his work, freed from the direct pressure of his social
environment though linked to it by his new habits. That will be
communism."[56]

Che concluded that to achieve freedom for the individual
and human fulfillment, people must produce without being
forced to sell themselves as commodities. To him, a socialist
needed vast inner resources, a sense of solidarity and service

to the people, and had to strive for total awareness.[57] Like Plato, Guevara believed that the realization of man lay within his community. He stressed that the socialist revolution need not extinguish the individual in favor of the state, and he emphasized the close dialectical unity between the individual and the mass, which are interrelated and also related to the leader.[58] Guevara's thinking thus preserves the individual's role in the state. He claimed that by adhering to the theory of moral rather than material incentives, the new socialist-humanist Cuban person could prevent the emergence of a state composed of avaricious bureaucrats.

Guevara's views on the new socialist person, adapted from the Chinese and Russian revolutions, have had considerable impact outside Cuba. During the late 1960s and early 1970s they were accepted by radical groups in North Vietnam, Latin America, and the United States. They influenced, in varying degrees, numerous younger communists, including the Colombian revolutionary priest Camilo Torres, who inspired the Christians for Socialism and liberation theology movements.[59] Guevara, not Castro, became the primary stimulus and guide to the Movimiento Izquierda Revolucionaria (Movement of the Revolutionary Left) (MIR), the far-left organization that worked with Salvador Allende's government in Chile. The MIR, and various factions in the Allende administration, approved of Guevara's emphasis on the spiritual element in Marxism—the fact that he was drawn to the humanism of the young Marx. Paradoxically, the most conservative groups in the Allende coalition felt that Guevara advocated communist totalitarianism—a non-Marxist concept.

Regardless of Che's theoretical strengths and weaknesses, he will be remembered as an opponent of Marxist sectarianism and as the existential socialist hero who gave his life for the revolution. He knew that the Cuban revolution often diverged from Marxist theory.[60] He understood that economic, political, and social circumstances differed from place to place in Latin America, and he implored revolutionaries to deal with theory and creative practice in accord with the special conditions of their respective countries while refraining from mechanical thinking. He considered all of Latin America his native country and viewed the Cuban revolution as the first part of a larger struggle to eventually embrace and emancipate the whole region.[61]

In *El socialismo y el hombre* (1966) (Socialism and Man) he visualized the future in the hands of youth and predicted that some day the Party, as the vanguard of the people, could give way to the latter when they were sufficiently educated for communism,[62] when they could comprehend the essence of Marxism. He urged his comrades to think of Marxism as ever changing, not static, as a system wherein the facts determine new concepts and the new concepts retain the segment of the truth held by the older concepts—thus producing a new synthesis.[63]

Che's ideas, but above all his romantic guerrilla-fighter image, appealed to young people all over the world. He believed that the Cuban revolution demonstrated the people's ability to rise up and cast off colonial domination, that it marked the beginning of the end for United States imperialism.[64] He may have inadvertently damaged scientific revolution by giving some naive young idealists the impression that all they need to do is take rifles to the mountains to start the process of societal change. On the other hand, he remains a major symbol of the value of combining theory with praxis.

Although Che Guevara came from a non-Cuban literary, intellectual, and ideological tradition, students of revolution will forever identify him primarily with Cuba. He will be remembered for his numerous contributions to the country that adopted him, to its ongoing revolution and to its present generation of *pensadores*.

Fidel Castro Ruz (1927–)

Since his youth, Fidel Castro, the son of an upper-middle-class family from Oriente province, has displayed radical tendencies and exceptional leadership ability. While a student leader at the University of Havana during the late 1940s, Castro read some Marx but also came under the influence of Eduardo Chibás, an ardent nationalist who convinced him that there existed revolutionary potential in Cuba's bourgeoisie and its student movements, whose support Castro subsequently used to achieve victory.[65] He joined Chibás's nationalistic Ortodoxo party in 1947 and helped organize its radical action wing, which worked for honest government, economic and political independence, and social reform.

Castro's speeches and writings, some of which may have been composed by others from his ideas, have always revealed a sense of history and the strong influence of José Martí, whose works he first read while in secondary school. Castro called Martí an anti-imperialist reformer, not a Marxist, but noted that conditions were not ripe for socialist revolution in Cuba during Martí's lifetime.

Until Castro took control of Cuba in 1959, he publicly stood for a humanist revolution. Lionel Martín, a political scientist and journalist who knows him well, indicated that behind the Cuban leader's reformist facade has always existed a revolutionary, and that from his religious background he has derived a social stance akin to primitive Christianity—the idea of justice and identification with the poor and humble. By the age of twenty, Castro had become familiar with the thinking of his countryman Julio Mella and admitted to being somewhat of a utopian socialist,[66] an admission he reiterated while fighting in the Sierra.[67]

Upon returning from Colombia in 1948, where he witnessed the *Bogotazo*, in which Colombia's liberal presidential aspirant

Jorge Gaitán was assassinated and his movement thwarted, Castro attended a Marxist study group, where he read Lenin's
The State and Revolution (1918) and *Imperialism: The Highest Stage of Capitalism* (1916) and developed a deeper appreciation of Marxist theory.[68]

After leading an abortive raid on the Moncada army barracks in 1953 that he hoped would spark a popular uprising to topple the Batista regime—which he spoke about as a step in a national liberation program, not a revolution[69]—Castro was imprisoned. In jail he wrote *History Will Absolve Me* (1954). The work was to some extent inspired by the thinking of Antonio Guiteras, who supported anti-imperialism and the idea that property is not an absolute right but a social function best guided by a state that controls the economy. Guiteras, one of the leaders of the 1933 rebellion that briefly brought democratic government to Cuba, advocated economic independence for the nation, supporting working-class interests and a vague kind of socialism without class dictatorship.[70] Maurice Halperin, who taught at the University of Havana and initially supported the Cuban revolution, believed that the thinking of Guiteras led to Castro's ideas on the nationalization of subsoil rights, public services, agrarian reform, expropriation of large estates, and the creation of agricultural cooperatives.[71]

Fidel, as everyone in Cuba calls him, based his early revolutionary activities on the belief in the legitimacy of revolution, a concept borrowed from the seventeenth- and eighteenth-century philosophers who challenged the "divine right of kings" and advocated bourgeois revolution. In a legal brief filed against the 1953 Batista takeover, he argued for "a new conception of the state, of society, of the judicial order based on profound historical and philosophical principles."[72] In 1953 he also spoke about adherence to Cuba's 1940 constitution, a move that would facilitate major social restructuring. For instance, that document declared that subsoil resources were public property and should be used for the public good.[73]

Even before the Moncada debacle, Castro believed in the masses and in the "irreducible force of great ideas," which adds up to the "Marxian dictum that when ideas take possession of the masses, they become a material force."[74] He reinforced these convictions while in prison for almost two years (1953–55) by rereading Marx and Lenin along with the works of Mariátegui, José Ingenieros, Weber, Balzac, Jorge Amado, Kant, Einstein, Descartes, Varela, Luz y Caballero, and Baliño. He also read a biography of longtime Brazilian Communist party leader Luiz Carlos Prestes.[75]

In a letter written while in prison on the Isle of Pines, he noted having read Victor Hugo's study of the 1848 revolution in France and its aftermath—*Napoléon le petit*—and Marx's *The Eighteenth of Brumaire of Louis Bonaparte*, and he commented that after comparing the two works "one could appreciate the enormous difference between a scientific and realistic conception of history and a purely romantic interpretation." For Hugo "history is chance, for Marx a process governed by laws."[76] While Hugo sees only a lucky adventurer, Marx sees the inevitable results of the social contradictions and the conflict of interests prevailing in those days."[77]

In the course of building an insurrectionary movement, Castro took cognizance of Cuba's lack of national identity, its legacies of Spanish authoritarianism, personalism, trade unionism, anarchism, radicalism, class conflict, and political instability. He assessed the need for radical domestic social and economic change in the nation and expressed the desire to eliminate all forms of subservience to the United States. He and his Twenty-sixth of July Movement cohorts also knew that their challenge to

United States dominance in Cuba would ultimately evoke Yankee opposition, and they moved quickly to build support for the movement among the masses.

The Programme Manifesto of the Twenty-sixth of July Movement issued in Mexico City in November 1956 stated: "With regard to ideological definitions, the 26th of July movement prefers to avoid abstract formulations or pre-established clichés. The ideology of the Cuban Revolution must arise from its own roots and the particular circumstances of the people and the country."[78] The manifesto maintained that the ideology of the Twenty-sixth of July Movement was native, embodied in what Nelson Valdés called the essentially populist thought of Martí.[79] Castro, after coming to power, blended these ideas with Marxist ideology to form *Fidelismo* or Castroism. He saw no contradictions between Martí's dream of a just society free of foreign domination, racism, and the power of the propertied interests and the socioeconomic teachings of Marx.

Castro has never denied his non-Marxist past, once stating, "If you ask me if I considered myself a revolutionary when I was in the Sierra, I'll say yes. If you ask me if I considered myself a classic communist, I'll say no."[80] Not until 2 December 1961 did he announce publicly: "I am a Marxist-Leninist, and I will be a Marxist-Leninist until the last days of my life." He dismissed charges of hypocrisy by declaring that his previous political stances were irrelevant to present conditions in Cuba, that one is entitled to change one's mind, and that intellectual growth can foster ideological and philosophical change in a person.[81]

Fidel underwent a metamorphosis. He learned that revolutions are not wrought by spontaneous uprisings, that "winning the war was not the Revolution, it gave us the right to make the revolution."[82] He assumed that Cuba's workers had acquired socialist spirit, attitudes, and virtues.[83] He found, through the use of Marxist methods, answers to some of Cuba's problems, but he realized that "Marxism is a science in constant change that has continually been enriched by historical reality."[84] Like C. Wright Mills, he did not believe that there existed a Marxist truth. Castro denied that Marx was a prophet but saw his thought as a link to the deeds of the Twenty-sixth of July Movement and the ideas of Martí, a means to continue the heroic epoch of Cuban liberation.

During the period of transition to communism, which Cuba is still in, Fidel, like Marx and Martí, has viewed the nation as a bearer of culture and a unifying element around which people work collectively for their freedom. When he talks about the "withering away of the state" he means the state as a coercive instrument controlled by the dominant class, not the abolition of the sovereign nation. To him the socialist state represents democracy because it serves and defends the interests of the majority, not merely because it holds elections. He noted that "for the oligarchic and bourgeois parties, elections were auctions for the highest bidder among those who had the most money for propaganda and vote buying."[85]

Throughout the revolution Castro has confronted remnants of Cuba's bourgeois past. Most noteworthy has been his treatment of the middle-class elements who supported the revolution. Fidel and his comrades have appealed to those people's deep sense of nationalism, their anger with the United States, which they blame for the rampant corruption that impeded Cuba's progress for decades.[86] He has encouraged Cubanness, which expands political consciousness, creates new loyalties, resolve, and unity, and eliminates alienation. Through revolutionary nationalism he has joined middle-class reformers, radicals, idealists, and Communists who support Cuba's independence from foreign control.

Castro came to believe, as the revolution progressed, that Marxism-Leninism means more than mere theory and philosophy, that it serves as a guide to daily considerations, to solving the practical problems that have faced humanity since classical times. He holds definite views on the role of intellectuals and artists in the search for solutions to society's problems, the elimination of alienation, and furthering the revolution. He conceives of intellectuals and those in the fine and applied arts as part of society, not outsiders, and condemns systems where the cultured people find ways to make the workers labor for them. He rejects the role of the intellectual as the "critical conscience of society." Therefore Cuba under Castro's leadership has resisted having an intellectual or artistic class and has at times discouraged writers and other artists from engaging in individual, anticollectivist criticisms of the revolution.[87]

Paradoxically, Fidel has displayed a reverence for Cuban and Western traditions and culture (both high and folk) and for the fruits of intellectual labor. He has, like Antonio Gramsci, stressed the role of intellectuals in strengthening the cultural superstructure. He views Cuba as a unified society wherein everyone relates equally to the same culture. Castro believes that culture, like education, cannot be apolitical or impartial but is an integral part of the revolutionary struggle and that socioeconomic revolution will produce a cultural revolution.[88]

Castro has courted writers such as Argentina's Julio Cortázar and Colombia's Gabriel García Márquez, whose revolutionary themes have inspired him. He has encouraged Cuba to develop its own literature in a style the masses can understand. Following the Marxist-Leninist principle that proletarian culture cannot be developed without assimilating the national and world cultural heritage, the government of Cuba initiated a book-publishing campaign to bring international and Cuban classics to the masses at low prices.[89] Fidel has strongly supported intellectual endeavors in Cuba. According to him, "All artists and intellectuals may find in the Revolution a field in which to work and create and in such a way that their creative spirit, even though they are not revolutionary writers or artists, may have the opportunity and the freedom to express themselves within the Revolution."[90] In his "Words to the Intellectuals," delivered at a meeting at Havana's National Library in June 1961, he stated that anyone could express ideas freely in any form, that all work would always be judged by revolutionary standards, and that only incorrigible counterrevolutionaries would be renounced.[91]

Castro knows that not everyone can be a political, economic, or social theorist, but he believes that theory can be derived from and predicated on the wants of the masses and expressed by their representatives. In other words, he follows Marx's contention that in a communist society a person is not just a thinker, but that there are people who, among other things, are thinkers.[92]

While working to build communism in Cuba, Castro has leaned heavily on the philosophy of education propounded by Argentina's Aníbal Ponce in the book *Educación y lucha de clases* (1936) (Education and the Class Struggle), which was discussed in chapter 3 in conjunction with the work of Juan Marinello.

Fidel called his own exposure to education and the opportunity to attend the university (one out of one thousand), a process of "social selection," not natural selection, since he came from a prosperous family.[93] He wished that all people could have a better life, including the chance to satisfy their educational and cultural needs, to develop their intellects, and to profit from the works produced by the intellects of others. Regarding that work, or intellectual property, Fidel stated that anything emanating from the intelligence of individuals—a book for example, fiction or nonfiction—ought to be the patrimony of all people. He believes, for instance, that authors deserve compensation, but he opposes copyrights, contending that books should be printed freely in all sections of the world.[94]

Despite his concern for the rights and responsibilities of Cuba's intellectual laborers, Castro does not consider himself one of them. Although his daily duties have precluded his devoting a great deal of time to theorizing, he has become somewhat of a pragmatic, sometimes impatient, philosopher and interpreter of Cuba's revolution for his people.[95] He has stated that "whoever stops to wait for ideas to triumph among the majority of the masses before initiating revolutionary action will never be a revolutionary,"[96] meaning that fighting may not be mandatory at a given time in a specific country but that it will ultimately have to be employed to foster revolution. He concluded, "Many times practice comes first and then theory," meaning that most people arrive at Marxism-Leninism by way of revolutionary struggle.[97] The Cuban revolution began with a basically nationalist orientation, but the struggle led to the development of a class consciousness, in turn leading to socialism.[98]

By the time the *Fidelistas* controlled Cuba, Castro understood that in a socialist society each person works according to his or her ability and receives compensation according to his or her work and needs. He concluded that to eliminate suffering and deprivation in Cuba during the socialist phase, communism must be built simultaneously.[99] The Russians believed it was necessary to build communism after the consolidation of socialism. Castro, on the other hand, realized that after a capitalist society falls there remain remnants of material incentives, commodity production, profit motives, and a system of socialist enterprises linked by market relations. Thus he urged the construction of communism free of the old order—a communist sector wherein there exists voluntary labor and a new attitude toward work before the existence of material abundance. In other words, he maintained that the elimination of poverty depended on sacrifice and communist attitudes.[100] In a way this corresponds to Trotsky's theory of permanent revolution and rejects the orthodox Marxist concept of consecutive stages of the revolutionary process.

Castro found that in Cuba, as everywhere in the socialist world, the market still existed. He then instituted measures to prevent the market from controlling the economy,[101] while facing the problem of maintaining production. In 1973, at the Thirteenth Congress of the Central Organization of Cuban Trade Unions, Fidel called for a return to wages tied to productivity.[102] Cuba thus instituted a policy of increased material incentives but retained moral incentives, a move that Castro saw not as a loss of revolutionary idealism but as a more realistic way of achieving socialism. Fidel deviated from some aspects of Soviet revolutionary theory, but he borrowed from Russia's policy of extending some material benefits and adhered to the Soviet idea of constructing a new technological base to increase production. Simultaneously, he strove to create the new socialist person advocated by Che Guevara. He believes that Cuba does not yet have the new man but no longer has the old one.[103]

Like Guevara, Castro initially rejected Lenin's idea of control of the revolution by a Marxist-Leninist party. At the beginning of the Cuban revolution Castro advocated the need for a vanguard that did not have to be Marxist-Leninist but could be made up of those who wanted a revolution even if they were independent of parties. Between 1962 and 1967 Latin America's Communist parties rejected Castro's thinking because he assigned leadership of the revolution to guerrillas, not Communist cadres, and praised the peasants rather than the industrial proletariat as the popular revolutionary army while downgrading urban political movements in favor of rural ones.[104] At the same time, he criticized leftist sectarianism, which he said fostered anticommunism,[105] and contended that minor differences of opinion should not be used to divide potential allies.

Fidel referred to the prerevolutionary Cuban Communist party as a sect in spirit, a group apart from the rest of society, which perhaps was necessary under capitalism.[106] But he came to understand the need for a Party, which orients but does not govern on all levels. To him the Party exists to build revolutionary consciousness, to serve as a link to the masses, to propagate socialist education, to encourage people to work, and to supervise and defend the revolution. He asserted that the Party should not weaken itself to buttress the state apparatus—that the latter must develop its own officials from the ranks.[107]

When Cuba's new Communist party formed in 1965, Fidel made it clear that the organization would follow Cuban ideas and methods. He supported Guevara's beliefs that in Latin America the peasantry constitutes a class that, because of its uncultured state and isolation, needs the revolutionary and political leadership of the urban working class and revolutionary intellectuals.[108] He also noted that Marx never anticipated a revolutionary transformation in an underdeveloped country like Cuba, which lacked industries and a class-conscious proletariat. Thus he justified Cuba's early non-Marxist revolutionary strategy whereby a small number of well-organized, dedicated people, at the propitious moment, seized the state and retained power by actions that drew the masses to the revolution. Whether one calls what initially happened in Cuba a socialist, Third World, or eclectic revolution is immaterial. What matters is that Cuba eliminated a neocolonial situation run by a corrupt and socially unresponsive government supported on all levels by the United States.[109]

Fidel has frequently remarked how much easier it was to destroy the old order than to create a new one that will work for Cuba. He has used Marxist thought as one of a number of devices to help create this new order. Also, over the years he has criticized and borrowed from Trotskyism, Maoism, and

Soviet communism. Castro's Marxism represents a conglomeration of native, European, and Latin American socialist and anti-imperialist thought.

By the early 1980s Castro and his colleagues had conceptualized a valid socialist ethos for Cuba, one that could both impose critical restraints on the society and heighten its consciousness. Simultaneously, they agreed with Marx that there can be no genuine revolution until there is a world revolution. "We are not stupid enough to believe that we can build a brave little communist state in splendid isolation,"[110] stated the Cuban leader whose government has actively tried to spread socialism in the Third World.

It is difficult to question the uniqueness of the Cuban revolution, where the old order was destroyed without a preconceived theory. Revolutionary left critics have accused the Cubans of turning from using theory as a guide to action, to action as a means of building theory and have noted that living intellectuals played only minor roles in the early stages of the revolution. After the *Fidelistas* took control of Cuba, the revolutionary government supported movements designed to replicate Cuba's achievements elsewhere in Latin America.[111] Cuba's inability to ignite and sustain similar revolutions in other parts of the Americas perhaps helped convince Castro of the value of theory as a guide.

Cuba turned its attention away from revolutionary forays into Latin America by the late 1960s and concentrated on domestic matters, which merit mention. Historically, democracy had rarely existed in Cuba, and Fidel was determined to forge a variety of it by interpreting the will of his people in Rousseau's fashion. With their deep faith in their fellow Cubans, Castro and his cohorts began to construct participatory democracy based on rational thought, reflection, and discussion. He contends that people's, or popular, democracy is enunciated not by democratic constitutions—all too often violated in Latin America—or by electoral parties, but through democratic institutions such as hospitals that serve all equally without cost differentials, through schools available to everyone, and through relatively equal living conditions.[112] He favors Marxist democracy, which achieves progress for society as a whole, rather than capitalist democracy, which he believes overemphasizes the accomplishments of electoral politics that primarily benefit those who control the means of production.

Democracy to Fidel connotes extending the benefits of life to all regardless of color or sex. He has reiterated Lenin's words that the full victory of the people could not be achieved without the complete liberation of women, that women must live as the equals of men, as comrades, and not at their feet as pretty toys.[113] He thinks that women must be respected for their labor, which shapes them as human beings, and not be seen merely as sex objects. They must not be part of carnival spectacles such as beauty contests. Theoretically women, in the eyes of the revolution, are equal, as individuals or as part of a couple.[114] Castro views the struggle for full integration of women into Cuban society as part of a historic battle, a revolution within the revolution.

Sexual and racial discrimination, in Fidel's estimation, emanates from the idea inherent in capitalism of exploitation of one human by another.[115] He condemns those who would relegate women to positions of virtual domestic slavery, wasting labor on unproductive, nerve-wracking drudgery.[116] He maintains that women should receive special treatment because they carry the extra burden of childbearing[117] To elevate the status of women in Cuban society, Castro endorsed the creation of the Federation of Cuban Women in 1960. By 1980 its membership had increased from 17,000 to 2,500,000, encompassing 80 percent of all women over the age of fourteen, and the status of women in Cuba has improved significantly.

The Cuban revolution has tried not only to establish equality for women, but to eliminate all tears in the fabric of society. The vehicle through which the revolution has moved toward this goal is democratic centralism, a system whereby the revolutionary leaders have organized a party composed of model workers who accept socialist ideology and cherish the responsibility of representing their *compañeros*, with whom they toil to build new class relations and social organizations.

To fabricate a socialist society, Castro believes it is necessary to have an administration that is well grounded in the technology and ideology of production and its human components. At the same time, he warns administrators against developing a petty bourgeois mentality.[118] He also asserts that as long as the nation's organization, administration, and policy are not communist, the danger of bureaucracy's becoming a special stratum exists.[119] He has called bureaucracy the most negative product of the division between manual and intellectual labor.[120] To him, bureaucracy and petty-bourgeois thinking perpetuate themselves and put a brake on the revolution. Castro would be likely to say that Cuba's revolutionary spirit is the antithesis of that represented by the bureaucratic mentality that gives rise to a new controlling class.[121]

He also rejects the Sovietization theory, that Cuba's socialism mirrors the Russian model and that Cuban foreign-policy decisions are made in Moscow. To him, Cuban foreign and domestic policy flows from the dynamics of Cuba's revolution. In his speeches he repudiates that Cuba is a Caribbean Russia or a Soviet satellite.

He also refutes the idea of a godless Cuban state dedicated to the persecution of the faithful. Like Martí, he has inveighed against cultural and spiritual oppression. He has averred that the struggle for economic and social change lessens religiousness, but that it is necessary to wage war on economic and political imperialism, not religion. Although Cuba's Communist party professes atheism, Cubans may be Christians, and it is not uncommon to find portraits of Christ and Che Guevara hanging side by side in their living rooms. Castro comprehends liberation theology and knows that initially Christianity was a humane religion of the poor. He believes that the socialist movement can benefit from honest leaders of the Catholic church who practice the fundamentals of Christian brotherhood. Castro recognizes the important role of Christian groups in Latin America revolutions and popular struggles such as that which occurred in Nicaragua in the late 1970s.[122]

Fidel takes a deep interest in Third World revolution. He believes strongly in the subordination of Cuban national interests to the higher objectives of socialist and communist progress, to the defeat of imperialism and the elimination of colonialism and neocolonialism. He views the Cuban revolution as an example, not a controlling influence, for sister revolutions such as those in Grenada, El Salvador, and Nicaragua and acknowledges that no two revolutions take place under identical conditions.[123]

Castro once called Cuba a Latin African as well as a Latin American nation. While Cuba endeavored to attain complete racial equality at home, at the request of Angola, as early as the 1960s, it dispatched troops there to assist in the struggle against racist South Africa. This move, like Cuba's support for the revolutionary New Jewel Movement that took over in primarily black Grenada in 1979, simultaneously strengthened nationalist sentiment among Cuba's people of African descent.

Fidel has continued the work of the Anti-imperialist League by joining forces with the Movement of Nonaligned Countries. He justifies this association by noting that Cuba does not belong to a military bloc and is not a signatory to the Warsaw Defense Pact. Under his leadership Cuba has not been closed off to outsiders. Foreigners can freely travel to and explore the island.

Cuba also maintains solid contacts with the Third World, Western and Eastern European states, Canada, and those Latin American nations that are not afraid of ignoring United States economic and political sanctions against the Caribbean island. Castro is quick to point out that it is the United States that has moved to isolate Cuba from the world.

Despite the United States blockade, and without the banking, industrial, landowning, professional, and business classes who formerly governed, Cuba, led by Castro, has undergone a successful social revolution, one he has sought to institutionalize so that it depends less and less on him. To those who claim that his actions have at times been precipitous or excessive, he replies, "each year that the liberation of America is speeded up will mean the lives of millions of children saved, millions of intelligences saved for culture, an indefinite quantity of pain spared the people".[124] Fidel Castro represents a rare species, the genuine revolutionary, one who has learned well from the lessons of Cuba's radical thinkers, a man with the courage to put theories into practice, to risk and to admit failure, a leader who has grown intellectually, mellowed, and matured as a statesman while in office.

I saw it in Havana.
I saw it, it was no dream.
Palaces of ancient marble
for those without shoes.
Castles where the worker rests
sitting protected by his own labor.
The country garden of the Duchess
for John's daughter who is ill.
The mountain, the beach, the vichy,
    the caviar
for those who had no place before.

Nicolás Guillén

CHAPTER 6

Reflections on the Past and Present

The following pages contain analyses of aspects of Cuba's rich
intellectual heritage omitted in previous chapters and fill in some
of the gaps in our knowledge of Cuban radicalism. This chapter
probes into the philosophy of Cuba's ongoing revolution, examines a few of its international facets, and assesses some of its
accomplishments.

   The political and social thought of Cuba's *pensadores,* from
José Agustín Caballero and the eighteenth-century rationalist-
eclectics through twentieth-century theory-praxis exponents
such as Che Guevara, has been pervaded by a belief in the
inherent worth of life. All of the Cuban thinkers studied in this
book believed or believe that humanity has advanced in the
past and will continue to do so. They hold a concept of progress
consonant with what in human terms could be called fulfillment.
They do not necessarily equate progress with what is new, nor
would they, for example, view as progress the improvement
of technology specifically designed to take human lives. Cuba's
radical thinkers have always understood the necessity of
organizing the people for beneficial change. They have shared

a form of secular millennialism that today emerges as a belief in socialism followed by intellectual and social development into communism.

Intellectual radicalism has existed for a long time in Cuba because thinkers there have traditionally had some opportunity to express their discontent. Writers have continually served the nation as a social conscience. They have assumed central roles in protest movements, especially giving voice to anti-imperialism and critiques of colonialism. They have, in diverse ways, always battled against alienation caused by class distinctions. Although most eighteenth- and ninteenth-century reformers did not refer to the class struggle per se, they railed against some of its manifestations.

Many of Cuba's radical thinkers have come from middle-class families, but their ideological orientations have been determined more by their social and political attitudes than by their backgrounds. They have for the most part exposed and fought for the needs of the masses, not the ruling class. At the same time, they have been products of their culture. For example, machismo and sexism have traditionally run rampant in Cuba, and until the revolution of the 1950s women, except for a few poets and novelists, were absent from the ranks of the intelligentsia. Ideally, a generation from now, when someone writes a sequel to this book, women will be included among Cuba's most distinguished political and social theorists.

To date, Cuba's radical *pensadores* have constituted a male antielitist elite. Despite their individual shortcomings, the members of this elite have been models of heroism and dignity. They have built a sense of community among themselves and within their audience and have created an atmosphere conducive to healthy skepticism, to debate, and to the development of ideas.

For the past two centuries every era has produced thinkers in Cuba who have generally considered themselves more progressive or radical than their forerunners. But they all have understood the essence of the work of their predecessors and its organic relationship to the present. They have all tended

to interpret knowledge and human experience in terms of historical change and have tried to comprehend the processes of change and to classify historical stages. Some of them, primarily the Marxists, have viewed history as a pseudoscience capable of establishing laws from the sweep of human experience. They agree with historian Harold Eugene Davis that "social power, both potential and effective, derives in large measure from man's historical consciousness, whether based upon true or false history. The role of political leadership is to convert this potential into effective power and to direct it to justifiable social ends."[1]

Cuba's radical thinkers have for generations attempted to understand power and to plot out a way to harness it for the common good. Unlike Cuba's prerevolutionary government leaders, who often merely gave lip service to the common good and who generally failed to comprehend their society in terms of scientific historical experience, Cuba's revolutionary government has used the historical work of the country's radicals as a foundation upon which to base programs directed toward social progress. Revolutionary Cuba has learned from the nation's radical thinkers about the mechanisms of sociopolitical equilibrium, their weaknesses, and how they can be strengthened to better serve society.

Since the nineteenth century, Cuban radical *pensadores* have followed a humanist tradition in their quest to improve the quality of life. Beauty and sensitivity have played a significant role in their search for a richer life. Many of them have written stories, verse, and plays. Their political and social writings often included forceful and eloquent phraseology promoting their ideas in an informative and creative fashion designed to embellish life and decrease alienation.

Cuba's quest to free itself psychologically, spiritually, culturally, politically and economically from Spain lasted longer than that of the other Latin American states, and Cubans lived through a protracted colonial era during which they constructed a cohesive current of radical and progressive thought. Independence from Spain did not bring freedom to the country, and radical currents gathered strength and direction for another six decades under various sorts of despotism. Every generation in Cuba during the nineteenth and twentieth centuries passed through some kind of revolutionary turmoil. Students and teachers began vehement social protests in the 1840s. Major political upheavals took place in the 1860s, 1870s, 1890s, 1920s, 1930s, and 1950s, and armed struggle became accepted as a legitimate form of protest.

During periods of internal strife Cuban intellectuals sought sustenance abroad. Since the period 1810–30, when most Latin American states won independence, Cuban thinkers have looked to neighboring nations for inspiration and insight. Their exploratory analyses helped develop an embryonic sense of internationalism and a healthy antipathy for the dictatorship and government corruption that pervaded their sister societies. Cuba's *pensadores* examined political and economic relationships in the newly formed American republics, then articulated the differences and similarities between colonialism as practiced in Cuba and the neocolonialism found in the other nations of Latin America. The investigations of Cuba's thinkers often resulted in findings that radicalized them and led them to affiliate with political movements. But for the most part, until the second quarter of the twentieth century the organizations they belonged to did not operate on the national level and could not reach beyond a small organized working class to the masses.

Although pre-Castro Cuba had radical working-class and anti-imperialist traditions, its economy was based on industrial capitalism and tied to the United States. According to economist

James O'Connor, it was an exceedingly regressive type of capitalism wherein the "relations and organization of production

190 stifled the further development of the forces of production."[2]
Cuba's *pensadores* understood this historical dilemma and
blamed many of their society's ills on capitalism and its imperialist components. Virulent anti-Americanism took root in nineteenth-century Cuba and never abated. Even some opponents
of Castro's revolution see his movement as the continuation
of the anti-imperialist struggle, albeit one they believe went
astray.

Cuba's nonsocialist nineteenth-century anti-imperialist thinkers reflected the philosophies of middle-class intellectuals such
as Locke, Descartes, Bacon, Condillac, Spencer, and Comte,
all of whom lived in strongly reformist epochs. The Cuban *pensadores* formed a vanguard that worked for radical political
change and was influenced to a degree by realism—the dispo-
sition to act on fact and experience and with skepticism.

During the nineteenth century, and at times in the twentieth,
Cuba's socialists have been at odds with its nonsocialist radicals
and have not always worked in concert with them. For example,
during the period 1928–34 the international Communist movement believed that anti-imperialist middle-class radical nationalists were counterrevolutionary because they were inextricably
tied to foreign capital and unable to complete the bourgeois-
democratic revolution. Cuba's Communists supported anti-
imperialism and opposed dictatorship but had little faith in
Cuba's liberal capitalists who shared these beliefs.[3] Thus we
must not misconstrue Cuba's radical intellectual tradition as
radical unity in thought and action.

Not until after 1933 did socialists, Communists, and populists
begin to cohere in Cuba. Young revolutionaries, representing
diverse interests, but often led by patient and tenacious radicals
such as Juan Marinello, Raúl Roa, Blas Roca, and Carlos Rafael

Rodríguez, built a left-wing intellectual cadre in Cuba between the 1930s and the 1950s. This radical intellectual coterie served as a well from which Fidel Castro drew ideological water and fashioned a political system to guide the revolution.

In addition to its radical intellectual tradition, Cuba had a long history of trade unionism and of mass participation in cooperative actions and worker uprisings. Worker movements in the country were strengthened because those employed in the sugar mills constituted more of a rural proletariat than a peasantry; their interests ran more to higher wages and better working conditions than to landownership, and they were compatible with urban proletarians with whom they formed class-based alliances.

For many workers *Fidelismo* and guerrilla warfare were extensions of the legacy of 1914–17 when rural folk took up arms against the foreign owners of the sugar plantations in Camaguey and Oriente provinces and against the government's rural guards who protected the *latifundistas*.[4] One might draw an analogy between the valiant peasant struggles of 1917 and those conducted in the 1950s by the Frente Obrero Nacional Unido (National United Workers' Front) in the "Free Territory of Las Villas" under the command of Camilo Cienfuegos. This workers' organization was part of the Twenty-sixth of July Movement, which its members viewed as engaged in a class and nationalist struggle.[5]

For centuries Cuba's radical intellectuals had sought to develop political and cultural nationalism among Cuba's workers. Radical groups representing the entire left spectrum historically endeavored to eradicate colonialism and neocolonialism and to create a nationalist ideology. By the 1960s their efforts bore fruit as diverse pieces of left-wing theory were woven into an ideological whole and nationalism, radicalism, and socialism joined forces in revolutionary Cuba.

The majority of Cuba's radical thinkers considered the defeat of Batista a result of the merger of Cuba's reform and revolutionary traditions. After Castro's victory most of Cuba's nonsocialist radicals concluded that reform and revolution are fundamentally incompatible, and they opted for the latter, with the belief that socialism represented the more humane choice.

Today's Cuban political and social thinkers, many of whom have grown up in the revolution, connect that movement to the island's historical past as well as to recently developed ideology, current events, and international alliances. They regard *Fidelismo* as the culmination of a century-long struggle with ideology, during which there developed a unique revolutionary character, one they say embodies the *Cubanidad* of Martí and Castro with all its variants. They continually assess the errors of the past to prevent their duplication. They constantly remind us of a bygone era when the predominant culture was tied to the privilege of the exploiting class, when many intellectuals were separated from the needs of the masses.

Cuba's contemporary political and social thinkers know that they were not essential elements in the insurrectionary phase of the revolution, but they have become part of the revolutionary intelligentsia. Under their guidance Cuba became the center of radical thought in the Americas from the 1960s until roughly the middle of the 1970s, when, after the overthrow of Salvador Allende's prosocialist government, most of the political exiles from Chile and Latin America's other national security states gathered in Mexico and made that nation the center for Marxist thought in the hemisphere.

Cuba's revolutionary intellectuals continue to make their ideas, and those of outstanding foreign thinkers, accessible and comprehensible to the Cuban people, to encourage and develop dialogue between the leaders and the masses.[6] They lend credence to Antonio Gramsci's concept of the role of intellectuals in building a revolution and to his view of the Communist party as an intellectual collective. They also believe in creating worker-intellectuals, because if mental workers constitute a privileged intellectual elite and dominate the society's thinking and planning, manual workers will remain exploited. Consequently, today's Cuban intellectuals cannot be located in society by their incomes or life-styles.

The Cuban government contends that a state is strong when the masses know about, and can form an opinion on, everything. Cuba approximates Mao's mass line by striving to develop workers capable of thinking and planning on day-to-day levels and participating intelligently in the construction of society. Cuba adheres to the thoughts of Lenin, who said that socialism cannot be built with illiterates, and the beliefs of Chile's Luis Emilio Recabarren (1876–1924), whose works have been reprinted in Cuba[7] and who insisted that the first step toward socialism was to educate the working masses.[8] On the other hand, this emphasis on developing worker-intellectuals helps explain why the Cuban revolution has not produced a great number of political and social theorists.

Cuba's thinkers strive to educate and impart revolutionary theory to their fellow citizens. But they believe and teach that ideas alone cannot make or sustain a revolution. They, like their radical predecessors, take a deep interest in students. They consider them academic apprentices, part of an intelligentsia dedicated to demystifying power by engaging in and promoting socialist self-criticism. Students of all ages are encouraged to understand the causes of social unrest, exploitation, poverty, illiteracy, disease, unemployment, and economic and political instability.

An element of romanticism exists in the way Cuba's intellectuals approach education. They project the belief that revolutionary goals can be attained through hard work, if it is combined with an awareness of the primacy of the worker in the world to be changed. They advise fellow Cubans to interpret

Marx creatively and flexibly, to adapt his ideas and those of his interpreters to the Cuban ethos. They also no longer view their revolution as an ideal model and know that one cannot expect to simply apply its lessons to other Latin American nations and have it succeed.

The hard realities of making a socialist revolution in the twentieth century have led Cuban intellectuals to comprehend why Marx did not accept the utopian view of humanity or the idea of voluntarism—that individual will has primacy over determinism in the historical process. They understand that his new science, based on class struggle and historical materialism, held out hope for human freedom and democracy derived from the study of economic, social, cultural, and political processes and their interconnections.

Cuba's revolutionary society faces myriad problems, and its thinkers must answer numerous questions in order to mold a more perfect socialist state. Included among them are how to transform the productive forces and social relations of society to enhance economic growth without preventing the development of socialist social relations. For example, if you provide worker incentives such as material benefits, do you hinder the socialist goal of equality?[9] How do you guard against the creation of vested interests, which diminsh democracy? Can you maintain a popular democracy that favors the interests of the working classes? Can this popular democracy initially stress sufficiency, full employment, universal literacy, access to education and health care and the government, and secondarily emphasize electoral processes and relative freedom of the press, without creating an image that people in representative electoral democracies will misconstrue as malevolent dictatorship?

During the 1970s Cuba's activist-intellectuals, going on the premise that many of the aforementioned initial objectives of the revolution were on the way to attainment—that the relation- ship between the people and the leadership no longer ensured that government policy corresponded to the interests and needs of the masses—helped institute formal election procedures. Cuba's 1975 constitution established guidelines to protect the rights of citizens and to permit them to choose their leaders and have access to them. It provided safeguards for proletarian democracy as well as avenues for expressing popular senti- ment.[10] Its implementation in 1976 led to a reduction in Castro's omnipotence and to a broader distribution of authority between the people and the government.

The constitution reflected the view that multiparty political systems are controlled by power brokers who only purport to represent the majority whereas Cuba's system supports the interests of the majority as well as the country's large minorities. To understand this position it is essential to know that Cuba's Communist party, which controls the revolution and whose members have been elected to most of the seats in the nation's National Assembly, does not run candidates for office and is not a political party in the middle-class democratic sense.

Since inaugurating electoral procedures in 1976, Cuba has tried to conserve and synthesize its collective experience within a more legalistic framework. At the same time, it has sought to distinguish between the old nationalism of the oppressed nation and the new nationalism of the sovereign internationalist state.[11] Simultaneously, Cuba strives for recognition of its revolution and culture as part of a world revolution and culture and thereby reconciles its nationalism with internationalism. The Cuban rev- olution encourages its intellectuals to assimilate the best tradi- tions of their culture while critically appropriating and redefining universal culture. The intelligentsia works to stimulate a forward-thinking outlook for the future, to reject absolute and antihumanist modes of analysis and expression, and to build solidarity with progressive and revolutionary movements everywhere.[12]

As they plan for the future of what they view as an increasingly secure revolution, Cuba's *pensadores* also express concern about protecting it from becoming resistant to criticism. Their warnings appear to be heeded by the government and the masses. Thus their role as social and political critics expands. At this time it is impossible to tell whether Cuba's radical intellectuals flourish more readily in an atmosphere of quest, searching for acceptance of their problem-solving approach as they did before the early 1960s, or in a society that has found its ideology and needs only to perfect the techniques necessary to follow and implement it.

To facilitate the transition from socialism to communism at home, where they believe they have made considerable progress in that direction, Cuba's intellectuals feel obligated to pursue socialism internationally. They view Cuban history as synonymous with that of Latin America, and they give moral support to other countries that have yet to reach the revolutionary stage. They maintain that revolution will take place, subsequently, all over Latin America and cite as a case in point the Nicaraguan revolution of 1979, which occurred twenty years after Cuba's.

Cuban social and political thinkers use Marxism-Leninism as an ideological base from which to lead Latin America's anticapitalist criticism of the United States. They designate imperialism, primarily that perpetrated by the United States, as the region's central problem. They contend that imperialism cannot be moderated or reformed, but only eliminated through revolution. They think that history has created opportunities for revolution all over, and they reject the orthodox Communist notion that it is necessary to wait for the correct moment in the historical process to begin the revolution. At the same time, they do not downplay the favorable conditions that enabled Castro to mobilize a broad segment of society for battle.

Cuban radical thinkers have been analyzing imperialism longer than their counterparts in most American nations. Emilio Roig de Leuchsenring, who devoted a lifetime to such analysis, called anti-imperialism directed at the United States a symbol of Cubanism. He placed the 1959 revolution in the vanguard of the world's struggle against United States–style imperialism.[13] Roig and his cohorts have not been so simplistic as to think that eliminating imperialism will, by itself, generate considerable social, political, and economic progress, but they have viewed it as a step toward achieving these goals. They have considered the anti-imperialist movement a vital component of the process of world revolution. They have contended that the elimination of Yankee imperialism from Cuba signified a break with the past when the United States could usually thwart revolutionary movements throughout Latin America. They have maintained that after Castro's victory the history of the region was altered, that the destiny of sister republics no longer remained in the hands of the leaders in Washington.

Cuban analysts point out that the transition to socialism resulted in the reduction of dependency, not its elimination. They also note that Cuba, as well as other states that opt for a revolutionary course, need not become subservient to a superpower. In every economic category except debt, Cuban dependency has declined substantially since 1959. The nation's economy does not respond directly to developments in the Soviet economy as it used to do with that of the United States, nor do the Russians own the means of production in Cuba as the United States did previously. The positive effects of Cuban-Russian politico-economic relations outweigh the negative.[14]

Cuban writers also tell fellow Latin Americans that Cuba does not operate under Soviet economic or political control, that even in the realm of foreign policy Havana frequently differs with Moscow. To illustrate the point, a high-ranking Cuban official confided to me in 1982 that while his government condemned Solidarity in Poland as antirevolutionary, it found the protracted Soviet presence in Afghanistan as objectionable as that of the United States in El Salvador. He added that Castro, who initially praised the Soviet action in Afghanistan, had subsequently communicated negative statements about it to the Kremlin. The official commented that as the Cuban revolution has gained strength it has been less inclined to accept Soviet positions. For example, the Havana government maintains that détente is crucial and criticizes the Soviets, as well as the United States, for squandering resources on nuclear weapons, which are in oversupply.[15] Also, Cuba claims to be a nonaligned nation and notes that it has no mutual defense agreement with Russia.

From these and similar observations there emerges a picture of Cuba analogous to that of Egypt under Gamal Abdul Nasser, with Castro and his *compañeros* very much their own policy-makers, playing off all political and economic power blocs against each other in the best interests of the nation.

By no means does Cuba represent a miniature USSR. It especially differs from Russia in the area of social and economic equality. The existence of relative equality in Cuba enables it to solve some ongoing problems of economic development and organization. Equality has helped solidify Cuba's worker-peasant alliance, under which both groups have taken control of, and improved, production and their political life.[16]

It is difficult to get across some of these concepts to people in the United States, where many of those who study Cuba are Cold War warriors and anti-Castro Cuban exiles with connections to the Defense Department or State Department and ties to right-wing think tanks, upon whom they rely for research funds. Such individuals sometimes even portray themselves as liberals while trying to hide their intellectually dishonest anti-communism under a cloak of academic respectability. In recent years a few progressive liberals, leftists, and pro-Castro Cubans have managed to win tenure battles in United States universities. They have conducted research without foundation money and have begun to open viable scholarly debates, which have deepened critical analysis of Cuba's past and present.

Conservative scholars in the United States, as well as United States government ideologues, have been obsessed with the unsubstantiated idea that the Soviet Union is using Cuba as a surrogate to foster and materially support Marxist subversion throughout the Caribbean and Central and South America. Initially Castro tried to export *Fidelismo* and stimulate guerrilla uprisings in the region. But by the late 1960s Cuba's limited efforts to incite insurrections had failed in Panama, Nicaragua, Haiti, the Dominican Republic, Venezuela, and Bolivia, and the Havana government concluded that socialist revolution could not be initiated from without but had to be homegrown to succeed. Cuba decided to refrain from attempting to ignite revolutionary fires in the hemisphere. It did not, however, desist from maintaining solidarity with oppressed people, and it continued to offer moral support and minimal training and advice to indigenous revolutions.[17]

Those who attribute all Latin American social and political upheavals to communism rather than to poverty, malnutrition, repression, corrupt government, imperialism, and racial and class strife have persisted in ascribing every move against the status quo in the region to some insidious plot orchestrated by Fidel Castro. Their evidence is minute. For example, Cuba often gets unearned credit for supplying the Tupamaro guerrillas who sought to replace capitalism in Uruguay during the late

1960s and early 1970s. That movement was not financed by Cuba or the Soviet Union and was not basically predicated on Guevara's and Castro's idea of *focos* forming in the mountains to conduct guerrilla warfare. Nor was it trained and led by Cuban cadres. The native insurrection in mountainless Uruguay was primarily based on the urban guerrilla warfare concepts articulated by a Spaniard, Abraham Guillén.

Salvador Allende's short-lived independent socialist-oriented government in Chile (1970–73) came to office democratically, through the ballot box, not guerrilla conflict. The leaders of the insurrection in Nicaragua, which sprang from an antidictator, anti-imperialist alliance started by Augusto Sandino in the 1920s and culminated in the ouster of the Somoza dynasty in 1979, were advised by Castro not to follow Cuba's example and become dependent on the Soviet Union. In fact, Nicaragua sought little attention from the Soviet Union until the United States mounted a campaign to topple the Sandinista government. The civil war in El Salvador that came to a head in 1979 emanated from centuries of repressive oligarchic rule, which created widespread impoverishment, alienation, and a sense of futility among the majority of the Central American country's people. It did not originate in Havana or Moscow.

The Cuban experience provided inspiration for the struggles in Uruguay, Chile, Nicaragua, and El Salvador as well as for revolutionary movements elsewhere in Latin America and the Caribbean, as it opened a new arena for class struggle. Its ideals and ideology have provided moral support for the mobilization of mass commitment to radical, social, political, and economic change.

Before the Cuban revolution some Latin American nations sought change through populist and generally nonviolent reform movements such as those begun or implemented in Bolivia, Guatemala, and Venezuela during the 1950s. Those efforts were virtually devoid of ideology and conscious self-regulation by the working class. They moved toward some state regulation of industry and commerce and tried to reduce dependence on foreign powers, but they did not socialize the means of production or eliminate private property. Eventually they all fell victim to the forces of reaction and failed to live up to their reformist potential.

The Cuban revolution, carried out by guerrilla insurrection, a method Marx and Engels considered a part of the larger concept of revolution, attained many of the reform or revolutionary objectives sought by other Latin American states and did so only ninety miles away from the world's most powerful capitalist nation. The neocolonial countries in the Americas and other exploited states in the world realize that Cuban socialism, albeit different from that envisioned and espoused by Marx and Lenin, has perhaps greater applicability to today's reality.[18]

Emerging nations in Africa, Asia, and Latin America often identify with the anti-imperialist struggle of Cuba and see similarities in their common histories, which have to a great extent been shaped by the relations between internal problems and external forces. Cuban intellectuals maintain contacts with their counterparts in these underdeveloped countries and keep them informed of the progress of the Cuban revolution.

Before Cuba's revolution and progress under socialism many Third World and Latin American intellectuals, tired of the unfulfilled promise of socialism, considered Marxism outdated or irrelevant. The Cuban revolution has forced them to reexamine scientific socialism, to delve more deeply into the vast store of Marxist theory for ideas, such as those of Gramsci and Mariátegui, which might be applied to conditions in their countries. Latin American intellectuals now reject the once popular myth that Latinos are too individualistic and lack the solidarity necessary to build socialism.[19]

Scholarly interchange between Cuba and its sister republics is not as strong as it was before the revolution. Cuban revolutionary thinkers are generally accepted in the Latin American states that remain free of reactionary political and military control. Conversely, Cuba welcomes foreign thinkers. Cubans believe that nationality is not the major influence on one's ideas. A Dane may be more revolutionary than a Russian. Thought can be significant on its own merits, not just in relation to a specific society's material level. Thus the ideas of foreign *pensadores* can be vital to Cuba even if they have not brought about change in the nations of their origin.[20]

Numerous foreign thinkers' theories have been used by Cuba's revolutionary leaders, and in turn many foreign *pensadores* have analyzed and commented on the significance of the Cuban revolution. A small sample of observations on the Cuban revolution by some of Latin America's outstanding radical writers is offered in the following paragraphs.

In the words of Mexican novelist and political activist Carlos Fuentes, the Cuban revolution represents "our reality, our hope" for the abandonment of misery and oppression. He sees Cuba reinvigorating the revolutionary zeal of Latin America. To him "Cuba is Mexico and the Cuban people are the Mexican people, the life of each Cuban is my life."[21] Fuentes, who has had some ideological and personal differences with a small segment of Cuba's literary intelligentsia, nevertheless has displayed considerable concern about United States imperialism and Washington's odious policies toward Cuba.

As long as Cuba comes under constant attack from the United States, liberals like Carlos Fuentes and nations like Mexico will assert their solidarity with the right of Cuban self-determination. Mexico, which lost half its territory to United States land hunger during the nineteenth century and lives under constant political, cultural, and economic threats and incursions from its neighbor to the north, understands the consequences of imperialism and gives moral and diplomatic support to Cuba's successful attempt to rid itself of United States overlordship. Mexico has tradition- ally been a haven for radical and liberal Cuban exiles. Martí, Mella, Marinello, Roa, Guevara, and Castro at one time or another received sanctuary there. Currently, most Mexican intellectuals agree with their esteemed political sociologist Pablo González Casanova, who views the Cuban revolution as Latin America's first example of a struggle for a different political and social system, for genuine structural change, socialism, and equality.[22]

Argentina, with roots in nineteenth-century anarchosyndicalism and European radicalism, has produced numerous socialist intellectuals in the twentieth century. Some of the most prominent have provided interesting insights into the Cuban phenomenon. Argentine writer, politician, lawyer, and professor Alfredo Palacios, a longtime opponent of United States control over Cuba under the Platt Amendment, traveled to the Caribbean island in 1960 and delighted in watching Cuba implement agrarian reform and defy Uncle Sam while building socialism in a "creative" fashion and fulfilling Martí's dream of liberty.[23]

Palacios's radical intellectual countryman Silvio Frondizi believed that the Cuban revolution, more than any event in Latin America during the twentieth century, demonstrated the potential to alter the dominion/dependence relationship. He saw the revolution beginning to destroy imperialism in the region, to replace capitalism with socialism. He claimed that some of Cuba's theories and strategies could work elsewhere in the Americas but that conditions in a comparatively small nonindustrial island did not approximate those in a large, industrially developing nation like Argentina.[24]

Argentine socialist *pensador* Jorge Abelardo Ramos asserted that the Cuban revolution provided psychological impetus for similar movements throughout the Americas. It proved that popular forces can defeat an army, that insurrectionist *focos* can create revolutionary conditions, and that in underdeveloped Latin America the place for struggle is in the countryside. He stated that Cuba successfully pursued Bolívar's and Martí's contention that national barriers can be broken down. Ramos advocated Marxism-Bolívarism, combining the two forms of struggle by utilizing parliamentary political action, unionization, guerrilla war, and propaganda as phases of a movement designed to create a United Socialist States of America.[25]

Upon viewing the Cuban revolution firsthand in 1961, Argentina's world-famous novelist Julio Cortázar noted that it made him a political person. He said: "I know that when I go to Cuba its leaders will turn to me—not to manipulate or use me, but to talk and to engage in dialogue. I would consider it manipulation if they told me what to say or not to say in a speech, but this has never happened."[26]

Colombian scholar José Consuegra Higgins, best known for refuting the neo-Malthusian pessimism found in capitalist developmentalism, drew analogies between Martí, Lenin, and Castro, all of whom understood imperialism and endeavored to eliminate it. He stated that for those men revolution organized and defined the strategy and tactics by which the people used their natural abilities to transform economic, social, and political conditions. Consuegra Higgins believed that Castro successfully adapted Marx to Cuba, that he represented to Latin America what Lenin was to the world.[27]

Marxist sociologist Diego Montaña Cuéllar concurred with his fellow Colombian Consuegra Higgins that the Cuban revolution emphasized the benefits of eliminating United States imperialism. To Montaña Cuéllar the Cuban situation illuminated the need for social revolution in Colombia, but he concluded that Colombia's national bourgeoisie, unlike that of

Cuba, could not begin to drive out the United States for fear such action would engender social revolution that would cost the bourgeoisie its power.[28]

As a result of the Cuban revolution, Chilean leftist thinkers Julio César Jobet and Oscar Waiss advocated gaining political control of their country through nonelectoral means or through armed struggle. Pardoxically, Chilean Communist party theoretician Luis Vitale saw the Cuban revolution as the major psychological impetus to the Allende movement in Chile, which came into power through a peaceful electoral process. Vitale asserted that the Cuban movement confirmed his belief that each revolution liberates new forces, accelerates the contradictions between workers and the bureaucratic leadership, and gives rise to centripetal and centrifugal tendencies, violent conflicts, and the birth of new organizations.[29]

Vitale's comrade, Communist party ideologue Luis Corvalán, wrote that the Cuban revolution enabled him to understand more clearly the dynamics of his own Chilean society. After studying Cuba, he decided that the Chilean revolutionary structure arose from a petty bourgeois foundation, one that tended to underestimate the proletariat, was nationalistic, and was inclined to use terrorism. But unlike the situation in Cuba, he maintained that violence could not erupt in the Chilean countryside but only in the cities, and he opted for a revolution without armed conflict for his nation.[30]

Nicaraguan revolutionary poet and priest Ernesto Cardenal compared the Cuban revolution to a "second conversion." He asserted that before witnessing Cuba's revolution he saw himself as a revolutionary with confused ideas, one trying to find a third way through the gospel. But when he saw that Cuba was "the gospel put into practice," he realized that only when he converted to Marxism could he "write religious poetry."[31]

Many Latin American *pensadores* eloquently attest the

importance and influence of the Cuban revolution and remind us how rarely enduring radical change has been effected in the Americas. They wonder why the quest for socialism succeeded in Cuba and failed in Chile. A partial answer can be found in the social structure of prerevolutionary Cuba, where there existed strong but not closely allied middle- and upper-class interest groups. It was easier to destroy these basically autonomous entities in Cuba than to break upper- and middle-class cohesion in Chile.

The Cuban revolution was unique in that Castro and his followers won the military phase of the revolution without building a mass base or movement, but one existed in the working class and soon joined forces with Castro's rebels. Subsequently the rebel army together with the working class demonstrated that a militant unorthodox Marxist revolution could succeed in a nonindustrialized society. The Cuban experience indicated that successful revolution in Latin America includes two phases. First, people mobilize to combat imperialism and forge democracy. Second, they learn that anti-imperialist and democratic objectives can be attained and defended only by building a viable socialist system.[32] Cuba also proved that noncommunists, with a strong progressive tradition, can overthrow capitalism and that a party, with its theory and discipline, is necessary to maintain the revolution.

Cuba's Marxist party has integrated society by promising equal abundance to all, giving scientific cohesion to Cuban policy and planning, implanting a philosophy and an identity in the nation, making work respectable, defending the concept of classlessness, and creating a national consensus by providing participation for most citizens.[33]

The Cuban revolution has illustrated the connection between imperialism and declining social and economic conditions and shown that the overall quality of life improves for the majority when native working-class interests assert control over institutions formerly controlled by the upper and middle classes and foreigners.

Through grassroots democracy, or the People's Power organs, Cubans participate in decision making and communicate their ideas and wants to their leaders, a system that has been far more effective than that based on elite-manipulated elections combined with rampant corruption, which prevailed before 1959. Very few observers without an ax to grind see Cuba as basically run by Castro's authority. Nor do they believe that the decisions of Cuba's leadership, which often borrows from Soviet models, primarily reflect the interests of a privileged bureaucracy as do the decisions of Soviet leaders. The consensus among those who have studied Cuba is that the performance record of the revolutionary government, the new nationalism, and increased mass participation have conferred legitimacy upon the regime and built mass support.[34]

Foreign analysts familiar with Cuba, as well as native political and social theorists, view the revolution as a distinct national proletarian movement that is internationally oriented. Cuban socialism differs in many ways from that set down by Karl Marx. For example, that German thinker relied on a technical vocabulary and presented his ideas in a ponderous fashion. Cuba's Marxists have put his thinking into a Cuban context and expressed them in terms readily understood by laymen. Marx in his *Thesis on Feuerbach* (1845) remarked, "The philosophers have only *interpreted* the world, the point is to *change* it." To him the purpose of understanding was to lay the foundation for change, not just understanding for its own sake. Cuba's revolutionary intellectuals follow his course as they establish in their nation a new cultural level, a greater popular love for reading, sharing, and implementing political and social ideas. They view critical evaluation rather than the rote memorization of data as the best way to learn. Millions more Cubans now read, and their ability to solve problems of diverse types has sharpened as their critical processes have improved under a system in which all citizens are exposed to some philosophical and economic theory.

Books, no longer the products of private business, are a part of Cuba's state-supported culture and education. They are inexpensive, published in huge quantities,[35] and they sell out rapidly. For instance, the ten-thousand-copy first Cuban printing of Gabriel García Márquez's *Cien años de soledad (A Hundred Years of Solitude)* quickly sold out, as did the immediate second printing of eighty thousand copies.[36] Books of all types, particularly novels, accounts of radical movements, biographies, and works that show how to apply theory to practice, are popular. The novels of world-famous Cuban Alejo Carpentier, director of the Imprenta Nacional (the National Printing Office), which were never published in his country before the triumph of the revolution, are especially in demand. Marxist-oriented histories such as Oscar Pino-Santos's *Historia de Cuba: Aspectos fundamentales* (1964) (History of Cuba: Fundamental Aspects), written on an intermediate level and stressing class struggle, racism, and slavery, sell very well, as do books about, and the collected works of, figures such as Varela, Martí, Mella, Marinello, and Rodríguez.

Cuba's Ministry of Culture and its major publishing house Casa de las Américas organize conferences of intellectuals and employ young writers who remain ever aware of Marx's dictum: "It is clear that the arm of criticism cannot replace the criticism of arms. Material force can only be overthrown by material force, but theory itself becomes a material force when it has seized the masses."[37]

The revolutionary government promotes popular comprehension of political and social theory. Cuba's new citizen is expected to understand a modicum of socialist theory in order to criticize constructively. Contrary to the general misconception in the United States, Cubans question their government's prac- tices. In 1982 I heard a member of Cuba's Supreme Court comment, when asked if genuine debate occurs in his country's National Assembly, that "critical debate is encouraged within the revolution. Just as Ronald Reagan would be thought a lunatic if he appeared before your Congress and presented ideas based on socialist theory, so too would we dismiss the thinking of a counterrevolutionary who wanted to bring back capitalism."

In light of the fact that Cuba remains vigilant against counterrevolution, especially the reappearance of direct cultural or political imperialism, its government and citizens show surprisingly little xenophobia. Cuban intellectuals know that the exchange of ideas on an international scale can foster growth in all spheres.

Cuban *pensadores* also understand that the revolution has disproved the hypothesis that their country was locked into a traditional political model and proved that European or Asian Marxist axioms can be altered and implemented successfully in light of local conditions. They point out that Castro's military victory surprised many Marxists, especially those from the Soviet Union, who thought that Latin America's class structure made progressive revolution unlikely there, that Castro-type rebellions would disintegrate in nonindustrialized nations without Communist party leadership. The success of the Cuban revolution disproved this basic premise of Marxism-Leninism and partially precipitated the Soviet Union's 1963 "revolutionary democracy theory" that the transition to socialism in the Third World might occur without the direction of a Communist party—that the military, peasantry, petty bourgeoisie, and intelligentsia might assume the position of a vanguard party.[38]

The Soviet willingness to articulate the "revolutionary

democracy theory" supports the contention of Cuba's intellectuals that they can theorize and try to interpret the world but that only the people have the power to change it. They realize that the best they can do is to unite theory and praxis, to test ideas and values against reality and try to create new conditions for human advancement in life and thought. They are proud that through these processes revolutionary Cuba has provided a more humane, though imperfect, society for the masses.

The Twenty-sixth of July Movement fought to attain Cuba's historical goals of political sovereignty, economic independence, and control over its own culture. Once the military phase of the revolution ended, the attention of Cuba's *pensadores* turned toward achieving these objectives completely. Since 1959 Cuba's intellectuals, those mentioned throughout this book and their younger colleagues whose recently published works are listed in its bibliography, have concentrated primarily on finding pragmatic answers to urgent social and economic questions. Secondarily, they have written "where do we go from here" articles, which have taken precedence over esoteric academic works. They have imparted to their fellow citizens a high degree of political consciousness, and they currently strive to develop their economic consciousness as well. Social scientists and humanists at the University of Havana emphasize teaching, not research. Their colleagues in the Social Science Division of Cuba's Academy of Science, who devote full time to research and writing, have produced more historical works and government policy studies than theoretical tracts. Many of their talented cohorts   have spent all their time in government ministries, while others have primarily engaged in journalism or writing for mass consumption.

Cuba cannot afford the luxury of many full-time political and social theorists while building a revolution. Stress on free universal education has led to neglect of quality specialized graduate studies. Since the early 1960s Cuba's institutions of higher learning have been restructured to emphasize technological skills and have allocated limited financial resources to the social sciences and humanities.[39] These developments give those interested in producing a new generation of *pensadores* cause for concern. So does the fact that Cuban intellectuals, though they have access to works by foreign scholars, do not travel abroad extensively and generally confer with their foreign counterparts only when the latter visit Havana.

Now for the first time in a quarter of a century, as the revolution gathers strength, one discerns a gradual increase in the number of Cubans who devote considerable time to sophisticated abstract thought. Radical thought represents too significant a part of Cuba's revolutionary past to be discarded in the present. With the encouragement of the older, presumably now wiser *pensadores,* a new breed of radical thinkers is emerging in Cuba, one without the intellectual and sectarian arrogance that has frequently split the left internally in Latin America and alienated potential converts and allies. Cuba's intellectuals now act as social critics from within the revolution, not as critical outsiders.

For over half a century Karl Marx and his disciples believed that revolutionary leadership, in terms of eliminating capitalism, would come from major capitalist states. Cuba's radical thinkers, as well as many of their Third World comrades, now contend, in light of the Cuban revolution, that all Marxists must accept the possibility that henceforth revolutionary leadership might emanate from peripheral nations, especially ones with substantial roots in radical thought.

NOTES

Introduction

1. Evidence for this can be found in the plethora of bibliographies and guides to archival collections published by government and private agencies in Cuba.

2. Robert J. Brym, *Intellectuals and Politics* (London: George Allen and Unwin, 1980), p. 59.

3. Ibid., p. 12.

4. C. Wright Mills, *Power, Politics and People: The Collected Essays of C. Wright Mills* (New York: Ballantine Books, 1963), p. 413.

5. Jean-Jacques Servan-Schreiber, *The Radical Alternative* (London: Macdonald, 1970), p. 44.

6. William H. Overholt, "Sources of Radicalism and Revolution: A Survey of the Literature," in *Radicalism in the Contemporary Age,* vol. 1, *Sources of Contemporary Radicalism,* ed. Seweryn Bialer and Sophia Sluzar (Boulder, Colo.: Westview Press, 1977), pp. 314–16.

7. Jacques Ellul, *Autopsy of Revolution* (New York: Alfred A. Knopf, 1971), pp. 299–300.

8. Sheldon B. Liss, *Marxist Thought in Latin America* (Berkeley: University of California Press, 1984), p. 6.

9. Melvin Rader, *Marx's Interpretation of History* (New York: Oxford University Press, 1979), p. 211.

10. Richard R. Fagen, *The Transformation of Political Culture in Cuba* (Stanford, Calif.: Stanford University Press, 1969), p. 2.

11. C. Wright Mills, *The Marxists* (New York: Delta Books, 1962), p. 96. Liss, *Marxist Thought*, p. 2.

12. Roberto Fernández Retamar, "Caliban," *Casa de las Américas* (September–October 1971), as translated in *Massachusetts Review* 15 (Winter–Spring 1974): 24.

Chapter 1

1. Arthur MacEwan, *Revolution and Economic Development in Cuba* (New York: St. Martin's Press, 1981), pp. 9–11.

2. Ramiro Guerra y Sánchez and others, *Historia de la nación cubana*, vol. 2, *Guerras coloniales conflictos y progresos, 1697–1790* (Havana: Editorial Historia de la Nación Cubana, 1952), p. 305.

3. Wyatt MacGaffey and Clifford R. Barnett, *Twentieth Century Cuba: The Background of the Castro Revolution* (Garden City, N.Y.: Doubleday, 1965), p. 256.

4. Ramiro Guerra y Sánchez and others, *Historia de la nación cubana*, vol. 3, *Ilustración libertad de comercio, 1790–1837* (Havana: Editorial Historia de la Nación Cubana, 1952), pp. 157–79.

5. Philip S. Foner, *A History of Cuba and Its Relations with the United States*, vol. 1, *1492–1845* (New York: International Publishers, 1962), p. 59.

6. Humberto Piñera Llera, *Panorama de la filosofía cubana* (Washington, D.C.: Pan American Union, 1960), p. 51.

7. Foner, *History of Cuba, 1492–1845*, p. 154.

8. Ramón Eduardo Ruiz, *Cuba: The Making of a Revolution* (New York: W. W. Norton, 1970), pp. 118–19.

9. Sheldon B. Liss, *Marxist Thought in Latin America* (Berkeley: University of California Press, 1984), p. 32.

10. José Antonio Portuondo, *El contenido social de la literatura cubana* (Mexico City: Colegio de México, Centro de Estudios Sociales, 1944), p. 38.

11. Joaquín Ordoqui, *Elementos para la historia del movimiento obrero en Cuba* (Havana: Comisión Nacional de Escuelas de Instrucción Revolucionaria, 1961), p. 10.

12. Ibid., pp. 10–11.

13. Leopoldo Zea, *The Latin American Mind* (Norman: University of Oklahoma Press, 1963), pp. 262–65.

14. Raimundo Menocal y Cueto, *Origen y desarrollo de pensamiento cubano* (Havana: Editorial Lex, 1945), 1:166.

15. Juan J. Remos, *Historia de la literatura cubana*, vol. 1, *Orígenes y clasicismo* (Havana: Cardénas y Compañia, 1945), p. 96.

16. Félix Lizaso, *Panorama de la cultura cubana* (Mexico City: Fondo de Cultura Económica, 1949), pp. 17–19.

17. Menocal y Cueto, *Origen y desarrollo*, 1:161–65.

18. Lizaso, *Panorama*, pp. 19–22.

19. Menocal y Cueto, *Origen y desarrollo*, 1:173.

20. Joseph McCadden and Helen McCadden, *Father Varela: Torch Bearer from Cuba* (New York: United States Catholic Historical Society, 1969), p. 25.

21. Menocal y Cueto, *Origen y desarrollo*, 1:172.

22. Max Henríquez Ureña, *Panorama histórico de la literatura cubana* (New York: Américas, 1963), 1:98–100.

23. Portuondo, *Contenido social*, pp. 19–20.

24. Remos, *Literatura cubana*, 1:179–83.

25. McCadden and McCadden, *Father Varela*, pp. 17–20.

26. Félix Varela, *Escritos políticos* (Havana: Editorial de Ciencias Sociales, 1977), pp. 260–67.

27. Ibid., p. 208.

28. Ibid., pp. 150–55.

29. Ibid., pp. 208–10.

30. Emilio Roig de Leuchsenring, ed., *Vida y pensamiento de Varela* (Havana: Municipio de la Habana, 1945), p. 240.

31. Varela, *Escritos*, p. 46.

32. Ibid., pp. 55–56.

33. Ibid., p. 38.

34. Ibid., pp. 120–21.

35. Ibid., p. 4.

36. Henríquez Ureña, *Panorama*, p. 100.

37. Remos, *Literatura cubana*, 1:176.

38. Ibid., p. 179.

39. Varela, *Escritos*, pp. 40–41.

40. Remos, *Literatura cubana*, 1:175.

41. Ibid., p. 184.

42. Medardo Vitier, *Las ideas en Cuba* (Havana: Editorial Trópico, 1938), 1:145–47.

43. Menocal y Cueto, *Origen y desarrollo*, 1:12.

44. Foner, *History of Cuba, 1492–1845*, p. 178.

45. Henríquez Ureña, *Panorama*, p. 141. See Saco's *Historia de la esclavitud de los indios en el nuevo mundo* (Barcelona, 1883).

46. Foner, *History of Cuba, 1492–1845*, pp. 214–20. See Saco's "La supresión del tráfico de esclavos en la isla de Cuba," in his *Colección de papeles científicos, históricos, políticos sobre la isla de Cuba* (Paris: d'Aubusson, 1859).

47. Remos, *Literatura cubana*, 1:229–30.

48. Franklin W. Knight, *Slave Society in Cuba during the Nineteenth Century* (Madison: University of Wisconsin Press, 1970), pp. 96–100.

49. Ibid., p. 139, and Gordon K. Lewis, *Main Currents in Caribbean Thought: The Historical Evolution of Caribbean Society in Its Ideological Aspects, 1492–1900* (Baltimore: Johns Hopkins University Press, 1983) pp. 108, 152–53.

50. Dennis B. Wood, "The Long Revolution: Class Relations

and Political Conflict in Cuba, 1868–1968," *Science and Society* 34 (Spring 1970):2–3.

51. Philip S. Foner, *A History of Cuba and Its Relations with the United States, vol. 2, 1845–1895* (New York: International Publishers, 1963), pp. 9–18.

52. Henríquez Ureña, *Panorama,* pp. 137–38.

53. See Ramiro Guerra y Sánchez and others, *Historia de la nación cubana,* vol. 4, *Ruptura con la metrópoli, 1837–1868* (Havana: Editorial Historia de la Nación Cubana, 1952.)

54. Leopoldo Zea, "The Struggle for Intellectual Emancipation," in *Man, State, and Society in Latin American History,* ed. Sheldon B. Liss and Peggy K. Liss (New York: Praeger, 1972), pp. 268–69.

55. José Manuel Pérez Cabrera, *Historiografía de Cuba* (México: Instituto Panamericano de Geografía e Historia, 1962), p. 197.

56. Lewis, *Main Currents,* p. 153.

57. Pérez Cabrera, *Historiografía,* p. 203.

58. Lewis, *Main Currents,* p. 150.

59. Henríquez Ureña, *Panorama,* pp. 144–45.

60. Ibid., p. 150.

61. Menocal y Cueto, *Origen y desarrollo,* 1:221.

62. Zea, *Latin American Mind,* pp. 113–14.

63. Ibid., p. 115.

64. Harold Eugene Davis, *Latin American Thought: A Historical Introduction* (New York: Free Press, 1974), p. 69.

65. Zea, *Latin American Mind,* pp. 115–16.

66. Juan J. Remos, *Historia de la literatura cubana,* vol. 2, *Romanticismo* (Havana: Cárdenas 1945), p. 243.

Chapter 2

1. Dennis B. Wood, "The Long Revolution: Class Relations and Political Conflict in Cuba, 1868–1968," *Science and Society* 34 (Spring 1970):4.

2. Juan Mier Febles, "Un siglo ideológico: Para llegar—correr el camino," *Cuba Internacional,* October 1968, p. 151.

3. From 70 to 90 percent of the sugar in the United States came from Cuba.

4. Oscar Pino-Santos, *Historia de Cuba: Aspectos fundamentales* (Havana: Editorial Nacional de Cuba, 1964), p. 207.

5. José Manuel Pérez Cabrera, *Historiografía de Cuba* (Mexico: Instituto Panamericano de Geografía e Historia, 1962), p. 249.

6. Ramón Eduardo Ruiz, *Cuba: The Making of a Revolution* (New York: W. W. Norton, 1970), p. 120.

7. Leopoldo Zea, *The Latin American Mind* (Norman: University of Oklahoma Press, 1963), pp. 264–66.

8. Philip S. Foner, *A History of*

Cuba and Its Relations with the United States, vol. 2, 1845–1895 (New York: International Publishers, 1963), p. 301.

9. United States investment reached $50 million by the 1890s, $160 million by 1906, $205 million by 1911, $1.2 billion by 1923, $7.5 billion by 1929, $11.8 billion by 1950, and $29.8 billion by 1958. Arthur MacEwan, *Revolution and Economic Development in Cuba* (New York: St. Martin's Press, 1981), pp. 12–13.

10. Paul Lafargue, *Socialism and the Intellectuals* (New York: New York Labor News, 1967), pp. 24–26.

11. See Raúl Roa, *Evocación de Pablo Lafargue* (Havana: Ministerio de Salud Pública, 1973).

12. Mier Febles, "Un siglo ideológico," p. 152.

13. Joaquín Ordoqui, *Elementos para la historia de movimiento obrero en Cuba* (Havana: Comisión Nacional de Escuelas de Instrucción Revolucionaria, 1961), p. 14.

14. See Roberto Fernández Retamar, "Caliban," *Casa de las Américas* (September–October 1971), as translated in *Massachusetts Review* 15 (Winter–Spring 1974):7–72.

15. Ramiro Guerra y Sánchez and others, *Historia de la nación cubana*, vol. 7, *Cambio de soberanía, 1868–1902* (Havana: Editorial Historia de la Nación Cubana, 1952), p. 266.

16. Aleida Plasencia, ed.,

Enrique Roig San Martín: Artículos publicados en el periódico "El Productor" (Havana: Biblioteca Nacional José Martí, 1967), pp. 37–40.

17. Ibid., pp. 30–38.

18. Rubén Pérez Chávez, "Biografía de Enrique Roig San Martín," *ISLAS* 12, no. 1 (1965): 62–63.

19. Plasencia, *Enrique Roig*, pp. 52–53.

20. Ibid., p. 31.

21. Pérez Chávez, "Biografía," pp. 62–63.

22. Plasencia, *Enrique Roig*, pp. 39, 167–71.

23. Ibid., p. 31.

24. Ibid., p. 142.

25. Ibid., p. 30.

26. Ibid., pp. 31–32.

27. Ibid., pp. 28–29.

28. Ibid., p. 367.

29. Ibid., p. 25.

30. Ibid., p. 27.

31. Ibid., p. 22.

32. Ibid., pp. 347–49.

33. Ordoqui, *Elementos para la historia*, p. 12.

34. Luis Gómez y Martínez, *Diego Vicente Tejera: Ensayo crítico-biográfico* (Havana: Bouza, 1928), p. 80.

35. Guerra y Sánchez, *Historia*, 7:324.

36. José Antonio Portuondo, *El contenido social de la literatura cubana* (Mexico City: Colegio de México, Centro de Estudios Sociales, 1944), pp. 45–50.

37. Diego Vicente Tejera, *Razón de Cuba* (Havana: Municipio de la Habana, 1948),

pp. 104–8.

38. Ibid., pp. 24–25, 58–64, 67–80.

39. José Rivero Muñiz, *El primer partido socialista cubano: Apuntes para la historia del proletariado en Cuba* (Santa Clara, Cuba: Universidad Central de Las Villas, 1962), pp. 36–37.

40. Eduardo J. Tejera, *Diego Vicente Tejera: Patriota-poeta y pensador cubano* (Madrid: Compañia de Impresores Reunidos, 1981), pp. 64–65, 169–78. Conference given at Key West, Florida, on 17 October 1897.

41. Ibid., pp. 66–68, 179–91. Conference given at Key West, Florida, in October 1897.

42. Ibid., pp. 69, 193–204, and Tejera, *Razón de Cuba*, pp. 98–107. Conference given at Key West, Florida, on 19 November 1897.

43. Ibid., pp. 72, 205–15. Conference given at Key West, Florida, in 1898.

44. Ibid., pp. 75–78, 217–25. Conference given at Key West, Florida, on 3 October 1897.

45. Ibid., pp. 78–80, 227–34. Conference given at Key West, Florida, on 12 December 1898.

46. Ibid., pp. 80–83, 235–46. Conference given at Key West, Florida, on 7 November 1897.

47. Ibid. pp. 83–85, 247–56. Conference given at Key West, Florida, in 1898.

48. Ibid., pp. 85–87, 257–66. Conference given at Key West,

Florida, on 10 October 1897.

49. C.A.M. Hennessy, "Cuba: The Politics of Frustrated Nationalism," in *Political Systems of Latin America*, ed. Martin Needler (Princeton, N.J.: D. Van Nostrand, 1964), pp. 25, 29.

50. Eduardo Tejera, *Diego Vicente Tejera*, pp. 87–90, 267–78. Conference given at Key West, Florida, on 21 November 1897.

51. Ibid., p. 96.

52. Sheldon B. Liss, *Marxist Thought in Latin America* (Berkeley: University of California Press, 1984), p. 239. Maurice Halperin, *The Rise and Decline of Fidel Castro* (Berkeley: University of California Press, 1974), p. 4.

53. Ruiz, *Cuba*, p. 120.

54. Eduardo Tejera, *Diego Vicente Tejera*, pp. 96–97.

55. Rivero Muñiz, *Primer partido socialista*, pp. 84–85, 118–19.

56. Ibid., pp. 75–78.

57. Miguel Jorrín and John D. Martz, *Latin-American Political Thought and Ideology* (Chapel Hill: University of North Carolina Press, 1970), p. 160.

58. *New York Sun*, 28 August 1880.

59. Fernández Retamar, "Caliban," pp. 37–41.

60. José Martí, *On Education: Articles on Educational Theory and Pedagogy and Writings for Children from The Age of Gold*, ed. Philip S. Foner (New York:

Monthly Review Press, 1979), p. 117.

61. Harold Eugene Davis, ed., *Latin American Social Thought: The History of Its Development since Independence, with Selected Readings* (Washington, D.C.: University Press of Washington, 1961), p. 264.

62. Gordon K. Lewis, *Main Currents in Caribbean Thought: The Historical Evolution of Caribbean Society in Its Ideological Aspects, 1492–1900* (Baltimore: Johns Hopkins University Press, 1983), p. 297.

63. Leonardo Acosta, *José Martí, la América precolombina y la conquista española* (Havana: Casa de las Américas, 1974), pp. 13, 24.

64. Lewis, *Main Currents,* p. 303.

65. Emilio Roig de Leuchsenring, *Martí: Anti-imperialist* (Havana: Ediciones Políticas, 1967), p. 9.

66. José Martí, *Inside the Monster: Writings on the United States and American Imperialism,* ed. Philip S. Foner (New York: Monthly Review Press, 1975), p. 42.

67. Ibid., pp. 261–62.

68. Roig, *Martí,* p. 17.

69. Martí, *Inside the Monster,* p. 295.

70. Roig, *Martí,* p. 22.

71. Ibid., pp. 10, 16.

72. José Martí, *Our America: Writings on Latin America and the Struggle for Cuban Independence,* ed. Philip S. Foner (New York: Monthly Review Press, 1977), p. 22.

73. Davis, *Latin American Social Thought,* p. 260.

74. Lewis, *Main Currents,* p. 299.

75. Jorge Ibarra, *José Martí: Dirigente político e ideologo revolucionario* (Havana: Editorial de Ciencias Sociales, 1980), p. 266.

76. Ibid., pp. 215–16.

77. John M. Kirk, *José Martí: Mentor of the Cuban Nation* (Tampa: University Presses of Florida, 1983), p. 86.

78. Liss, *Marxist Thought,* p. 240.

79. Martí, *Inside the Monster,* p. 38.

80. Ibid.

81. José Martí, *Obras completas* (Havana: Editorial Lex, 1946), 1:1518.

82. Herbert L. Matthews, *Revolution in Cuba* (New York: Charles Scribner's Sons, 1975), p. 223.

83. Richard Butler Gray, "José Martí and Social Revolution in Cuba," *Journal of Inter-American Studies* 5 (April 1963): 249–56.

84. Richard Butler Gray, *José Martí, Cuban Patriot* (Gainesville: University of Florida Press, 1962), p. 60.

85. José Antonio Portuondo, *Bosquejo histórico de las letras cubanas* (Havana: Ministerio de Relaciones Exteriores, 1960), p. 36.

86. Jorrín and Martz, *Latin American Political Thought*, p. 156.

87. Harold Eugene Davis, *Latin American Thought: A Historical Introduction* (New York: Free Press, 1974), pp. 130–31.

88. *Times of the Americas*, 29 March 1978, p. 2.

89. Liss, *Marxist Thought*, p. 241.

90. Acosta, *José Martí*, p. 88.

Chapter 3

1. Jaime Suchliki, *Cuba: From Columbus to Castro* (New York: Charles Scribner's Sons, 1974), p. 105.

2. Jorge I. Domínguez, *Cuba: Order and Revolution* (Cambridge: Harvard University Press, 1978), pp. 53–54.

3. Martin S. Stabb, *In Quest of Identity: Patterns in the Spanish American Essay of Ideas, 1890–1960* (Chapel Hill: University of North Carolina Press, 1967), pp. 35–37.

4. Domínguez, *Cuba: Order and Revolution*, p. 51.

5. Ibid., p. 52.

6. James O'Connor, *The Origins of Socialism in Cuba* (Ithaca, N.Y.: Cornell University Press, 1970), p. 178.

7. J. A. Hobson, *Imperialism: A Study* (London: Allen and Unwin, 1902), p. 106.

8. Carlos Baliño, *Documentos y artículos* (Havana: Instituto de Historia del Movimiento Comunista y de la Revolución Socialista de Cuba, 1976), p. 233.

9. Suchliki, *Cuba: From Columbus to Castro*, pp. 106–7.

10. Duvon C. Corbitt, "Cuban Revisionist Interpretations of Cuba's Struggle for Independence," *Hispanic American Historical Review* 43 (August 1963): 396.

11. Max Henríquez Ureña, *Panorama histórico de la literatura cubana* (New York: Américas, 1963), 2:272–74.

12. Wyatt MacGaffey and Clifford R. Barnett, *Twentieth Century Cuba: The Background of the Castro Revolution* (Garden City, N.Y.: Doubleday, 1965), pp. 262–63.

13. José Antonio Portuondo, *El contenido social de la literatura cubana* (Mexico City: Colegio de México, Centro de Estudios Sociales, 1944), p. 79.

14. Jorge García Montes and Antonio Alonso Avila, *Historia del partido comunista de Cuba* (Miami: Ediciones Universal, 1970), pp. 27–29.

15. Portuondo, *Contenido social*, p. 397; Enrique Anderson-Imbert, *Spanish American Literature: A History* (Detroit: Wayne State University Press, 1962), 2:387; Juan J. Remos, *Historia de la literatura cubana*, vol. 3, *Modernismo* (Havana: Cárdenas y Compañia, 1945), pp. 302–6.

16. Sheldon B. Liss, *Marxist Thought in Latin America* (Berke-

ley: University of California Press, 1984), pp. 129–37.

17. Ibid., pp. 7–8. Recabarren's works were reissued by the Castro government. See Luis Emilio Recabarren, *Obras* (Havana: Casa de las Américas, 1976).

18. Jules Robert Benjamin, *The United States and Cuba: Hegemony and Dependent Development, 1880–1934* (Pittsburgh: University of Pittsburgh Press, 1977), p. 58; Luis E. Aguilar, *Cuba 1933: Prologue to Revolution* (New York: W. W. Norton, 1974), pp. 70–71.

19. Trinidad Pérez and others, *Recopilación de textos sobre Juan Marinello* (Havana: Ediciones Casa de las Américas, 1979), p. 35.

20. Rosario Rexach, "La Revista de Avance publicada en Habana 1927–1930," *Caribbean Studies* 3 (October 1963): 8.

21. Mañach (1898–1961), a middle-class intellectual, gradually became more conservative, and after the Castro takeover he left Cuba for exile.

22. Félix Lizaso, *Panorama de la cultura cubana* (Mexico City: Fondo de Cultura Económica, 1949), p. 130.

23. Jules Robert Benjamin, "The Machadato and Cuban Nationalism, 1928–1932," *Hispanic American Historical Review* 55 (February 1975): 82.

24. Hugh Thomas, *Cuba: The Pursuit of Freedom* (New York:

Harper and Row, 1971), p. 578.

25. Robert J. Alexander, *Organized Labor in Latin America* (New York: Free Press, 1965), p. 154.

26. Suchliki, *Cuba: From Columbus to Castro*, pp. 117–19.

27. Portuondo, *Contenido social*, p. 70.

28. Emilio Roig de Leuchsenring, ed., *Curso de introducción a la historia de Cuba* (Havana: Municipio de la Habana, 1938), pp. 422–23.

29. Rexach, "Revista de Avance," pp. 15–16.

30. Aguilar, *Cuba 1933*, pp. 71–72.

31. Lizaso, *Panorama*, pp. 131–33.

32. Ibid., pp. 139–40.

33. Aguilar, *Cuba 1933*, pp. 118–20.

34. José Martí, *Our America: Writings on Latin America and the Struggle for Cuban Independence*, ed. Philip S. Foner (New York: Monthly Review Press, 1977), p. 31.

35. Liss, *Marxist Thought*, p. 241; Gaspar Jorge García Galló and others, eds., *Carlos B. Baliño: Apuntes históricos sobre sus actividades revolucionarias* (Havana: Partido Comunista de Cuba, 1967), pp. 42–43.

36. Baliño, *Documentos y artículos*, p. 36.

37. Ibid., p. 28.

38. Ibid., p. 49.

39. Martí, *Our America*, p. 32.

40. Carlos Baliño, *Documentos de Carlos Baliño* (Havana: Departmento "Colección Cubana" de la Biblioteca Nacional José Martí, 1964), pp. 33, 36.

41. Baliño, *Documentos y artículos*, p. 215.

42. García Galló, *Carlos B. Baliño: Apuntes*, p. 85.

43. Baliño, *Documentos y artículos*, p. 15.

44. Boris Kozolchyk, *The Political Biographies of Three Castro Officials* (Santa Monica, Calif.: Rand Corporation, 1966), p. 6.

45. Baliño, *Documentos y artículos*, pp. 223–24.

46. Baliño, *Documentos de Carlos Baliño*, pp. 43–53.

47. García Galló, *Carlos B. Baliño: Apuntes*, pp. 55–59.

48. Liss, *Marxist Thought*, p. 242.

49. Ibid.

50. Baliño, *Documentos de Carlos Baliño*, p. 64. The Cuban government reissued his translation in 1961.

51. Baliño, *Documentos y artículos*, p. 190.

52. Ibid., p. 262.

53. García Galló, *Carlos B. Baliño: Apuntes*, pp. 35–37.

54. Baliño, *Documentos de Carlos Baliño*, p. 33; Liss, *Marxist Thought*, p. 243.

55. Baliño, *Documentos y artículos*, pp. 197–202.

56. Emilio Roig de Leuchsenring, ed., *Vida y pensamiento de Varela* (Havana: Municipio de la Habana, 1945), pp. 217–20.

57. Corbitt, "Cuban Revisionist," p. 397.

58. Henríquez Ureña, *Panorama*, 2:327–28.

59. Corbitt, "Cuban Revisionist," p. 399.

60. Robert F. Smith, "Twentieth Century Cuban Historiography," *Hispanic American Historical Review* 44 (February 1964): 49. Roig also worked for the Cuban Society of International Law, helped create the Friends of the National Library, the magazine *Gráfico (Graphic)*, the Conference Society, and Cuba's Film Society.

61. See Emilio Roig de Leuchsenring, ed., *La guerra hispano-cubano-americana fue ganada por el lugarteniente general del ejército libertador Calixto García Iñiguez* (Havana: Oficina del Historiador de la Ciudad de la Habana, 1955).

62. See Emilio Roig de Leuchsenring, *La guerra libertadora cubana de los treinta años 1868–1898: Razón de su victoria* (Havana: Oficina del Historiador de la Ciudad de la Habana, 1952).

63. See Emilio Roig de Leuchsenring, *Revolución y república en Maceo* (Havana: P. Fernández, 1945).

64. See Emilio Roig de Leuchsenring, *Médicos y medicina en Cuba: Historia, biografía y costumbrismo* (Havana: Museo

Histórico de las Ciencias Médicas Carlos J. Finlay, 1965).

65. Roig, *Guerra libertadora*, pp. 105–9.

66. Félix Lizaso, *Ensayistas contemporáneos, 1900–1920* (Havana: Editorial Trópico, 1938), p. 170.

67. Emilio Roig de Leuchsenring, *Males y vicios de Cuba republicana: Sus causas y sus remedios* (Havana: Oficina del Historiador de la Ciudad de la Habana, 1959), pp. 168–69.

68. Roig, *Guerra libertadora*, p. 44.

69. Emilio Roig de Leuchsenring, *Martí: Anti-imperialist* (Havana: Ediciones Políticas, 1967), p. 41.

70. See Emilio Roig de Leuchsenring, *Hostos, apóstol de la independencia y de la libertad de Cuba y Puerto Rico* (Havana: Municipio de la Habana, 1939).

71. Roig, *Martí*, p. 43.

72. Roig, *Males y vicios*, p. 21.

73. Robin Blackburn, "Prologue to the Cuban Revolution," *New Left Review* 4 (October 1963):74.

74. Emilio Roig de Leuchsenring, ed., *Defensa de Cuba: Vida y obra de Manuel Sanguily* (Havana: Oficina del Historiador de la Ciudad de la Habana, 1948), pp. 93–97.

75. Ibid., pp. 99–105.

76. Ibid., pp. lxvi–vii.

77. Ibid., pp. 76–77.

78. Ibid., pp. 88–89.

79. Ibid., lxx; Roig, *Males y vicios*, p. 272.

80. Roig, *Curso de introducción*, pp. 168–70.

81. Roig, *Martí*, p. 54.

82. Emilio Roig de Leuchsenring, *Historia de la enmienda Platt: Una interpretación de la realidad cubana* (Havana: Cultural, 1935), 1:15.

83. Ibid., 2:174.

84. Roig, *Historia de la enmienda Platt*, 1:301–4.

85. Roig, *Males y vicios*, p. 262.

86. Roig, *Martí*, p. 58.

87. Roig, *Males y vicios*, p. 255.

88. Roig, *Martí*, pp. 62–63.

89. Ibid., p. 60.

90. Roig, *Curso de introducción*, p. 412.

91. Roig, *Martí*, p. 62.

92. Emilio Roig de Leuchsenring, *Tradición antiimperialista de nuestra historia* (Havana: Oficina del Historiador de la Ciudad de la Habana, 1962), pp. 11–87.

93. J. P. Morray, *The Second Revolution in Cuba* (New York: Monthly Review Press, 1962), p. 60.

94. Lizaso, *Panorama*, p. 130.

95. Emilio Roig de Leuchsenring, *El Groupo Minorista de intelectuales y artistas habaneros* (Havana: Oficina del Historiador de la Ciudad de la Habana, 1961), p. 36.

96. Ibid., pp. 35–36.

97. Ibid., p. 22.

98. Ibid., p. 33.

99. Roig, *Males y vicios,* p. 98.

100. Roig, *Historia de la enmienda Platt,* 2:210.

101. Roig, *Males y vicios,* p. 199.

102. Ibid., pp. 93–94.

103. Corbitt, "Cuban Revisionist," p. 403.

104. Roig, *Males y vicios,* p. 279.

105. See Julio Antonio Mella, *Escritos revolucionarios* (Mexico City: Siglo XXI, 1978).

106. Liss, *Marxist Thought,* p. 243.

107. Julio Antonio Mella, *Mella: Documentos y artículos* (Havana: Editorial de Ciencias Sociales, 1975), pp. 5–7.

108. Erasmo Dumpierre, *J. A. Mella: Biografía* (Havana: Editorial de Ciencias Sociales, 1977), p. 15.

109. Mella, *Escritos,* p. 17.

110. Dumpierre, *J. A. Mella,* pp. 29–30.

111. Mella, *Escritos,* pp. 22–23.

112. Julio Antonio Mella, *Julio Antonio Mella en el Machete: Antología parcial de un luchador y su momento histórico* (Mexico: Fondo de Cultura Popular, 1968), pp. 244–46.

113. Mella, *Escritos,* pp. 44–45.

114. Ibid., p. 24; García Montes and Alonso Avila, *Historia del partido comunista,* pp. 47–49.

115. Mella, *Escritos,* pp. 58–59; Liss, *Marxist Thought,* p. 244.

116. García Montes and Alonso Avila, *Historia del partido comunista,* p. 44.

117. Mella, *Mella en el Machete,* pp. 256–57.

118. Mella, *Escritos,* pp. 49–50.

119. Ibid., p. 243: Dumpierre, *J. A. Mella,* p. 105.

120. Mella, *Escritos,* pp. 157–58; Mella, *Mella en el Machete,* p. 276.

121. Ibid., p. 22.

122. Ibid., p. 23.

123. Mella, *Documentos,* p. 107.

124. Blas Roca, *Los fundamentos del socialismo en Cuba* (Havana: Ediciones Populares, 1962), p. 95.

125. Mella, *Escritos,* p. 70; Mella, *Documentos,* pp. 181–83.

126. Mella, *Escritos,* pp. 74–77.

127. Mella, *Documentos,* pp. 174–79.

128. Dumpierre, *J. A. Mella,* pp. 110–11.

129. Kozolchyk, *Political Biographies,* p. 9.

130. Mella, *Documentos,* p. 197.

131. Dumpierre, *J. A. Mella,* pp. 53–54, 97.

132. Mella, *Documentos,* p. 8.

133. Carleton Beals, *The Crime of Cuba* (Philadelphia: J. B. Lippincott, 1933), p. 266.

134. Dumpierre, *J. A. Mella,* p. 77.

135. Ibid., pp. 102–3.

136. Mella, *Escritos*, p. 26.

137. Ibid., pp. 28–29; Dumpierre, J. A. *Mella*, p. 101.

138. Mella, *Escritos*, p. 28.

139. Dumpierre, J. A. *Mella*, pp. 99–100.

140. Julio Antonio Mella, *La lucha revolucionaria contra el imperialismo: ¿Que es el APRA?* (Mexico City, 1928), p. 5.

141. Ibid., pp. 12–17.

142. Ibid., pp. 16–19.

143. Mella, *Escritos*, p. 25.

144. Mella, *Documentos*, p. 199.

145. Dumpierre, J. A. *Mella*, p. 143.

146. Juan Marinello, *Ensayos* (Havana: Editorial Arte y Literatura, 1977), p. 146.

147. Ibid., p. 24.

148. Juan Marinello, *Contemporáneos* (Havana: Universidad Central de las Villas, 1964), p. 169; see Juan Marinello, *Ocho notas sobre Aníbal Ponce* (Buenos Aires: Cuadernos de Cultura, 1958).

149. Pérez, *Recopilación*, p. 57.

150. Ibid., p. 54.

151. Ibid., p. 558.

152. Aníbal Ponce, *Humanismo burgués y humanismo proletario* (Havana: Imprenta Nacional, 1962), pp. 18–21.

153. Liss, *Marxist Thought*, p. 50; Juan Antonio Salceda, *Aníbal Ponce y el pensamiento de mayo* (Buenos Aires: Editorial Lautaro, 1957), pp. 210–13.

154. Aníbal Ponce, *Educación y lucha de clases* (Havana: Imprenta Nacional de Cuba, 1961), pp. 12–14.

155. Ibid., pp. 147–49.

156. Liss, *Marxist Thought*, pp. 50–51.

157. See Aníbal Ponce, *Obras escogidas de Aníbal Ponce* (Havana: Casa de las Américas, 1975); Ponce, *Educación*; and Ponce, *Humanismo*.

158. See Juan Marinello, *Literatura hispanoamericana: Hombres, meditaciones* (Mexico City: Universidad Nacional, n.d.).

159. See Juan Marinello, *Once ensayos maritianos* (Havana: Comisíon Nacional Cubana de la UNESCO, 1964).

160. Ibid., p. 193.

161. Pérez, *Recopilación*, pp. 74–75.

162. Ibid., pp. 468–72.

163. Richard Butler Gray, *José Martí, Cuban Patriot* (Gainesville: University of Florida Press, 1962), pp. 173–74.

164. See Juan Marinello, *José Martí, escritos americano: Martí y el modernismo* (Mexico City: Editorial Grijalbo, 1958).

165. Harold Eugene Davis, *Latin American Thought: A Historical Introduction* (New York: Free Press, 1974), p. 130.

166. Marinello, *Contemporáneos*, p. 229.

167. Ibid.

168. Liss, *Marxist Thought*, p. 249.

226

169. Robert J. Alexander, *Communism in Latin America* (New Brunswick: Rutgers University Press, 1957), p. 281.

170. Pérez, *Recopilación,* p. 724.

171. Juan Marinello, *Cuba contra la guerra imperialista* (Havana: Ediciones Sociales, 1940), pp. 8–9.

172. Ibid., pp. 22–23.

173. Liss, *Marxist Thought,* p. 249.

174. Ibid., pp. 249–50.

175. Marinello, *Cuba contra,* pp. 24–27.

176. See Marinello, *Once ensayos.*

177. Pérez, *Recopilación,* p. 176.

178. Ibid., pp. 575–76.

179. Ibid., pp. 560–64.

180. Ibid., p. 170.

181. Ibid., pp. 203–4.

182. Ibid., p. 14.

183. Ibid., pp. 15–16.

184. Marinello, *Ensayos,* p. 41.

185. Ibid., pp. 265–79.

186. Ibid., p. 76.

187. Ibid., pp. 208–23.

188. See Juan Marinello, *Conversación con nuestros pintores-abstractos* (Santiago de Cuba: Universidad de Oriente Departamento de Extensión y Relaciones Culturales, 1960).

189. Marinello, *Ensayos,* pp. 393–94.

190. Ibid., p. 452.

191. Ibid., pp. 567–68.

Chapter 4

1. Jorge I. Domínguez, *Cuba: Order and Revolution* (Cambridge: Harvard University Press, 1978), p. 109.

2. Ibid., p. 54.

3. Jules Robert Benjamin, "The Machadato and Cuban Nationalism, 1928–1932," *Hispanic American Historical Review* 55 (February 1975): 90–91.

4. Robin Blackburn, "Prologue to the Cuban Revolution," *New Left Review* 4 (October 1963): 88.

5. Partido Aprista Cubano, *El aprismo ante la realidad cubana* (Havana: Editorial APRA, 1934), pp. 5–34.

6. Dennis B. Wood, "The Long Revolution: Class Relations and Political Conflict in Cuba, 1868–1968," *Science and Society* 34 (Spring 1970): 37.

7. C.A.M. Hennessy, "The Roots of Cuban Nationalism," *International Affairs* 39 (July 1963): 354.

8. Félix Lizaso, *Panorama de la cultura cubana* (Mexico City: Fondo de Cultura Económica, 1949), p. 141.

9. Blackburn, "Prologue," p. 77.

10. Nelson P. Valdés, "Ideological Roots of the Cuban Revolutionary Movement," in *Contemporary Caribbean: A Sociological Reader,* ed. Susan Craig (Maracas, Trinidad and

Tobago: Susan Craig, 1982), 2:213.

11. Ibid.

12. Ibid.

13. Arthur P. Whitaker and David C. Jordan, *Nationalism in Contemporary Latin America* (New York: Free Press, 1966), p. 151. Since the depression United States companies had withdrawn from ownership in the sugar industry, primarily because of unfavorable labor conditions.

14. Samuel Farber, "The Cuban Communists in the Early Stages of the Cuban Revolution: Revolutionaries or Reformists?" *Latin American Research Review* 18, no. 1 (1983): 61.

15. Hugh Thomas, *Cuba: The Pursuit of Freedom* (New York: Harper and Row, 1971), p. 851.

16. Calixta Guiteras Holmes, *Biografía de Antonio Guiteras* (Havana: Municipio de la Habana, 1960), p. 5: Olga Cabrera, Guiteras, la época, el hombre (Havana: Editorial de Arte y Literatura, 1974), pp. 12, 30–31.

17. Olga Cabrera, ed., *Antonio Guiteras: Su pensamiento revolucionario* (Havana: Editorial de Ciencias Sociales, 1974), pp. 241–42. The statements appeared in an article by Beals in *Common Sense*, July 1935.

18. See ibid.

19. Guiteras Holmes, *Biografía*, pp. 5, 7.

20. Cabrera, *Guiteras, la época*, pp. 245–57.

21. Maurice Halperin, *The Rise and Decline of Fidel Castro* (Berkeley: University of California Press, 1974), p. 9, as cited in Pedro Luis Padrón, "Guiteras," *Granma Weekly Review, 19 May 1968; Guiteras Holmes, Biografía,* p. 12.

22. Cabrera, *Guiteras, la época*, p. 284.

23. Ibid., p. 380. The program of *Joven Cuba* was published as a pamphlet and reproduced in the newspaper *Ahora*, 24 October 1934.

24. Ibid., pp. 383–87: Cabrera, *Antonio Guiteras,* pp. 183–98.

25. Cabrera, *Antonio Guiteras*, p. 43.

26. Ibid., pp. 43–44, 178–82. The article appeared in *Bohemia*, vol. 26 (1 April 1934).

27. Cabrera, *Guiteras, la época*, pp. 349–54.

28. Cabrera, *Antonio Guiteras*, p. 129.

29. Boris Kozolchyk, *The Political Biographies of Three Castro Officials* (Santa Monica, Calif.: Rand Corporation, 1966), pp. 21–22.

30. Ibid., p. vii.

31. Ibid., p. vi.

32. Raúl Roa Kourí, "Cuba in the United Nations: An Interview with Ambassador Raúl Roa Kourí," *Cuba Update* 4 (November 1983): 3.

33. Ibid.

34. Raúl Roa, *15 años después* (Havana: Editorial Librería

Selecta, 1950), p. 32.

35. Raúl Roa, *Historia de las doctrinas sociales* (Havana: Universidad de la Habana, 1949), p. 8.

36. Jorge García Montes and Antonio Alonso Avila, *Historia del partido comunista de Cuba* (Miami: Ediciones Universal, 1970), p. 489.

37. Ernesto Cardenal, *In Cuba* (New York: New Directions, 1974), p. 273.

38. Roa Kourí, "Cuba in the United Nations," p. 3.

39. Ibid., p. 1.

40. Roa, *Historia de las doctrinas sociales*, p. 37.

41. Kozolchyk, *Political Biographies*, pp. 28–29.

42. Roa, *Historia de las doctrinas sociales*, p. 25.

43. Raúl Roa, *Retorno a la alborado* (Havana: Universidad de las Villas, 1964), 1:265–75.

44. Ibid., p. 303.

45. Roa, *Historia de las doctrinas sociales*, p. 61.

46. Ibid., p. 70.

47. Raúl Roa, *En pie, 1953–1958* (Havana: Universidad Central de las Villas, 1959), pp. 316–17.

48. Roa, *15 años*, pp. 462–67.

49. Raúl Roa, *Viento sur* (Havana: Editorial Selecta, 1953), pp. 80–85.

50. Roa, *Retorno a la alborado*, 1:27.

51. Roa, *Viento sur*, p. 60.

52. Roa, *15 años*, p. 94.

53. Roa, *Viento sur*, p. 72.

54. Roa, *Historia de las doctrinas sociales*, p. 143.

55. Roa, *Viento sur*, p. 71.

56. Roa, *15 años*, pp. 470–71.

57. Ibid., p. 569; Kozolchyk, *Political Biographies*, pp. 31–33.

58. Ibid., p. 33.

59. Ibid., pp. 29–31; Roa, *Retorno a la alborado*, 2:249.

60. Roa, *Viento sur*, pp. 334–38.

61. Roa, *15 años*, p. 277.

62. Roa, *En pie*, pp. 63, 249–51.

63. Raúl Roa, *Evocación de Pablo Lafargue* (Havana: Ministerio de Salud Pública, 1973) pp. 37, 42–43.

64. Kozolchyk, *Political Biographies*, p. 31.

65. Roa, *15 años*, p. 403.

66. Roa, *Viento sur*, pp. 389–95.

67. Ibid., p. 121.

68. Roa, *15 años*, p. 92.

69. Raúl Roa, *Martí y el fascismo* (Havana: Ucar, García, 1937), p. 31.

70. Roa, *15 años*, pp. 104–8.

71. Roa, *En pie*, p. 34.

72. Roa, *15 años*, p. 305.

73. Ibid., p. 308.

74. Ibid., pp. 336–37.

75. Roa, *Viento sur*, p. 415.

76. Roa, *Retorno a la alborado*, 1:214.

77. Roa, *Viento sur*, pp. 405–15.

78. Roa, *Retorno a la alborado*, 1:232–33.

79. Raúl Roa, "Utopia, ideología y mito en la política con-

temporánea," in *Los mejores ensayistas cubanos*, ed. Salvador Bueno, (Lima: Imprenta Torres Aguirre, 1959), pp. 103–4.

80. Ibid., pp. 111-12.

81. Roa, *Historia de las doctrinas sociales*, p. 224.

82. Kozolchyk, *Political Biographies*, p. 37.

83. Roa, *15 años*, p. 461.

84. Kozolchyk, *Political Biographies*, p. 50.

85. Roa, *Retorno a la alborado*, 2:255–57.

86. Ibid., p. 590.

87. Ibid., pp. 591, 599–600.

88. Roa, *15 años*, pp. 211–12.

89. Ibid., pp. 480–81.

90. See Roa, *En pie*.

91. Ibid., pp. 418–20.

92. Roa, *Retorno a la alborado*, 2:141.

93. Ibid., pp. 585–86.

94. Ibid.

95. Cardenal, *In Cuba*, p. 272.

96. David Gallagher, "The Literary Life of Cuba," *New York Review of Books* 10 (5 May 1968): 37.

97. As a tribute to Baliño he wrote the prologue to *Verdades socialistas* (1941), which consisted of three of the Communist party founder's works.

98. Terence Cannon, *Revolutionary Cuba* (New York: Thomas Y. Crowell, 1981), p. 252.

99. Blas Roca, *29 artículos sobre la revolución cubana* (Havana: Partido Socialista Popular, 1960), p. 94.

100. Ibid., pp. 227–31.

101. Ibid., p. 150.

102. Blas Roca, *Los fundamentos del socialismo en Cuba* (Havana: Ediciones Populares, 1962), p. 98.

103. Blas Roca, *The Cuban Revolution: Report to the Eighth National Congress of the Popular Socialist Party of Cuba* (New York: New Century, 1961), p. 90.

104. Roca, *29 artículos*, pp. 15–18.

105. Blas Roca, "The Cuban Revolution in Action," *World Marxist Review* 2 (August 1959): 18.

106. García Montes, *Historia del partido comunista*, pp. 307–9.

107. Carlos Rafael Rodríguez, *Cuba en el tránsito al socialismo (1953–1963): Lenin y la cuestión colonial* (Mexico City: Siglo XXI, 1978), pp. 30–45.

108. Roca, *Fundamentos*, p. 60.

109. Ibid., pp. 16–22.

110. Sheldon B. Liss, *Marxist Thought in Latin America* (Berkeley: University of California Press, 1984), p. 252.

111. Roca, *29 artículos*, pp. 191–92.

112. Roca, *Fundamentos*, p. 109.

113. Ramón Eduardo Ruiz, *Cuba, The Making of a Revolution* (New York: W. W. Norton, 1970), p. 17.

114. Roca, *Fundamentos*, pp. 50–56.

115. Roca, "Cuban Revolution

in Action," p. 17.

116. Roca, *29 artículos,* pp. 77–78.

117. Roca, *Cuban Revolution: Report,* pp. 77–83.

118. Ibid., p. 118.

119. Blas Roca, "El desarrollo histórico de la revolución cubana," *Cuba Socialista* 4 (January 1964): 15.

120. Roca, *29 artículos,* pp. 74–75.

121. Ibid., pp. 96–104.

122. Ibid., pp. 173–74.

123. Ibid., pp. 79–80.

124. Roca, *Cuban Revolution: Report,* p. 112.

125. Roca, "Desarrollo," p. 14.

126. Roca, *Cuban Revolution: Report,* pp. 40–52.

127. Cole Blasier, *The Giant's Rival: The USSR and Latin America* (Pittsburgh: University of Pittsburgh Press, 1983), p. 102.

128. Roca, *Cuban Revolution: Report,* p. 26.

129. Ibid., pp. 38–40.

130. Roca, *29 artículos,* pp. 177–78, 182.

131. Arthur MacEwan, *Revolution and Economic Development in Cuba* (New York: St. Martin's Press, 1981), pp. 39–40.

132. Roca, *29 artículos,* pp. 156–58.

133. Blas Roca, "Sobre algunos aspectos del desarrollo de la lucha de clases en Cuba," *Cuba Socialista* 11 (April 1965): 33–35.

134 Roca, "Desarrollo," p. 11.

135. Ibid., p. 23.

136. Blas Roca, "New Stage in the Cuban Revolution," *World Marxist Review* 9 (October 1961): 4.

137. Roca, "Cuban Revolution in Action," p. 18.

138. Reynaldo González, "Interview with Carlos Rafael Rodríguez," *Cuba Update* 4 (November 1983): 12.

139. Carlos Rafael Rodríguez, *Letra con filo* (Havana: Editorial de Ciencias Sociales, 1983), 1:v.

140. González, "Interview," p. 12.

141. Ibid.

142. Rodríguez, *Letra,* pp. 5–11.

143. Herbert L. Matthews, *Revolution in Cuba* (New York: Charles Scribner's Sons, 1975), p. 225.

144. Rodríguez, *Letra,* p. 94.

145. Ibid., pp. 383–85.

146. Ibid., p. xv.

147. Liss, *Marxist Thought,* p. 254.

148. García Montes, *Historia del partido comunista,* pp. 334–35.

149. Carlos Rafael Rodríguez, *El marxismo y la historia de Cuba* (Havana: Editorial Páginas, 1944), pp. 3–24.

150. Ibid.

151. Emilio Roig de Leuchsenring, ed., *Curso de introducción a la historia de Cuba* (Havana: Municipio de la Habana, 1938), pp. 243–55.

152. Sergio Aguirre, *Seis actitudes de la burguesía cubana*

en el siglo XIX (Havana: Editorial Páginas, 1944), pp. 25–47.

153. Rodríguez, Cuba en el tránsito, p. 13.

154. Ibid., p. 16.

155. Rodríguez, Letra, pp. 15–22.

156. Rodríguez, Cuba en el tránsito, p. 137.

157. Ibid., pp. 104–5.

158. Ibid., p. 103.

159. Lionel Martín, The Early Fidel: Roots of Castro's Communism (Secaucus, N.J.: Lyle Stuart, 1978), p. 198.

160. Rodríguez, Cuba en el tránsito, p. 107.

161. Martín, Early Fidel, p. 220.

162. Rodríguez, Cuba en el tránsito, pp. 130–35.

163. Ibid., pp. 146–54.

164. Rodŕguez, Letra, p. 256.

165. Carlos Rafael Rodríguez, "The Cuban Revolution and the Peasantry," World Marxist Review 8 (October 1965): 63.

166. Ibid., pp. 69–70.

167. Ibid., p. 71.

168. Michael Taber, ed., Fidel Castro: Speeches, vol. 2, Building Socialism in Cuba (New York: Pathfinder Press, 1983), p. 22.

169. Ibid., pp. 320–21.

170. Frank T. Fitzgerald, "The Direction of Cuban Socialism: A Critique of the Sovietization Thesis," in Contemporary Caribbean: A Sociological Reader, ed. Susan Craig, (Maracas, Trinidad and Tobago: Susan Craig, 1982), 2:254–56.

171. Barry B. Levine, ed., The New Cuban Presence in the Caribbean (Boulder, Colo.: Westview Press, 1983), p. 204.

172. Rodríguez, Letra, p. 388.

173. Ibid., pp. 294–95.

174. Rodríguez, Cuba en el tránsito, p. 166.

175. Ibid., pp. 232–33.

176. José Consuegra Higgins, Lenin y la América Latina (Barranquilla, Colombia: Ediciones Cruz del Sur, 1972), pp. 111–24.

177. González, "Interview," p. 18.

178. Rodríguez, Letra, pp. 141–45.

179. Ibid., pp. 77–87.

180. Ibid., p. 375.

181. Lynn Darrell Bender, The Politics of Hostility: Castro's Revolution and United States Policy (Hato Rey, Puerto Rico: Inter-American University Press, 1975), p. 50; Granma, 15 June 1969.

182. Rodríguez, Letra, p. 375.

Chapter 5

1. Fidel Castro, Osvaldo Dorticós, and Raúl Roa, Así se derrotó al imperialismo, vol. 1, Preparando la defensa (Mexico City: Siglo XXI, 1981), p. 81.

2. Fidel Castro, La primera revolución socialista en América (Mexico City: Siglo XXI, 1980), p. 24.

3. Samuel Farber, Revolution and Reaction in Cuba, 1933–

232

1960: A Political Sociology from Machado to Castro (Middletown, Conn.: Wesleyan University Press, 1976), p. 208.

4. Dennis B. Wood, "The Long Revolution: Class Relations and Political Conflict in Cuba, 1868–1968," Science and Society 34 (Spring 1970): 24.

5. Arthur MacEwan, Revolution and Economic Development in Cuba (New York: St. Martin's Press, 1981), p. x.

6. Hugh Thomas, Cuba: The Pursuit of Freedom (New York: Harper and Row, 1971), p. 1080.

7. Ibid., p. 1343.

8. "Che" is Argentine slang for "pal."

9. Pablo Neruda, Memoirs, trans. Hardie St. Martin (New York: Penguin, 1978), p. 323.

10. Maurice Halperin, The Taming of Fidel Castro (Berkeley: University of California Press, 1981), p. 115.

11. Ernesto Guevara, "Notes for the Study of the Ideology of the Cuban Revolution," in Revolution, ed. Bruce Mazlish, Arthur D. Kaledin, and David B. Ralston (New York: Macmillan, 1971), pp. 401–2.

12. Ernesto Guevara, Che Guevara Speaks (New York: Pathfinder Press, 1967), p. 80.

13. Michael Lowy, The Marxism of Che Guevara (New York: Monthly Review Press, 1973), p. 23.

14. Ibid., p. 33.

15. Ernesto Guevara, "On Art and Revolution," Praxis, Winter 1976, p. 396.

16. Sheldon B. Liss, Marxist Thought in Latin America (Berkeley: University of California Press, 1984), pp. 257–58.

17. Guevara, Che Guevara Speaks, p. 74.

18. Donald C. Hodges, The Latin American Revolution: Politics and Strategy from Apro-Marxism to Guevarism (New York: William Morrow, 1974), p. 165.

19. Nils Castro, Cultura nacional y cultura socialista (Havana: Casa de las Américas, 1978), p. 164.

20. Jay Mallin, ed., "Che" Guevara on Revolution (Coral Gables, Fla.: University of Miami Press, 1969), pp. 11–12.

21. Donald C. Hodges, ed., The Legacy of Che Guevara: A Documentary Study (London: Thames and Hudson, 1977), p. 58.

22. Ibid., pp. 20–21.

23. Harry E. Vanden, "Marxism and the Peasantry in Latin America: Marginalization or Mobilization?" Latin American Perspectives 9 (Fall 1982): 86.

24. Liss, Marxist Thought, p. 258.

25. Nelson P. Valdés, "Ideological Roots of the Cuban Revolutionary Movement," in Contemporary Caribbean: A Sociological Reader, vol. 2, ed. Susan Craig (Maracas, Trinidad and Tobago: Susan Craig, 1982).

26. Castro, *Cultura nacional,* p. 64.

27. Hodges, *Legacy,* p. 20.

28. Hartmut Ramm, *The Marxism of Régis Debray: Between Lenin and Guevara* (Lawrence, Kans.: Regents Press of Kansas, 1978), pp. 7–9.

29. Valdés, "Ideological Roots," pp. 214–15.

30. Ernesto Guevara, "The Philosophy of Che Guevara," taped interview (Hollywood, Calif.: Center for Cassette Studies, 1965).

31. Mallin, *"Che" Guevara,* p. 13.

32. Ramm, *Marxism of Régis Debray,* pp. vii–viii.

33. Boris Goldenberg, *The Cuban Revolution and Latin America* (New York: Praeger, 1966), p. 26.

34. Guevara, "Notes for the Study," p. 406.

35. Guevara, "Philosophy."

36. Liss, *Marxist Thought,* p. 259.

37. Joseph Hansen, *The Leninist Strategy of Party Building: The Debate on Guerrilla Warfare in Latin America* (New York: Pathfinder Press, 1979), pp. 296–97. The Cuban revolution received moral support from the Fourth International, which viewed Cuba as a workers' state, while other Trotskyists labeled the revolution "bourgeois." Che referred to Cuba's Trotskyists as "not inside the revolution, but only devisionists." Robert J. Alexander, *Trotskyism in Latin America* (Stanford, Calif.: Hoover Institution Press, 1973), pp. 231–33.

38. Liss, *Marxist Thought,* p. 260.

39. John Gerassi, ed., *The Coming of the New International* (New York: World, 1971), p. 57.

40. John Gerassi, *Towards Revolution* (London: Weidenfeld and Nicolson, 1971), 2:425.

41. Hodges, *Legacy,* pp. 26–27.

42. Liss, *Marxist Thought,* p. 261.

43. Vanden, "Marxism and the Peasantry," p. 92.

44. Liss, *Marxist Thought,* p. 261.

45. Andrew Sinclair, *Che Guevara* (New York: Viking Press, 1970), p. 30.

46. Jacques Ellul, *Autopsy of Revolution* (New York: Alfred A. Knopf, 1971), p. 169.

47. Guevara, *Che Guevara Speaks,* p. 61.

48. Ibid., p. 66.

49. Sinclair, *Che Guevara,* pp. 67–68.

50. Ibid., p. 67.

51. Liss, *Marxist Thought,* p. 262.

52. Ibid.

53. Michael Harrington, *The Twilight of Capitalism* (New York: Simon and Schuster, 1976), pp. 177–78.

54. Michael Albert and Robin Hahnel, *Socialism Today and Tomorrow* (Boston: South End

Press, 1981), p. 197.

55. Liss, *Marxist Thought*, p. 263.

234

56. Ernesto Guevara, "Notes on Socialism and Man," *International Socialist Review* 27 (Winter 1966): 21.

57. Lowy, *Marxism of Che Guevara*, pp. 27–28.

58. Bertram Silverman, ed., *Man and Socialism in Cuba* (New York: Atheneum, 1973), p. 340.

59. Hodges, *Legacy*, pp. 48–49.

60. See Guevara, "Notes on Socialism and Man."

61. Liss, *Marxist Thought*, p. 264.

62. Harold Eugene Davis, *Latin American Thought: A Historical Introduction* (New York: Free Press, 1974), p. 199; Ernesto Guevara, *El socialismo y el hombre* (Montevideo: Nativa Libros, 1966), p. 13.

63. Guevara, "Notes for the Study," p. 401.

64. Guevara, *Che Guevara Speaks*, p. 24.

65. Liss, *Marxist Thought*, p. 265.

66. Martin, *Early Fidel*, pp. 28–30.

67. Herbert L. Matthews, *Fidel Castro* (New York: Simon and Schuster, 1969), p. 186.

68. Martin, *Early Fidel*, p. 64.

69. Castro, *Primera revolución*, p. 34.

70. Valdés, "Ideological Roots," pp. 222–24.

71. Maurice Halperin, *The Rise and Decline of Fidel Castro* (Berkeley: University of California Press, 1974), pp. 10–12.

72. Martin, *Early Fidel*, p. 101.

73. Maurice Zeitlin and Robert Scheer, *Cuba: Tragedy in Our Hemisphere* (New York: Grove Press, 1963), pp. 52–53.

74. Martin, *Early Fidel*, p. 107.

75. Carlos Franqui, *Diary of the Cuban Revolution* (New York: Viking Press, 1980), p. 66.

76. Martin, *Early Fidel*, p. 154.

77. Franqui, *Diary*, p. 71.

78. Valdés, "Ideological Roots," p. 216.

79. Ibid.

80. Ernesto Cardenal, *In Cuba* (New York: New Directions, 1974), p. 275.

81. Liss, *Marxist Thought*, p. 267.

82. Terence Cannon, *Revolutionary Cuba* (New York: Thomas Y. Crowell, 1981), p. 107.

83. James O'Connor, *The Origins of Socialism in Cuba* (Ithaca, N.Y.: Cornell University Press, 1970), p. 314.

84. Loree A. R. Wilkerson, *Fidel Castro's Political Programs: From Reformism to Marxism-Leninism* (Gainesville: University of Florida Press, 1965), p. 80.

85. William LeoGrande, "The Theory and Practice of Socialist Democracy in Cuba: Mechanisms of Elite Accountability," *Studies in Comparative Communism* 12 (Spring 1979): 41.

86. Gerhard Masur, *National-*

ism in Latin America (New York: Macmillan, 1966), p. 207.

87. Liss, *Marxist Thought,* p. 267.

88. Fidel Castro, "Words to the Intellectuals," in *Radical Perspectives in the Arts,* ed. Lee Baxandall (Baltimore: Penguin Books, 1972), p. 268.

89. See José Portuondo, "The Cuban Revolution and the Intellectual," *New World Review* 32 (October 1964): 37–44.

90. Cardenal, *In Cuba,* p. 189.

91. José Antonio Portuondo, "Literature and Society," in *Latin America in its Literature,* ed. César Fernández Moreno, Julio Ortega, and Ivan A. Schulman (New York: Holmes and Meier, 1980), pp. 287–88.

92. Cynthia McClintock, *Cuban Revolutionary Ideology and the Cuban Intellectual* (Cambridge: Center for International Studies, Massachusetts Institute of Technology, 1975), pp. 36–37.

93. Castro, "Words to the Intellectuals," p. 292.

94. Fidel Castro, "On Intellectual Property," in *Writing in Cuba since the Revolution,* ed. Andrew Salkey (London: Bogle-L'Overture 1977), pp. 150–51.

95. Liss, *Marxist Thought,* p. 267.

96. Martin Kenner and James Petras, eds., *Fidel Castro Speaks* (New York: Grove Press, 1969), p. 146.

97. Ramm, *Marxism of Régis Debray,* p. 58.

98. Liss, *Marxist Thought,* p. 268.

99. Hodges, *Legacy,* pp. 152–53.

100. Ibid. pp. 49–50.

101. Edward Boorstein, *The Economic Transformation of Cuba* (New York: Monthly Review Press, 1968), pp. 253–54.

102. Michael Taber, ed., *Fidel Castro: Speeches,* vol. 2, *Building Socialism in Cuba* (New York: Pathfinder Press, 1983), p. 155.

103. Jan Knippers Black and others, *Area Handbook for Cuba* (Washington, D.C.: Foreign Area Studies of the American University, 1976), p. 140.

104. Liss, *Marxist Thought,* pp. 268–69.

105. Taber, *Fidel Castro,* 2:57.

106. Ibid., p. 51.

107. Ibid., pp. 48–49.

108. Herbert L. Matthews, *Revolution in Cuba* (New York: Charles Scribner's Sons, 1975), pp. 255–56.

109. Liss, *Marxist Thought,* p. 269.

110. K. S. Karol, *Guerrillas in Power* (New York: Hill and Wang, 1970), p. 384.

111. Liss, *Marxist Thought,* p. 270.

112. Barry Reckord, ¿ *Does Fidel Eat More Than Your Father? Conversations in Cuba* (New York: Praeger, 1971), p. 35.

113. Elizabeth Stone, ed., *Women and the Cuban Revolution* (New York: Pathfinder Press, 1981), pp. 71–72.

114. Ibid., pp. 102–3.

115. Ibid., pp. 48–52.

116. Ibid., p. 99.

117. Ibid., pp. 67–68.

118. Taber, *Fidel Castro*, 2:84.

119. Ibid., p. 75.

120. Ibid., pp. 68–70.

121. Taber, *Fidel Castro*, 2:81.

122. Michael Taber, ed., *Fidel Castro: Speeches*, vol. 1, *Cuba's Internationalist Foreign Policy, 1975–80* (New York: Pathfinder Press, 1981), p. 320; *Granma*, 26 July 1980.

123. Ibid., p. 300; *Granma*, 5 August 1979.

124. Albert, *Socialism Today*, p. 174.

Chapter 6

1. Harold Eugene Davis, *History and Power: The Social Relevance of History* (Lanham, Md.: University Press of America, 1983), p. 146.

2. James O'Connor, *The Origins of Socialism in Cuba* (Ithaca, N.Y.: Cornell University Press, 1970), p. 11.

3. Jules Robert Benjamin, "The Machadato and Cuban Nationalism, 1928–1932," *Hispanic American Historical Review* 55 (February 1975): 87.

4. Louis A. Pérez, Jr., "La Chambelona: Political Protest, Sugar, and Social Banditry in Cuba, 1914–1917," *Inter-American Economic Affairs* 31 (Spring 1978): 26–27; also see Louis A.

Pérez, Jr., *Intervention, Revolution, and Politics in Cuba, 1913–1921* (Pittsburgh: University of Pittsburgh Press, 1978), chap. 5.

5. Joaquín Ordoqui, *Elementos para la historia del movimiento obrero en Cuba* (Havana: Comisión Nacional de Escuelas de Instrucción Revolucionaria, 1961), pp. 40–41.

6. Cynthia McClintock, *Cuban Revolutionary Ideology and the Cuban Intellectual* (Cambridge: Center for International Studies, Massachusetts Institute of Technology, 1975), p. 37.

7. See Digna Castañeda Fuertes, ed., *Luis Emilio Recabarren: Obras* (Havana: Casa de las Américas, 1976).

8. Sheldon B. Liss, *Marxist Thought in Latin America* (Berkeley: University of California Press, 1984), pp. 75–78.

9. Arthur MacEwan, *Revolution and Economic Development in Cuba* (New York: St. Martin's Press, 1981), p. 127.

10. William LeoGrande, "The Theory and Practice of Socialist Democracy in Cuba: Mechanisms of Elite Accountability," *Studies in Comparative Communism* 12 (Spring 1979): 60.

11. Nils Castro, *Cultura nacional y cultura socialista* (Havana: Casa de las Américas, 1978), pp. 5–8.

12. Jaime Saruske and Gerardo Mosquera, *The Cultural Policy of Cuba* (Paris: UNESCO, 1979), pp. 22–23.

13. Emilio Roig de Leuchsenring, *Martí: Anti-imperialist* (Havana: Ediciones Políticas, 1967), pp. 67–68.

14. William LeoGrande, "Cuban Dependency: A Comparison of Pre-revolutionary and Post-revolutionary International Economic Relations," *Cuban Studies* 9 (July 1979): 23–28.

15. Wayne S. Smith, "Cuba: Time for a Thaw," *New York Times Magazine*, 29 July 1984, p. 54.

16. MacEwan, *Revolution*, pp. 224–27.

17. See Carla Anne Robbins, *The Cuban Threat* (New York: McGraw-Hill, 1983).

18. Liss, *Marxist Thought*, pp. 238–39.

19. Ibid., p. 278.

20. McClintock, *Cuban Revolutionary Ideology*, p. 18.

21. Casa de las Américas, *Cuba: Transformación del hombre* (Havana: Casa de las Américas, 1961), p. 102.

22. Liss, *Marxist Thought*, p. 231.

23. Ibid., pp. 48–49; see Alfredo L. Palacios, *Una revolución: La reforma agraria en Cuba* (Buenos Aires: Editorial Palestra, 1961).

24. See Silvio Frondizi, *La revolución cubana: Su significación histórica* (Montevideo: Editorial Ciencias Políticas, 1961).

25. Jorge Abelardo Ramos, *Bolivarismo y marxismo* (Buenos Aires: A Peña Lillo, 1969), pp. 110–11, 131–33.

26. Alan Riding, "Revolution and the Intellectual in Latin America," *New York Times Magazine*, 13 March 1983, pp. 33, 40.

27. José Consuegra Higgins, *El control de la natalidad como arma del imperialismo* (Buenos Aires: Editorial Galerna, 1969), pp. 38, 48.

28. Diego Montaña Cuéllar, *Colombia: País formal y país real* (Buenos Aires: Editorial Platina, 1963), p. 283.

29. Liss, *Marxist Thought*, pp. 84–89; Luis Vitale, *Los discursos de Clotario Blest y la revolución chilena* (Santiago: Editorial Por, 1961); Luis Vitale, "Fidelismo and Marxism," *International Socialist Review* 24 (Winter 1963): 23.

30. Luis Corvalán, *Nuestra vía revolucionaria* (Santiago: Impresora Horizonte, 1964), p. 40.

31. Riding, "Revolution and the Intellectual," p. 33.

32. William Bollinger, "Revolutionary Strategy in Latin America," *Monthly Review* 24 (February 1983): 31.

33. Martin Weinstein, ed., *Revolutionary Cuba in the World Arena* (Philadelphia: Institute for the Study of Human Issues, 1979), pp. 152–53.

34. Center for Cuban Studies, *Cuba Update*, February–March 1983, p. 5.

35. During the twenty-five years of the revolution, 19,600

238

titles (585 million copies) have been published in Cuba. Cuba Resource Center, *Cuba Times*, July–August 1984, p. 8.

36. Ernesto Cardenal, *In Cuba* (New York: New Directions, 1974), p. 76.

37. T. B. Bottomore, *Karl Marx,* *Early Writings* (New York: McGraw-Hill, 1964), p. 52.

38. Robbins, *Cuban Threat,* p. 149.

39. Miles D. Wolpin, "Cuban Political Science in the Seventies: Some Observations," *Caribbean Quarterly* 21 (June 1975): 20.

BIBLIOGRAPHY

Aaron, Daniel. *Writers on the Left*. New York: Oxford University Press, 1977.

Acosta, Leonardo. *Jose Martí, la América precolombina y la conquista española*. Havana: Casa de las Américas, 1974.

Aguilar, Luis E. *Cuba 1933: Prologue to Revolution*. New York: W. W. Norton, 1974.

———, ed. *Marxism in Latin America*. 2d ed. Philadelphia, Temple University Press, 1978. (Originally published 1968.)

Aguirre, Sergio. *Seis actitudes de la burguesía cubana en el siglo XIX*. Havana: Editorial Páginas, 1944.

Alba, Víctor. *Historia del Comunismo en América Latina*. Mexico City: Ediciones Occidentales, 1954.

Albert, Michael, and Robin Hahnel. *Socialism Today and Tomorrow*. Boston: South End Press, 1981.

Alexander, Robert J. *Communism in Latin America*. New Brunswick: Rutgers University Press, 1957.

———. *Organized Labor in Latin America*. New York: Free Press, 1965.

———. *Trotskyism in Latin America*. Stanford, Calif.: Hoover Institution Press, 1973.

Alvarez Ríos, Baldomero. *Cuba: Revolución e imperialismo*. Havana: Editorial de Ciencias Sociales, 1969.

Anderson-Imbert, Enrique. *Spanish American Literature: A History*. 2 vols. Detroit: Wayne State University Press, 1962.

Baliño, Carlos. *Documentos y artículos*. Havana: Instituto de

240

Historia del Movimiento Comunista y de la Revolución Socialista de Cuba, 1976.

———. *Documentos de Carlos Baliño.* Havana: Departmento "Colleción Cubana" de la Biblioteca Nacional José Martí, 1964.

Bambirra, Vania. *La revolución cubana.* Mexico City: Editorial Nuestro Tiempo, 1974.

Barkin, David P., and Nita R. Manitzas, eds. *Cuba: The Logic of the Revolution.* Andover, Mass.: Warner Modular Publications, 1973.

Baxandall, Lee, and Stefan Morawski, eds. *Marx and Engels on Literature and Art.* Saint Louis and Milwaukee: Telos Press, 1973.

Beals, Carleton. *The Crime of Cuba.* Philadelphia: J. B. Lippincott, 1933.

Beals, Carleton, and Clifford Odets. *Rifle Rule in Cuba.* New York: Provisional Committee for Cuba, 1935.

Beauvais, Jean-Pierre. "Achievements and Contradictions of the Cuban Workers' State." In *Crisis in the Caribbean,* ed. Fitzroy Ambursely and Robin Cohen. New York: Monthly Review Press, 1983.

Bender, Lynn Darrell. *The Politics of Hostility: Castro's Revolution and United States Policy.* Hato Rey, Puerto Rico: Inter-American University Press, 1975.

Benedetti, Mario. *El escritor lati-noamericano y la revolución posible.* Buenos Aires: Editorial Alfa Argentina, 1974.

———. "Relaciones entre el hombre de acción y el intelectual." *Casa de las Américas* 7 (March–April 1968): 116–20.

Benjamin, Jules Robert. "The Machadato and Cuban Nationalism, 1928–1932." *Hispanic American Historical Review* 55 (February 1975): 66–91.

———. *The United States and Cuba: Hegemony and Dependent Development, 1880–1934.* Pittsburgh: University of Pittsburgh Press, 1977.

Bernardo, Robert M. *The Theory of Moral Incentives in Cuba.* University: University of Alabama Press, 1971.

Bialer, Seweryn. "On the Meanings, Sources and Carriers of Radicalism in Contemporary Industrialized Societies: Introductory Remarks." In *Radicalism in the Contemporary Age,* vol. 1, *Sources of Contemporary Radicalism,* ed. Seweryn Bailer and Sophia Sluzar. Boulder, Colo.: Westview Press, 1977.

Black, Jan Knippers, and others. *Area Handbook for Cuba.* Washington, D.C.: Foreign Area Studies of the American University, 1976.

Blackburn, Robin. "Prologue to the Cuban Revolution." *New*

Left Review 4 (October 1963): 53–91.

Blanksten, George I. "Fidel Castro and Latin America." In *Latin American Politics,* ed. Robert D. Tomasek. Garden City, N.Y.: Anchor Books, 1966.

Blasier, Cole. *The Giant's Rival: The USSR and Latin America.* Pittsburgh: University of Pittsburgh Press, 1983.

Bollinger, William. "Revolutionary Strategy in Latin America." *Monthly Review Press* 24 (February 1983): 27–33.

Bonachea, Ramón L., and Marta San Martín. *The Cuban Insurrection, 1952–1959.* New Brunswick, N.J.: Transaction Books, 1974.

Bonachea, Rolando E., and Nelson P. Valdés, eds. *Cuba in Revolution.* Garden City, N.Y.: Anchor-Doubleday, 1972.

——, eds. *Revolutionary Struggle, 1947–1958: The Selected Works of Fidel Castro.* Cambridge: MIT Press, 1972.

Bonsal, Philip W. *Cuba, Castro and the United States.* Pittsburgh: University of Pittsburgh Press, 1971.

"Book Industry Flourishes." *Cuba Times* 4 (July–August. 1984): 8.

Boorstein, Edward. *The Economic Transformation of Cuba.* New York: Monthly Review Press, 1968.

Bosch, Juan. *Cuba, la isla fascinante.* Santiago de Chile: Editorial Universitaria, 1955.

Bottomore, T B. *Karl Marx, Early Writings.* New York: McGraw-Hill, 1964.

Bray, Donald W., and Timothy F. Harding. "Cuba." In *Latin America: The Struggle with Dependency and Beyond,* ed. Ronald H. Chilcote and Joel C. Edelstein. New York: Schenkman, 1974.

Brym, Robert J. *Intellectuals and Politics.* London: George Allen and Unwin, 1980.

Bueno, Salvador. *Medio siglo de literatura cubana (1902-1952).* Havana: Comisión Nacional Cubana de la UNESCO, 1953.

——, ed. *Los mejores ensayistas cubanos.* Lima: Imprenta Torres Aguirre, 1959.

Cabrera, Olga, ed. *Antonio Guiteras: Su pensamiento revolucionario.* Havana: Editorial de Ciencias Sociales, 1974.

——. *Guiteras, la época, el hombre.* Havana: Editorial de Arte y Literatura, 1974.

Cannon, Terence. *Revolutionary Cuba.* New York: Thomas Y. Crowell, 1981.

Cardenal, Ernesto. *In Cuba.* New York: New Directions, 1974.

Casa de las Américas. *Cuba: Transformación del hombre.* Havana: Casa de las Américas, 1961.

Casal, Lourdes. "Literature and Society." In *Revolutionary Change in Cuba,* ed. Carmelo

242

Mesa-Lago. Pittsburgh: University of Pittsburgh Press, 1971.

Castañeda Fuertes, Digna, ed. *Luis Emilio Recabarren: Obras.* Havana: Casa de las Américas, 1976.

Castellanos, Jorge. *Raíces de la ideología burguesa en Cuba.* Havana: Editorial Páginas, 1944.

Castro, Fidel. *Fidel in Chile.* New York: International Publishers, 1972.

———. *José Martí: El autor intelectual.* Havana: Editorial Política, 1983.

———. *La primera revolución socialista en América.* Mexico City: Siglo XXI, 1980.

———. "Words to the Intellectuals." In *Radical Perspectives in the Arts,* ed. Lee Baxandall. Baltimore: Penguin Books, 1972.

———. *The World Economic and Social Crisis.* Havana: Publishing Office of the Council of State, 1983.

Castro, Fidel, Osvaldo Dorticós, and Raúl Roa. *Así se derrotó al imperialismo.* Vol. 1. *Preparando la defensa.* Mexico City: Siglo XXI, 1981.

Castro, Fidel, and Álvaro Prendes. *Así se derrotó al imperialismo.* Vol. 2. *El combate y la victoria.* Mexico City: Siglo XXI, 1978.

Castro, Nils. *Cultura nacional y cultura socialista.* Havana: Casa de las Américas,1978.

Casuso, Teresa. *Cuba and Castro.* New York: Random House, 1961.

Central Committee of the Communist Party of Argentina. "A 'Revolution in the Revolution' Is Impossible (1967)." In *Models of Political Change in Latin America,* ed. Paul Sigmund. New York: Praeger, 1970.

Chaliand, Gérard. *Revolution in the Third World.* New York: Penguin Books, 1978.

Chang-Rodríguez, Eugenio. *La literatura política de González Prada, Mariátegui y Haya de la Torre.* Mexico City: Ediciones de Andrea, 1957.

Chapman, Charles E. *A History of the Cuban Republic.* New York: Octagon Books, 1969. (Originally published 1927.)

Chilcote, Ronald H., and Joel C. Edelstein, eds. *Latin America: The Struggle with Dependency and Beyond.* New York: Schenkman, 1974.

Childs, David. *Marx and the Marxists.* London: Ernest Benn, 1973.

Codovilla, Victorio. "The Ideas of Marxism-Leninism in Latin America." *World Marxist Review* 7 (August 1964): 40–49.

Cole, G.D.H. *A History of Socialist Thought.* Vol. 3, part 2. *The Second International, 1889–1914.* London: Macmillan, 1956.

Comisión de Activistas de Historia, Provincial del Partido de la Habana. "Antonio Guiteras, un precursor de nuestra revolución (1906–1935)." *Bohemia* 63 (7 May 1971): 98–101.

Consuegra Higgins, José. *El control de la natalidad como arma del imperialismo.* Buenos Aires: Editorial Galerna, 1969.

———. *Lenin y la América Latina.* Barranquilla, Colombia: Ediciones Cruz del Sur, 1972.

Corbitt, Duvon C. "Cuban Revisionist Interpretations of Cuba's Struggle for Independence." *Hispanic American Historical Review* 43 (August 1963): 395–404.

———. "Historical Publications of the Oficina Del Historiador de la Cuidad de la Habana." *Hispanic American Historical Review* 35 (November 1955): 492–98.

Corvalán, Luis. *Nuestra vía revolucionaria.* Santiago: Impresora Horizonte, 1964.

Coser, Lewis A. *Men of Ideas.* New York: Free Press, 1965.

Crawford, William Rex. *A Century of Latin-American Thought.* New York: Praeger, 1966.

D'Angelo, Edward, ed. *Cuban and North American Marxism.* Amsterdam: B. R. Grüner, 1984.

Davis, Harold Eugene. *History and Power: The Social Relevance of History.* Lanham,

Md.: University Press of America, 1983.

———, ed. *Latin American Social Thought: The History of Its Development since Independence, with Selected Readings.* Washington, D.C.: University Press of Washington, 1961.

———. *Latin American Thought: A Historical Introduction.* New York: Free Press, 1974.

———. *Revolutionaries, Traditionalists, and Dictators in Latin America.* New York: Cooper Square, 1973.

———. *Social Science Trends in Latin America.* Washington, D.C.: American University Press, 1950.

Davis, Horace B. *Nationalism and Socialism: Marxist and Labor Theories of Nationalism to 1917.* New York: Monthly Review Press, 1967.

Debray, Régis. *Che's Guerrilla War.* Baltimore: Penguin Books, 1975.

———. *Prison Writings.* London: Allen Lane, 1973.

———. *Revolution in the Revolution.* New York: Grove Press, 1967.

———. *Strategy for Revolution: Essays on Latin America.* New York: Monthly Review Press, 1970.

Del Duca, Gemma R. "Creativity and Revolution: Cultural Dimensions of the New Cuba." *Cuba, Castro, and Revolution,* ed. Jaime Suchliki. Coral Gables, Fla.: University of Miami Press, 1972.

Dolgoff, Sam. *The Cuban Revolution: A Critical Perspective.* Montreal: Black Rose Books, 1976.

Domínguez, Jorge I., ed. *Cuba: Internal and International Affairs.* Beverly Hills, Calif.: Sage Publications, 1982.

——. *Cuba: Order and Revolution.* Cambridge: Harvard University Press, 1978.

Draper, Theodore. *Castroism: Theory and Practice.* New York: Praeger, 1965.

Dumont, René. *Cuba: Socialism and Development.* New York: Grove Press, 1970.

Dumpierre, Erasmo. *J. A. Mella: Biografía.* Havana: Editorial de Ciencias Sociales, 1977.

Duncan, W. Raymond. "Nationalism in Cuban Politics." *Cuba, Castro and Revolution,* ed. Jaime Suchliki. Coral Gables, Fla.: University of Miami Press, 1972.

Eddy, W.H.C. *Understanding Marxism.* Totowa, N.J.: Rowan and Littlefield, 1979.

Ellul, Jacques. *Autopsy of Revolution.* New York: Alfred A. Knopf, 1971.

Fagen, Richard R. "Enemies, Friends, and Cuban Nationalism." In *Nationalism in Latin America,* ed. Samuel Baily. New York: Knopf, 1971.

——. *The Transformation of Political Culture in Cuba.* Stanford, Calif.: Stanford University Press, 1969.

Farber, Samuel. "The Cuban Communists in the Early Stages of the Cuban Revolution: Revolutionaries or Reformists?" *Latin American Research Review* 18, no. 1 (1983): 59–83.

——. *Revolution and Reaction in Cuba, 1933–1960: A Political Sociology from Machado to Castro.* Middletown, Conn.: Wesleyan University Press, 1976.

Fernández Bulté, Julio. *Historia de las ideas políticas y jurídicas.* Havana: Editorial de Ciencias Sociales, 1977.

Fernández Moreno, César, Julio Ortega, and Ivan A. Schulman. *Latin America in Its Literature.* New York: Holmes and Meier, 1980.

Fernández Retamar, Roberto. "Caliban." *Casa de las Américas* (September–October 1971), translated in *Massachusetts Review* 15 (Winter–Spring 1974): 7–72.

——. "Hacia una intelectualidad revolucionaria en Cuba." *Casa de las Américas* 7 (January–February 1967): 4–18.

Fitzgerald, Frank T. "The Direction of Cuban Socialism: A Critique of the Sovietization Thesis." In *Contemporary Caribbean: A Sociological Reader,* vol. 2, ed. Susan Craig. Maracas, Trinidad and Tobago: Susan Craig, 1982.

Foner, Philip S. *Antonio Maceo: The "Bronze Titan" of Cuba's*

Struggle for Independence. New York: Monthly Review Press, 1977.

―――. A History of Cuba and Its Relations with the United States. Vol. 1. 1492–1845. Vol. 2. 1845–1895. New York: International Publishers, 1962, 1963.

―――. The Spanish-Cuban-American War and The Birth of American Imperialism, 1895–1902. Vol. 1. 1895–1898. New York: Monthly Review Press, 1972.

Franco, Jean. An Introduction to Spanish-American Literature. Cambridge: Cambridge University Press, 1969.

―――. Spanish American Literature since Independence. London: Ernest Benn, 1973.

Frank, André Gunder. World Accumulation, 1492–1789. New York: Monthly Review Press, 1978.

Frank, Waldo. Cuba: Prophetic Island. New York: Marzani and Munsell, 1961.

Franqui, Carlos, Diary of the Cuban Revolution. New York: Viking Press, 1980.

―――. Family Portrait with Fidel: A Memoir. New York: Random House, 1984.

Frondizi, Silvio. La revolución cubana: Su significación histórica. Montevideo: Editorial Ciencias Políticas, 1961.

Gallagher, David. "The Literary Life of Cuba." New York Review of Books 10 (5 May 1968): 37–41.

García Galló, Gaspar Jorge, and others, eds. Carlos B. Baliño: Apuntes históricos sobre sus actividades revolucionarias. Havana: Partido Comunista de Cuba, 1967.

García Montes, Jorge, and Antonio Alonso Avila. Historia del partido comunista de Cuba. Miami: Ediciones Universal, 1970.

Gellman, Irwin F. Roosevelt and Batista: Good Neighbor Diplomacy in Cuba, 1935–1945. Albuquerque: University of New Mexico Press, 1973.

Gerassi, John, ed. The Coming of the New International. New York: World, 1971.

―――. Towards Revolution. Vol. 2. London: Weidenfeld and Nicolson, 1971.

―――, ed. Venceremos: The Speeches and Writings of Che Guevara. New York: Simon and Schuster, 1968.

Gilio, Maria Esther. The Tupamaro Guerrillas: The Structure and Strategy of the Urban Guerrilla Movement. New York: Saturday Review Press, 1972.

Gilly, Adolfo. Inside the Cuban Revolution. New York: Monthly Review Press, 1964.

Goldenberg, Boris. The Cuban Revolution and Latin America. New York: Praeger, 1966.

Gómez y Martínez, Luis. Diego Vicente Tejera: Ensayo crítico-

biográfico. Havana: Bouza, 1928.

González, Edward. *Cuba under Castro: The Limits of Charisma.* Boston: Houghton Mifflin, 1974.

González, Manuel Pedro. *José Martí: Epic Chronicler of the United States in the Eighties.* Chapel Hill: University of North Carolina Press, 1953.

González, Reynaldo. "Interview with Carlos Rafael Rodríguez." *Cuba Update* 4 (November 1983): 12, 18–19.

González Carbajal, Ladislao. *Mella y el Movimiento Estudiantil.* Havana: Editorial de Ciencias Sociales, 1977.

Goodsell, James Nelson, ed. *Fidel Castro's Personal Revolution in Cuba, 1959–1973.* New York: Knopf, 1975.

Gorman, Robert A. *Neo-Marxism: The Meanings of Modern Radicalism.* Westport, Conn.: Greenwood Press, 1982.

Gray, Richard Butler. "José Martí and Social Revolution in Cuba." *Journal of Inter-American Studies* 5 (April 1963): 249–56.

——. *José Martí, Cuban Patriot.* Gainesville: University of Florida Press, 1962.

Green, Gil. *Cuba at 25: The Continuing Revolution.* New York: International Publishers, 1983.

——. *Revolution Cuban Style.* New York: International Publishers, 1970.

Guerra y Sánchez, Ramiro, and others. *Historia de la nación cubana.* Vol. 1. *Culturas primitivas, descubrimiento, conquista y colonización (desde la época precolombiana hasta 1697).* Vol. 2. *Guerras coloniales, conflictos y progresos (desde 1697 hasta 1790).* Vol.3. *Ilustración libertad de comercio (desde 1790 hasta 1837).* Vol. 4. *Ruptura con la metrópoli (desde 1837 hasta 1868).* Vol. 5. Guerra de los diez años y otras actividades revolucionarios (desde 1868 hasta 1902) (1). Vol. 6. *Autonomismo guerra de independencia (desde 1868 hasta 1902 (2).* Vol. 7. *Cambio de soberanía (desde 1868 hasta 1902) (3).* Vol. 8. *Advenimiento de la república organización institucional (desde 1902 hasta 1951) (1).* Vol. 9. *Desarrollo económico y proceso social (desde 1902 hasta 1951) (2).* Vol. 10. *Consolidación de la república (desde 1902 hasta 1951) (3).* Havana: Editorial Historia de la Nación Cubana, 1952.

Guevara, Ernesto. *Che Guevara Speaks.* New York: Pathfinder Press, 1967.

——. "Notes for the Study of the Ideology of the Cuban Revolution." In *Revoltuion,* ed. Bruce Mazlish, Arthur D. Kaledin, and David B. Ralston. New York: Macmillan, 1971.

———. "Notes on Socialism and Man." *International Socialist Review* 27 (Winter 1966): 18–23.

———. *Obra revolucionaria.* Mexico City: Ediciones Era, 1979.

———. "On Art and Revolution." *Praxis,* Winter 1976, 396.

———. "The Philosophy of Che Guevara." Taped interview. Hollywood, Calif.: Center for Cassette Studies, 1965.

———. *Reminiscences of the Cuban Revolutionary War.* New York: Grove Press, 1968.

———. *Socialism and Man in Cuba and Other Works.* London: Stage I, 1968.

———. *El socialismo y el hombre.* Montevideo: Nativa Libros, 1966.

Guiteras Holmes, Calixta. *Biografía de Antonio Guiteras.* Havana: Municipio de la Habana, 1960.

Hagopian, Mark N. *The Phenomenon of Revolution.* New York: Dodd Mead, 1975.

Halebsky, Sandor, and John Kirk, eds. *Cuba: Twenty-five Years of Revolution, 1959–1984.* New York: Praeger, 1985.

Halévy, Elie. *The Growth of Philosophic Radicalism.* Boston: Beacon Press, 1966.

Halperin, Ernest. *Nationalism and Communism in Chile.* Cambridge: MIT Press, 1965.

Halperin, Maurice. *The Rise and Decline of Fidel Castro.* Berkeley: University of California Press, 1974.

———. *The Taming of Fidel Castro.* Berkeley: University of California Press, 1981.

Hamaliam, Leo, and Frederick R. Karl, eds. *The Radical Vision: Essays for the Seventies.* New York: Thomas Y. Crowell, 1970.

Hansen, Joseph. *Dynamics of the Cuban Revolution.* New York: Pathfinder Press, 1978.

———. "Ideology of the Cuban Revolution." *International Socialist Review,* Summer 1960, 74–78.

———. *The Leninist Strategy of Party Building: The Debate on Guerrilla Warfare in Latin America.* New York: Pathfinder Press, 1979.

Harrington, Michael. *The Twilight of Capitalism.* New York: Simon and Schuster, 1976.

Hennessy, C.A.M. "Cuba: The Politics of Frustrated Nationalism." In *Political Systems of Latin America,* ed. Martin Needler. Princeton, N.J.: D. Van Nostrand, 1964.

———. "The Roots of Cuban Nationalism." *International Affairs* 39 (July 1963): 345–59.

Henríquez Ureña, Max. *Panorama histórico de la literatura cubana.* 2 vols. New York: Américas, 1963.

Henríquez Ureña, Pedro. *Literary Currents in Hispanic America.* Cambridge: Harvard University Press, 1945.

Herman, Donald L., ed. *The*

Communist Tide in Latin America. Austin: University of Texas Press, 1973.

248

Hobsbawm, E. J. *Revolutionaries.* New York: Meridian Books, 1973.

Hobson, J. A. *Imperialism: A Study.* London: Allen and Unwin, 1902.

Hodges, Donald C. *The Latin American Revolution: Politics and Strategy from Apro-Marxism to Guevarism.* New York: William Morrow, 1974.

———, ed. *The Legacy of Che Guevara: A Documentary Study.* London: Thames and Hudson, 1977.

Hodges, Donald C., and Robert Elias Abu Shanab, eds. *National Liberation Fronts, 1960/1970.* New York: William Morrow, 1972.

Holt-Seeland, Inger. *Women of Cuba.* Westport, Conn.: Lawrence Hill, 1981.

Horowitz, Irving L., ed. *Cuban Communism.* New Brunswick: Transaction Books, 1970, 1977, 1981.

Horowitz, Irving L., and others, eds. *Latin American Radicalism: A Documentary Report on Left and Nationalist Movements.* New York: Random House, 1969.

Howe, Irving, ed. *The Radical Imagination.* New York: New American Library, 1967.

Huberman, Leo, and Paul M. Sweezy. *Socialism in Cuba.* New York: Monthly Review Press, 1969.

Hyams, Edward. *A Dictionary of Modern Revolution.* New York: Taplinger, 1973.

Ibarra, Jorge. *Ideología mambisa.* Havana: Instituto Cubano del Libro, 1972.

———. *José Martí: Dirigente político e ideologo revolucionario.* Havana: Editorial de Ciencias Sociales, 1980.

Instituto de Literatura Lingüística de la Academia de Ciencias de Cuba. *Perfil histórico de las letras cubanas: Desde los orígenes hasta 1898.* Havana: Editorial Letras Cubanas, 1983.

Jorrín, Miguel, and John D. Martz. *Latin-American Political Thought and Ideology.* Chapel Hill: University of North Carolina Press, 1970.

Judson, C. Fred. *Cuba and the Revolutionary Myth: The Political Education of the Cuban Rebel Army, 1953–1963.* Boulder, Colo.: Westview Press, 1984.

Karol, K. S. *Guerrillas in Power.* New York: Hill and Wang, 1970.

Keniston, Kenneth. *Young Radicals: Notes on Committed Youth.* New York: Harcourt Brace and World, 1968.

Kenner, Martin, and James Petras, eds. *Fidel Castro Speaks.* New York: Grove Press, 1969.

Kettle, Arnold. *Communism and the Intellectuals.* London:

Lawrence and Wishert, 1965.

Kiernan, V. G. *Marxism and Imperialism*. New York: St. Martin's Press, 1974.

Kirk, John M. *José Martí: Mentor of the Cuban Nation*. Tampa: University Presses of Florida, 1983.

Knight, Franklin W. *Slave Society in Cuba during the Nineteenth Century*. Madison: University of Wisconsin Press, 1970.

Kozolchyk, Boris. *The Political Biographies of Three Castro Officials*. Santa Monica, Calif.: Rand Corporation, 1966.

Lafargue, Paul. *Socialism and the Intellectuals*. New York: Labor News, 1967.

Lazo, Raimundo. *La teoría de las generaciones y su aplicación al estudio histórico de la literatura cubana*. Cuadernos del Centro de Estudios Literarios, no. 5. Mexico City: Universidad Nacional Autónoma de México, 1972.

Lens, Sidney. *Radicalism in America*. New York: Thomas Y. Crowell, 1969.

———. *Unrepentant Radical*. Boston: Beacon Press, 1980.

Leo Grande, William. "Cuba." In *Communism in Central America and the Caribbean*, ed. Robert Wesson. Stanford, Calif.: Hoover Institution Press, 1982.

———. "Cuban Dependency.: A Comparison of Pre-revolutionary and Post-revolutionary International Economic Relations." *Cuban Studies* 9 (July 1979): 1–29.

———. "The Theory and Practice of Socialist Democracy in Cuba: Mechanisms of Elite Accountability." *Studies in Comparative Communism* 12 (Spring 1979): 39–62.

———. "Two Decades of Socialism in Cuba." *Latin American Research Review* 16, no. 1 (1981): 187–206.

Lévesque, Jacques. *The USSR and the Cuban Revolution*. New York: Praeger, 1978.

Levine, Barry B., ed. *The New Cuban Presence in the Caribbean*. Boulder, Colo.: Westview Press, 1983.

Lewis, Gordon K. *Main Currents in Caribbean Thought: The Historical Evolution of Caribbean Society in Its Ideological Aspects, 1492–1900*. Baltimore: Johns Hopkins University Press, 1983.

Lewis, Oscar, Ruth M. Lewis, and Susan M. Rigdon. *Four Men: Living the Revolution: An Oral History of Contemporary Cuba*. Urbana: University of Illinois Press, 1977.

Lifton, Robert Jay, ed. *Explorations in Psychohistory*. New York: Simon and Schuster, 1974.

Liss, Sheldon B. *Marxist Thought in Latin America*. Berkeley: University of California Press, 1984.

Liss, Sheldon B., and Peggy K.

Liss, eds. *Man, State, and Society in Latin American History.* New York: Praeger, 1972.

Lizaso, Félix. *Ensayistas contemporáneos, 1900–1920.* Havana: Editorial Trópico, 1938.

———. *Martí: Martyr of Cuban Independence.* Albuquerque: University of New Mexico Press, 1953.

———. *Panorama de la cultura cubana.* Mexico City: Fondo de Cultura Económica, 1949.

Llerena, Mario. *The Unsuspected Revolution: The Birth and Rise of Castroism.* Ithaca, N.Y.: Cornell University Press, 1978.

Lowy, Michael. *The Marxism of Che Guevara.* New York: Monthly Review Press, 1973.

McCadden, Joseph, and Helen McCadden. *Father Varela: Torch Bearer from Cuba.* New York: United States Catholic Historical Society, 1969.

McClintock, Cynthia. *Cuban Revolutionary Ideology and the Cuban Intellectual.* Cambridge: Center for International Studies, Massachusetts Institute of Technology, 1975.

Macdonald, Dwight. "The Root Is Man." In *Radical Perspectives on Social Problems,* ed. Frank Lindenfeld. New York: Macmillan, 1973.

MacEwan, Arthur. *Revolution and Economic Development in Cuba.* New York: St. Martin's Press, 1981.

MacGaffey, Wyatt, and Clifford R. Barnett. *Twentieth Century Cuba: The Background of the Castro Revolution.* Garden City, N.Y.: Doubleday, 1965.

McLennan, Gregor. *Marxism and the Methodologies of History.* London: Verso Editions, 1981.

Maier, Charles S. "Beyond Revolution? Resistance and Vulnerability to Radicalism in Advanced Western Societies." In *Radicalism in the Contemporary Age,* vol. 3, *Strategies and Impact of Contemporary Radicalism,* ed. Seweryn Bialer and Sophia Sluzar. Boulder, Colo.: Westview Press, 1977.

Mallin, Jay, ed. *"Che" Guevara on Revolution.* Coral Gables, Fla.: University of Miami Press, 1969.

Mañach, Jorge. *Martí: Apostle of Freedom.* New York: Devin-Adair, 1950.

Marinello, Juan. *Comentarios al arte.* Havana: Editorial Letras Cubanas, 1983.

———. *Contemporáneos.* Havana: Universidad Central de las Villas, 1964.

———. *Conversación con nuestros pintoresabstractos.* Santiago de Cuba: Universidad de Oriente Departamento de Extensión y Relaciones Culturales, 1960.

———. *Cuba contra la guerra imperialista.* Havana: Ediciones Sociales, 1940.

———. *Ensayos.* Havana: Editorial Arte y Literatura, 1977.

———. *José Martí, escritor americano: Martí y el modernismo.* Mexico City: Editorial Grijalbo, 1958.

———. *Literatura hispanoamericana: Hombres, meditaciones.* Mexico City: Universidad Nacional, n. d.

———. *Ocho notas sobre Aníbal Ponce.* Buenos Aires: Cuadernos de Cultura, 1958.

———. *Once ensayos martianos.* Havana: Comisión Nacional Cubana de la UNESCO, 1964.

Martí, José. *The America of José Martí: Selected Writings.* Translated by Juan de Onís. New York: Minerva Press, 1968.

———. "Homage to Marx." In *The Quest for Change in Latin America,* ed. W. Raymond Duncan and James Nelson Goodsell. New York: Oxford University Press, 1970. Also in José Martí, *Obras completas,* vol. 1. Havana: Editorial Lex, 1946.

———. *Inside the Monster: Writing on the United States and American Imperialism.* Edited by Philip S. Foner. New York: Monthly Review Press, 1975.

———. *Obras completas.* Vol. 1. Havana: Editorial Lex, 1946.

———. *On Art and Literature.* Edited by Philip S. Foner. New York: Monthly Review Press, 1982.

———. *On Education: Articles on Educational Theory and Pedagogy and Writings for Children from The Age of Gold.* Edited by Philip S. Foner. New York: Monthly Review Press, 1979.

———. *Our America: Writings on Latin America and the Struggle for Cuban Independence.* Edited by Philip S. Foner. New York: Monthly Review Press, 1977.

Martin, Lionel. *The Early Fidel: Roots of Castro's Communism.* Secaucus, N.J.: Lyle Stuart, 1978.

Martínez Bello, Antonio. *Ideas sociales y económicas de José Martí.* Havana: La Verónica, 1940.

Martínez de la Torre, Ricardo. *De la reforma universitaria al partido socialista: Apuntes para una interpretación marxista de historia social del Perú.* Lima: Ediciones Frente, 1945.

Masur, Gerhard. *Nationalism in Latin America.* New York: Macmillan, 1966.

Matthews, Herbert L. *The Cuban Story.* New York: George Braziller, 1961.

———. *Fidel Castro.* New York: Simon and Schuster, 1969.

———. *Revolution in Cuba.* New York: Charles Scribner's Sons, 1975.

Mazlish, Bruce. *The Revolutionary Ascetic: Evolution of a Political Type.* New York:

Basic Books, 1976.

Mella, Julio Antonio. *Escritos revolucionarios*. Mexico City: Siglo XXI, 1978.

———. *Julio Antonio Mella en el Machete: Antología parcial de un luchador y su momento histórico*. Mexico: Fondo de Cultura Popular, 1968.

———. *La lucha revolucionaria contra el imperialismo. ¿Qué es el APRA?* Mexico City, 1928.

———. *Mella: Documentos y artículos*. Havana: Editorial de Ciencias Sociales, 1975.

Menocal y Cueto, Raimundo. *Origen y desarrollo del pensamiento cubano*. 2 vols. Havana: Editorial Lex, 1945, 1947.

Mesa-Lago, Carmelo. "Building Socialism in Cuba: Romantic versus Realistic Approach." *Latin American Perspectives* 3 (Fall 1976): 117–21.

———. *Cuba in the 1970s*. Albuquerque: University of New Mexico Press, 1978.

———. "Ideological, Political and Economic Factors in the Cuban Controversy on Material versus Moral Incentives." *Journal of Inter-American Studies and World Affairs* 14 (February 1972): 49–111.

———, ed. *Revolutionary Change in Cuba*. Pittsburgh: University of Pittsburgh Press, 1971.

Mestre, José Manuel. *De la filosofía en la Habana*. Havana:

Ministerio de Educación, Dirección de Cultura, 1952.

Mier Febles, Juan. "Un siglo ideológico: Para llegar—correr el camino." *Cuba Internacional*, October 1968, 150–54.

Mills, C. Wright. *Listen Yankee: The Revolution in Cuba*. New York: Ballantine Books, 1960.

———. *The Marxists*. New York: Delta Books, 1962.

———. *Power, Politics and People: The Collected Essays of C. Wright Mills*. New York: Ballantine Books, 1963.

Montaña Cuéllar, Diego. *Colombia: País formal y país real*. Buenos Aires: Editorial Platina, 1963.

Morray, J. P. *The Second Revolution in Cuba*. New York: Monthly Review Press, 1962.

Nash, June, Juan Corradi, and Hobart Spalding, Jr., eds. *Ideology and Social Change in Latin America*. New York: Gordon and Breach Science Publishers, 1977.

Neruda, Pablo. *Memoirs*. Translated by Hardie St. Martin. New York: Penguin Books, 1978.

Nisbet, Robert. "The Function of the Vision of the Future in Radical Movements." In *Radicalism in the Contemporary Age*, vol. 2, *Radical Visions of the Future*, ed. Seweryn Bialer and Sophia Sluzar. Boulder, Colo.: Westview Press, 1977.

———. *History of the Idea of*

Progress. New York: Basic Books, 1980.

———. *The Social Philosophers: Community and Conflict in Western Thought.* New York: Thomas Y. Crowell, 1973.

Nizan, Paul. *The Watchdogs: Philosophers of the Established Order.* New York: Monthly Review Press, 1971.

O'Connor, James. "The Foundations of Cuban Socialism." *Studies on the Left* 4 (Fall 1964): 97–117.

———. *The Origins of Socialism in Cuba.* Ithaca, N.Y.: Cornell University Press, 1970.

Ordoqui, Joaquín. *Elementos para la historia del movimiento obrero en Cuba.* Havana: Comisión Nacional de Escuelas de Instrucción Revolucionaria, 1961.

Ortiz, Fernando. *Cuban Counterpoint: Tobacco and Sugar.* New York: Vintage Books, 1970.

Overholt, William H. "Sources of Radicalism and Revolution: A Survey of the Literature." In *Radicalism in the Contemporary Age.* Vol. 1. *Sources of Contemporary Radicalism,* ed. Seweryn Bialer and Sophia Sluzar. Boulder, Colo.: Westview Press, 1977.

Page, Charles Albert. "The Development of Organized Labor in Cuba." Ph.D. diss. University of California, Berkeley, 1952.

Palacios, Alfredo L. *Una revolu-*
ción: La reforma agraria en Cuba. Buenos Aires: Editorial Palestra, 1961.

Pando, Magdalen M. *Cuba's Freedom Fighter, Antonio Maceo: 1845–1896.* Gainesville, Fla.: Felicity Press, 1980.

Partido Aprista Cubano. *El aprismo ante la realidad cubana.* Havana: Editorial APRA, 1934.

Peña, Alcira de la. "Cuba and Marxism." *World Marxist Review* 6 (June 1963): 75–78.

Pérez, Louis A., Jr. *Army Politics in Cuba, 1898–1958.* Pittsburgh: University of Pittsburgh Press, 1976.

———. "La Chambelona: Political Protest, Sugar, and Social Banditry in Cuba, 1914–1917." *Inter-American Economic Affairs* 31 (Spring 1978): 3–27.

———. *Cuba between Empires, 1878–1902.* Pittsburgh: University of Pittsburgh Press, 1983.

———. *Intervention, Revolution, and Politics in Cuba, 1913–1921.* Pittsburgh: University of Pittsburgh Press, 1978.

———. "Scholarship and the State: Notes on a History of the Cuban Republic." *Hispanic American Historical Review* 54 (November 1974): 682–90.

———. "Toward a New Future, from a New Past: The Enterprise of History in Socialist Cuba." *Cuban Studies* 15

(Winter 1985): 1–13.

Pérez, Trinidad, and others. *Recopilación de textos sobre Juan Marinello.* Havana: Ediciones Casa de las Américas, 1979.

Pérez Cabrera, José Manuel. *Historiografía de Cuba.* Mexico: Instituto Panamericano de Geografía e Historia, 1962.

Pérez Chávez, Rubén. "Biografía de Enrique Roig San Martín." *ISLAS* 12, no. 1 (1965): 41–77.

Petras, James F. *Class, State and Power in the Third World.* Montclair, N.J.: Allanheld, Osmun, 1981.

———. *Critical Perspectives on Imperialism and Social Class in the Third World.* New York: Monthly Review Press, 1978.

Piñera Llera, Humberto. *Panorama de la filosofía cubana.* Washington, D.C.: Pan American Union, 1960.

Pino-Santos, Oscar. *Historia de Cuba: Aspectos fundamentales.* Havana: Editorial Nacional de Cuba, 1964.

Plasencia, Aleida, ed. *Enrique Roig San Martín: Artículos publicados en el periódico "El Productor."* Havana: Biblioteca Nacional José Martí, 1967.

Pomeroy, William J., ed. *Guerrilla Warfare and Marxism.* New York: International Publishers, 1968.

Ponce, Aníbal. *Educación y lucha de clases.* Havana: Imprenta Nacional de Cuba, 1961.

———. *Humanismo burgués y humanismo proletario.* Havana: Imprenta Nacional, 1962.

———. *Obras escogidas de Aníbal Ponce.* Havana: Casa de las Américas, 1975.

Ponte Domínguez, Francisco J. *La masonería en la independencia de Cuba.* Havana: Editorial "Modas Magazine," 1954.

Portuondo, Fernando. *Historia de Cuba hasta 1898.* Havana: Editorial Nacional de Cuba, 1965.

Portuondo, José Antonio. *Bosquejo histórico de las letras cubanas.* Havana: Ministerio de Relaciones Exteriores, 1960.

———. *El contenido social de la literatura cubana.* Mexico City: Colegio de México, Centro de Estudios Sociales, 1944.

———. "The Cuban Revolution and the Intellectual." *New World Review* 32 October 1964): 37–44.

———. "Literature and Society." In *Latin America in Its Literature,* ed. César Fernández Moreno, Julio Ortega, and Ivan A. Schulman. New York: Holmes and Meier, 1980.

Poyo, Gerald E. "The Anarchist Challenge to the Cuban Independence Movement," 1885–1890." *Cuban Studies* 15

(Winter 1985): 29–42.

Radosh, Ronald, ed. *The New Cuba: Paradoxes and Potentials*. New York: William Morrow, 1976.

Rama, Carlos M. *Mouvements ouvrières et socialistes: L'Amérique Latine (1492–1936)*. Paris: Editions Ouvrières, 1959.

Ramm, Hartmut. *The Marxism of Régis Debray: Between Lenin and Guevara*. Lawrence, Kans.: Regents Press of Kansas, 1978.

Ramos, Jorge Abelardo. *Bolivarismo y Marxismo*. Buenos Aires: A. Peña Lillo, 1969.

Ratliff, William E. *Castroism and Communism in Latin America, 1959–1976: The Varieties of Marxist-Leninist Experience*. Washington, D.C.: American Enterprise Institute, 1976.

Reckord, Barry. *¿Does Fidel Eat More Than Your Father? Conversations in Cuba*. New York: Praeger, 1971.

Rejai, Mostafa, ed. *Mao Tsetung: On Revolution and War*. Garden City, N.Y.: Doubleday, 1969.

Remos, Juan J. *Historia de la literatura cubana*. Vol. 1. *Orígenes y clasicismo*. Vol. 2. *Romanticismo*. Vol. 3. *Modernismo*. Havana: Cárdenas y Compañía, 1945.

———. "Historiadores de Cuba." *Revista de la Biblioteca Nacional José Martí* 1 (Jan.–March 1955): 45–92.

———. *Proceso histórico de las letras cubanas*. Madrid: Ediciones Guadarrama, 1958.

Rexach, Rosario. "La Revista de Avance publicada en Habana 1927–1930." *Caribbean Studies* 3 (October 1963): 3–16.

Riding, Alan. "Revolution and the Intellectual in Latin America." *New York Times Magazine*, 13 March 1983, 28–40.

Riera Hernández, Mario. *Cuba política, 1899–1955*. Havana: Impresora Modelo, 1955.

———. *Historial obrero cubano, 1574–1965*. Miami: Rema Press, 1965.

Ripoll, Carlos. *José Martí, the United States, and the Marxist Interpretation of Cuban History*. New Brunswick, N.J.: Transaction Books, 1984.

Rivero Muñiz, José. *El primer partido socialista cubano: Apuntes para la historia del proletariado en Cuba*. Santa Clara, Cuba: Universidad Central de las Villas, 1962.

Roa, Raúl. *En Pie, 1953–1958*. Havana: Universidad Central de las Villas, 1959.

———. *Evocación de Pablo Lafargue*. Havana: Ministerio de Salud Pública, 1973.

———. *El fuego de la semilla en el surco*. Havana: Editorial Letras Cubanas, 1982.

———. *Historia de las doctrinas sociales*. Havana: Universidad de la Habana, 1949.

———. *Martí y el fascismo*. Havana: Ucar, García, 1937.

———. *15 años después*. Havana: Editorial Librería Selecta, 1950.

——— *Retorno a la alborada*. 2 vols. Havana: Universidad de las Villas, 1964.

———. "Utopia, ideología y mito en la política contemporánea." In *Los mejores ensayistas cubanos*, ed. Salvador Bueno. Lima: Imprenta Torres Aguirre, 1959.

———. *Viento sur*. Havana: Editorial Selecta, 1953.

Roa Kourí, Raúl. "Cuba in the United Nations: An Interview with Ambassador Raúl Roa Kourí." *Cuba Update* 4 (November 1983): 1, 3, 6, 28.

Robbins, Carla Anne. *The Cuban Threat*. New York: McGraw-Hill, 1983.

Roca, Blas. *The Cuban Revolution: Report to the Eighth National Congress of the Popular Socialist Party of Cuba*. New York: New Century, 1961.

———. "The Cuban Revolution in Action." *World Marxist Review* 2 (August 1959): 16–22.

———. *El desarrollo histórico de la revolución cubana."* *Cuba Socialista* 4 (January 1964): 8–27.

———. *Los fundamentos del socialismo en Cuba*. Havana: Ediciones Populares, 1962. (Originally published 1943.)

———. "New Stage in the Cuban Revolution." *World Marxist Review* 9 (October 1961): 3–10.

———. "Sobre algunas aspectos del desarrollo de la lucha de clases en Cuba." *Cuba Socialista* 11 (April 1965): 31–44.

———. *29 artículos sobre la revolución cubana*. Havana: Partido Socialista Popular, 1960.

Rodríguez, Carlos Rafael. *Cuba en el tránsito al socialismo (1953–1963): Lenin y la cuestión colonial*. Mexico City: Siglo XXI, 1978.

———. "The Cuban Revolution and the Peasantry." *World Marxist Review* 8 (October 1965): 62–71.

———. *Letra con filo*. Vol. 1. *Pensar y hacer*. Vol. 2. *Análisis y defensa de la economía, de viva voz (1959–1983)*. Havana: Editorial de Ciencias Sociales, 1983.

———. *El marxismo y la historia de Cuba*. Havana: Editorial Páginas, 1944.

———. *Palabras en los setenta*. Havana: Editorial de Ciencias Sociales, 1984.

Roig de Leuchsenring, Emilio. *Cuba: No debe su independencia a los Estados Unidos*. Havana: Sociedad Cubana de Estudios Históricos e Internacionales, 1950.

———, ed. *Curso de introducción a la historia de Cuba*. Havana: Municipio de la Habana, 1938.

———, ed. *Defensa de Cuba:*

Vida y obra de Manuel San-guily. Havana: Oficina del Historiador de la Ciudad de la Habana, 1948.

——, ed. *Los Estados Unidos contra Cuba libre*. 2 vols. Santiago de Cuba: Editorial Oriente, 1982.

——. *El Groupo Minorista de intelectuales y artistas haba-neros*. Havana: Oficina del Historiador de la Ciudad de la Habana, 1961.

——, ed. *La guerra hispano-cubano-americana fue ga-nada por el lugarteniente general del ejército liberata-dor Calixto García Iñiguez*. Havana: Oficina del Historia-dor de la Ciudad de la Habana, 1955.

——. *La guerra libertadora cubana de los trienta años 1868–1898: Razón de su victoria*. Havana: Oficina del Historiador de la Ciudad de la Habana, 1952.

——. *Historia de la enmienda Platt: Una interpretación de la realidad cubana*. 2 vols. Havana: Cultural, 1935.

——. *Hostos, apóstol de la independencia y de la liber-tad de Cuba y Puerto Rico*. Havana: Municipio de la Habana, 1939.

——. *La lucha cubana por la república, contra la anexión y la enmienda Platt, 1899–1902*. Havana: Oficina del Historiador de la Ciudad de la Habana, 1952.

——. *Males y vicios de Cuba republicana: Sus causas y sus remedios*. Havana: Oficina del Historiador de la Ciudad de la Habana, 1959.

——. *Martí: Anti-imperialist*. Havana: Ediciones Políticas, 1967.

——. *Médicos y medicina en Cuba: Historia, biografía y costumbrismo*. Havana: Museo Histórico de las Cien-cias Médicas Carlos J. Finlay, 1965.

——. *Revolución y república en Maceo*. Havana: P. Fer-nández, 1945.

——. *Tradición antiimperialista de nuestra historia*. Havana: Oficina del Historiador de la Ciudad de la Habana, 1962.

——. *Tres estudios martianos*. Havana: Editorial de Ciencias Sociales, 1983.

——, ed. *Vida y pensamiento de Varela*. Havana: Municipio de la Habana, 1945.

Rojo, Ricardo. *My Friend Che*. New York: Grove Press, 1968.

Ruiz, Ramón Eduardo. *Cuba: The Making of a Revolution*. New York: W. W. Norton, 1970.

Salceda, Juan Antonio. *Aníbal Ponce y el pensamiento de mayo*. Buenos Aires: Editorial Lautaro, 1957.

Salkey, Andrew, ed. *Writing in Cuba since the Revolution*. London: Bogle-L'Overture, 1977.

Sánchez, Luis Alberto. "The University Reform Movement." In *Man, State, and Society in Latin American History*, ed. Sheldon B. Liss and Peggy K. Liss. New York: Praeger, 1972.

Sanguily, Manuel. *Defensa de Cuba*. Havana: Municipio de la Habana, 1948.

Saruski, Jaime, and Gerardo Mosquera. *The Cultural Policy of Cuba*. Paris: UNESCO, 1979.

Seers, Dudley, ed. *Cuba: The Economic and Social Revolution*. Chapel Hill: University of North Carolina Press, 1964.

Servan-Schreiber, Jean-Jacques. *The Radical Alternative*. London: Macdonald, 1970.

Silverman, Bertram, ed. *Man and Socialism in Cuba*. New York: Atheneum, 1973.

Sims, Harold D. "Cuban Labor and the Communist Party, 1937–1958: An Interpretation." *Cuban Studies* 15 (Winter 1985): 43–58.

Sinclair, Andrew. *Che Guevara*. New York: Viking Press, 1970.

Smith, Robert F., ed. *Background to Revolution: The Development of Modern Cuba*. New York: Robert F. Krieger, 1979.

———. "Twentieth Century Cuban Historiography." *Hispanic American Historical Review* 44 (February 1964): 44–73.

Smith, Wayne S. "Cuba: Time for a Thaw." *New York Times Magazine*, 29 July 1984, 22–24, 54–56.

Somerville, John. *The Philosophy of Marxism: An Exposition*. Minneapolis: Marxist Education Press, 1983.

Spalding, Hobart A., Jr. *Organized Labor in Latin America: Historical Case Studies of Urban Workers in Dependent Societies*. New York: Harper and Row, 1977.

Stabb, Martin S. *In Quest of Identity: Patterns in the Spanish American Essay of Ideas, 1890–1960*. Chapel Hill: University of North Carolina Press, 1967.

Stavrianos, L. S. *Global Rift: The Third World Comes of Age*. New York: William Morrow, 1981.

Stone, Elizabeth, ed. *Women and the Cuban Revolution*. New York: Pathfinder Press, 1981.

Suchliki, Jaime. *Cuba: From Columbus to Castro*. New York: Charles Scribner's Sons, 1974.

———. "The Intellectual Background of the Cuban Revolution." *Annals of the Southeastern Conference on Latin American Studies* 3 (March 1972): 105–20.

———. *University Students and Revolution in Cuba, 1920–1968*. Coral Gables, Fla.: University of Miami Press, 1969.

Taber, Michael, ed. *Fidel Castro: Speeches*. Vol. 1. *Cuba's Internationalist Foreign Policy, 1975–1980*. Vol. 2. *Build-*

ing Socialism in Cuba. Vol. 3. *War and Crisis in the Americas.* New York: Pathfinder Press, 1981–85.

Tejera, Diego Vicente. "Autonomistas y anexionistas." *Revista Bimestre Cubana* 47 (May–June 1941): 367–80.

———. "Los futuros partidos políticos de la república cubana." In *Razón de Cuba.* Havana: Municipio de la Habana, 1948.

———. *Razón de Cuba.* Havana: Municipio de la Habana, 1948.

———. "Un párrafo de la historia de Cuba." *Revista Bimestre Cubana* 51 (May–June 1943): 395–417.

Tejera, Eduardo J. *Diego Vicente Tejera: Patriota-poeta y pensador cubano.* Madrid: Compañia de Impresores Reunidos, 1981.

Thomas, Hugh. *Cuba: The Pursuit of Freedom.* New York: Harper and Row, 1971. The second half of this book was published as *The Cuban Revolution.* New York: Harper and Row, 1977.

Torres-Rioseco, Arturo. *Historia de la literatura iberoamericana.* New York: Américas, 1965.

Valdés, Nelson P. "Ideological Roots of the Cuban Revolutionary Movement." In *Contemporary Caribbean: A Sociological Reader,* vol. 2, ed. Susan Craig. Maracas,

Trinidad and Tobago: Susan Craig, 1982.

Vanden, Harry E. "Mariátegui: Marxismo, Comunismo, and Other Bibliographic Notes." *Latin American Research Review* 14 (1979): 61–86.

———. "Marxism and the Peasantry in Latin America: Marginalization or Mobilization?" *Latin American Perspectives* 9 (Fall 1982): 74–98.

Varela, Félix. *Escritos políticos.* Havana: Editorial de Ciencias Sociales, 1977.

Varona, Enrique José. *El imperialismo a la luz de la sociología.* Havana: Editorial Apra, 1933.

Villares, Ricardo. "Precursores de la revolución." *Bohemia,* 11 October 1968, 74–78.

Vitale, Luis. *Los discursos de Clotario Blest y la revolución chilena.* Santiago: Editorial Por, 1961.

———. "Fidelismo and Marxism." *International Socialist Review* 24 (Winter 1963): 23–24, 31.

Vitier, Medardo. *Las ideas en Cuba.* 2 vols. Havana: Editorial Trópico, 1938.

Weinstein, Martin, ed. *Revolutionary Cuba in the World Arena.* Philadelphia: Institute for the Study of Human Issues, 1979.

Whitaker, Arthur P., and David C. Jordan. *Nationalism in Contemporary Latin America.* New York: Free Press, 1966.

Wilkerson, Loree A. R. *Fidel Castro's Political Programs: From Reformism to Marxism-Leninism.* Gainesville: University of Florida Press, 1965.

Williams, William Appleman. *The United States, Cuba, and Castro.* New York: Monthly Review Press, 1962.

Winn, Peter. "The Cuban State and the Arts." In *Cuban Communism,* ed. Louis Irving Horowitz. New Brunswick, N.J.: Transaction Books, 1981.

Wolpin, Miles D. *Cuban Foreign Policy and Chilean Politics.* Lexington, Mass.: Lexington Books, 1972.

———. "Cuban Political Science in the Seventies: Some Observations." *Caribbean Quarterly* 21 (June 1975): 20–34.

Wood, Dennis B. "The Long Revolution: Class Relations and Political Conflict in Cuba, 1868–1968." *Science and Society* 34 (Spring 1970): 1–41.

Yglesias, José. *In the Fist of the Revolution: Life in a Cuban Country Town.* New York: Pantheon, 1968.

Zalamea, Jorge. *Antecedentes históricos de la revolución cubana.* Bogotá: Ediciones Suramérica, 1961.

Zea, Leopoldo. *The Latin American Mind.* Norman: University of Oklahoma Press, 1963.

———. "The Struggle for Intellectual Emancipation." In *Man, State, and Society in Latin American History,* ed. Sheldon B. Liss and Peggy K. Liss. New York: Praeger, 1972.

Zeitlin, Maurice. *Revolutionary Politics and the Cuban Working Class.* New York: Harper and Row, 1970.

Zeitlin, Maurice, and Robert Scheer. *Cuba: Tragedy in Our Hemisphere.* New York: Grove Press, 1963.

INDEX

265